LIBRARY OF RELIGIOUS BIOGRAPHY

Edited by Mark A. Noll, Nathan O. Hatch,
and Allen C. Guelzo

The LIBRARY OF RELIGIOUS BIOGRAPHY is a series of original
biographies on important religious figures throughout American and
British history.

The authors are well-known historians, each a recognized authority in the period of religious history in which his or her subject
lived and worked. Grounded in solid research of both published and
archival sources, these volumes link the lives of their subjects — not
always thought of as "religious" persons — to the broader cultural
contexts and religious issues that surrounded them. Each volume
includes a bibliographical essay and an index to serve the needs of
students, teachers, and researchers.

Marked by careful scholarship yet free of footnotes and academic
jargon, the books in this series are well-written narratives meant to be
read and *enjoyed* as well as studied.

LIBRARY OF RELIGIOUS BIOGRAPHY

Emily Dickinson
and the Art of Belief

Roger Lundin

WILLIAM B. EERDMANS PUBLISHING COMPANY
GRAND RAPIDS, MICHIGAN / CAMBRIDGE, U.K.

To Matthew, Kirsten, and Thomas

© 1998 Wm. B. Eerdmans Publishing Co.
255 Jefferson Ave. S.E., Grand Rapids, Michigan 49503 /
P.O. Box 163, Cambridge CB3 9PU U.K.

Printed in the United States of America

03 02 01 00 99 98   7 6 5 4 3 2 1

Library of Congress Cataloging-in-Publication Data

Lundin, Roger.
    Emily Dickinson and the art of belief / Roger Lundin.
        p.   cm. — (Library of religious biography)
    Includes bibliographical references and index.
    ISBN 0-8028-3857-X (cloth : alk. paper)
    ISBN 0-8028-0157-9 (pbk. : alk. paper)
    1. Dickinson, Emily, 1830-1886 — Religion. 2. Women and
literature — New England — History — 19th Century. 3. Christian
poetry, American — History and criticism. 4. Women poets, American —
19th century — Biography. 5. Belief and doubt in literature.
I. Title. II. Series.
PS1541.Z5L86   1998
811'.4 — dc21   97-53055
                                                             CIP

Contents

96522

Foreword

ONE OF THE TRAGEDIES of modern life is the division of intellectual labor into disciplines. "Tragedy," though, is probably not
the right word, for, while this situation is self-inflicted and filled with
irony, it allows neither expiation for practitioners nor catharsis for
readers. Rather, the rendering of thought and writing into discrete fields
of study appears to be welcomed since it affords multiplied opportunities for *cognoscenti* to exclude uninitiated outsiders, aspiring authorities
to set up fiefdoms, and the programs of annual learned societies to
parade the latest fashionable clichés. The greatest loss occasioned by
acquiescing to rigid disciplinary boundaries is the distortion of reality.
In fact, poets pray, biophysicists take their kids to the movies, novelists
cash their checks, financiers bake bread, missionaries propagate the
species as well as the gospel, jocks read books. No single vocabulary,
no single set of intellectual insights, can encompass the breadth and
depth of lived existence. When academic discourses deny or underesti-
mate the wholeness of life, they cheat their adepts. And they cheat the
rest of us, for readers need all the help we can get, and from every
resource imaginable, if we expect to have even a chance to understand
even a portion of the world that whirls about us.

Thankfully, there are many exceptions to the short-sightedness of disciplinary despotism. Thankfully, many authors do exist who write out of broad learning and who do not consider it beneath themselves to be understood by a general audience. Thankfully, many books are still being published whose authors, however accomplished they may be in the latest and most technical questions of their disciplines, are able to bring that learning to bear on questions that transcend the narrow concerns of any one guild of scholars.

A surprisingly large number of such books that reach out beyond the boundaries of particular disciplines are biographies. Almost always, the subjects of biographies are written up because they have achieved distinction in a particular field — Feynman in physics, Ruth in baseball, Lippman in public discourse, Madame Curie in radioisotopes. To be sure, distinguished biographies provide authoritative translations for the laity of the particulars that made the subject renowned. Yet they also go much beyond to show how their subject's life course illuminates the subject's work. Usually they also relate the achievements of the person in his or her own sphere to parallel events, influences, trends, movements, and achievements connected to the subject's times and places. The best biographies, in other words, combine learning in particulars with a concern for the general, and do so while also slaking our inexhaustible curiosity about the personal.

The life of Emily Dickinson, the reclusive poet of Amherst, Massachusetts, might seem less likely than other noteworthy subjects for a well-rounded biography. The woman, who was never comfortable in society and who spent the last half of her life within the confines of one relatively secluded house, does not at first appear to be a subject worth connecting to other things occurring throughout the American nineteenth century in which she lived. Moreover, her poetry is remarkable for its ability to translate with lightening metaphorical leaps the barest of particular observations into the loftiest and most abstract generalizations about The Human Condition. Concreteness abounds in her poems — the fall of snow, the flutter of a bird's wing, a bridge spanning chasms. But those concrete images seem more devoted to Grand Conclusions than to a particular life.

The singular achievement of Roger Lundin's biography is to show how profoundly connected Emily Dickinson actually was to so many of the grand developments of her century. Through his own remarkable range of interests as literary theorist, intellectual historian, and cultural critic, Lundin offers persuasive readings of her poems, but also opens them up as striking evocations of her age.

And what an age it was. Emily Dickinson witnessed firsthand the transformation of a rural New England village into a cog in a new world of international commerce and its stoutly Congregational college into a cosmopolitan institution participating fully in the great changes that transformed American higher education during the last half of the century. Through her family she experienced the newfound possibilities and perils of professionalization. Through a wider network of friends and correspondents she experienced the Civil War. Most importantly, she was a fully informed participant in the revolution of sensibility that overtook American letters during her lifetime. When she was born, the novels of James Fenimore Cooper, with their pioneering patriotism, and the poetry of Henry Wadsworth Longfellow, with its optimistic pieties, spoke for an intellectual landscape still ruled by a benevolent Deity. By the time of her death, the urban realism of Theodore Dreiser and the sublime egotism of Walt Whitman were pushing aside earlier literary conventions, and the Argument from Design lay shattered on the altar of Darwinian evolution.

In such a world, Emily Dickinson was a magnifying glass: her meticulously crafted poems force readers to see the aching depths created by that shift of sensibility; they are also devices focusing the rays of the sun into a fire of emotion.

By not treating Emily Dickinson as just a poet, or a trophy to be won in the literati wars, or just a symbol of an era — but by treating Emily Dickinson and her times whole, and by doing so in prose as refined as the learning on which it rests, *Emily Dickinson and the Art of Belief* will doubtless earn a place in the ranks of distinguished biographies. As such a biography of such a person, its appearance also strikes a welcome blow against the artificial academic divisions that so disfigure the intellectual life of our age.

MARK A. NOLL

Acknowledgments

I would not have been able to write this book without the generous support of the Pew Evangelical Scholarship Initiative. The grant from the Pew Charitable Trusts freed me to do a year of research and writing at the start of this project. I am grateful to Nathan Hatch for the pioneering work he has done on behalf of Christian scholarship and to Michael Hamilton for his excellent administration of the Pew ESI program.

In like manner, I wish to thank Wheaton College for a sabbatical leave in 1995, which enabled me to do further research and to revise my first draft, and for its generous support of my travel and research needs over the past several years.

Over the course of this project, librarians at a number of institutions were unfailingly helpful. I thank the staffs at the Yale University Library, the Houghton Library of the Harvard College Library, the Amherst College Library, and the Jones Library of the town of Amherst. Daniel Lombardo, curator of special collections at the Jones Library, was especially generous in giving of his time during my several visits to that collection. Here at Wheaton, Paul Snezek and John Fawcett, of the Buswell Memorial Library, gave timely support and assistance in securing materials and answering questions about sources. As always, Jennifer Hoffman, my editor at Eerdmans, was prompt and judicious in shepherding my manuscript through the publication process.

A number of student assistants at Wheaton have provided invaluable help along the way. At the start, Lynn Dixon spent endless hours tracking down and photocopying obscure articles and reading many reels of microfilmed documents. Lynn did her work flawlessly, as did Jennifer Siebersma at the project's close; Jennifer had the unenviable task of checking every citation in the book and of reconciling all inconsistencies in documentation. In addition, Tim Lindgren, Robin Reames, and Matt Lundin assisted me with any number of details at different stages of my work. And finally, my thanks go to Tom Lundin, who gave a week of his summer's time to the proofreading of every Dickinson poem I have cited in the text.

Allen Guelzo, Sue Lundin, Mark Noll, and Chuck Van Hof all read sizable portions of the manuscript at different stages. Their criticism was always timely and constructive. They made me see obvious things that I had missed and opened to me new possibilities that I needed to explore. I am thankful for such astute friends — and for such an astute wife — and for the generosity with which they treated my work, even in its unformed, early stages.

At crucial points in my work on the biography, two doctors offered timely help in making sense of Dickinsonian medical mysteries. For insight into Dickinson's eyesight problems, Dr. David Giesur of the Wheaton Eye Clinic provided important information both about her condition (*exotropia*) and about the probable causes of her anxieties over her condition. And for my understanding of the poet's final illness, Dr. Thomas Meloy of the Mayo Clinic offered an astute assessment of her condition.

Though reading and writing are by nature solitary practices, scholarship is a communal enterprise. In addition to the persons I have already mentioned, there are many other friends at Wheaton and elsewhere who have deepened my work through their conversation and writing. I am also grateful to the larger community of scholars whose work on Dickinson and American culture has informed my own thinking and writing every step of the way. At the end of this book, in a section called "A Note on the Sources," I document this debt, but I would like to single out for thanks the following individuals, some of whom I know well and others whom I have not yet been privileged to meet: Karen Dandurand, Jane Donahue Eberwein, Albert Gelpi, Allen Guelzo, George Marsden, Mark Noll, Dorothy Huff Oberhaus, Richard Sewall, and James Turner.

I have dedicated this book to Sue's and my three children, Matthew, Kirsten, and Thomas. In large measure, they have grown up with this work and have shared time with it as a kind of fourth child in our family. They have always been eager to ask "How's Emily?" and to endure my sometimes convoluted responses to that simple question. Matt, Kiri, and Tom have traveled with me to Amherst, have heard me talk about Dickinson in any number of venues, public and private, and have shared with me a delight in the mysterious intricacies of this extraordinary poet. But most of all, with gracious good cheer and creative individuality, each of them has enabled me to fathom more completely the sense of what Dickinson meant when she told a friend, "I find ecstasy in living — the mere sense of living is joy enough." For Sue and me, these three children have brought — and continue to bring — "ecstasy in living" and joy beyond all measure.

ROGER LUNDIN

A note on citations: To avoid interrupting the narrative of Emily Dickinson's life, the text of this biography contains no footnotes or reference marks. At the back of the book, however, readers will find a bibliographical essay on the sources as well as notes annotating every quotation or reference in the book.

Chronology

1828 (May 6)	Edward Dickinson and Emily Norcross married
1829 (April 16)	William Austin Dickinson born
1830 (December 10)	Emily Elizabeth Dickinson born
1833 (February 28)	Lavinia Norcross Dickinson born
1840	Dickinson family moves from Homestead to Pleasant Street home
1840-47	ED attends Amherst Academy
1847-48	ED spends one year at Mount Holyoke Female Seminary
1850	Revival in Amherst
1853 (March 24)	Benjamin Franklin Newton dies
1855 (Winter)	ED and Lavinia travel to Washington to visit their father, Congressman Edward Dickinson; return trip via Philadelphia, home of Charles Wadsworth
1855	Dickinson family moves back to Homestead on Main Street
1856 (July 1)	Austin Dickinson and Susan Gilbert married

1858-65	Period of ED's greatest poetic productivity (more than 1,000 poems)
1858-61	ED writes three "Master Letters"
1861	Civil War begins
1862 (April 15)	ED writes first letter to Thomas Wentworth Higginson
1864, 1865	ED travels twice to Boston for eye care
1865	Civil War ends
1870 (August 16)	Higginson visits Homestead, meets ED for first time
1874 (June 16)	Edward Dickinson dies
1875 (June 15)	Emily Norcross Dickinson suffers stroke
1878 (January 16)	Samuel Bowles dies
1878-84	ED develops relationship with Otis Phillips Lord, considers marriage
1882 (April 1)	Charles Wadsworth dies
1882 (November 14)	Emily Norcross Dickinson dies
1883 (October 5)	Thomas Gilbert Dickinson (nephew) dies; ED leaves home for first time in at least fifteen years
1884 (March 13)	Otis Phillips Lord dies
1884 (June 14)	ED collapses; first stages of renal failure
1885 (August 12)	Helen Hunt Jackson dies
1886 (May 15)	ED dies; funeral held May 19
1890 (November 12)	First edition of ED's *Poems* published
1894 (November 21)	First edition of *Letters of Emily Dickinson* published

Introduction

THE FAMILY AND FRIENDS who gathered for Emily Dickinson's funeral in Amherst, Massachusetts, on a sunny May afternoon in 1886 had no idea that the woman they mourned was one of the greatest lyric poets in the English language. To the members of the group that had assembled at the Dickinson home that day, Emily was a beloved sister and a dynamic, albeit eccentric, friend. All of the mourners knew that their reclusive neighbor had written poetry of a kind. Some were even aware that a very few of those poems had been published anonymously during her lifetime. None of them, however, had any notion of the enormous scope of this woman's genius or the abiding significance of the work that lay upstairs in a box in Emily's room. Yet within a matter of decades, those poems were to earn her a place in the top echelon of poets in the English language.

Dickinson had wanted it this way. From the time that she began seriously writing poetry in her late twenties until her death almost thirty years later, she had sought to develop her art in virtual anonymity. At death she left behind close to 1,800 poems, only a handful of which had been published against her will or with her grudging permission. Not only did she not seek fame in her own lifetime, but she positively shunned publicity of any kind, securing for herself by her early thirties a solitude that was so complete that few were ever to see her again.

1

Yet at the same time, Dickinson did not exactly hide her poetic light under a bushel. She carried on a voluminous correspondence and freely sent copies of her poems along with her letters throughout her adult life. We know that she mailed to friends and family over 575 copies of her poems, and given the number of her letters that were lost or destroyed before her fame was secured, the total number is probably much higher than that. She intended her poems to do any number of things for their recipients — to bring comfort to a grieving acquaintance, to revive the flagging spirits of a neighbor, or perhaps simply to entertain or delight a treasured friend.

What Dickinson did not seek in her own lifetime was a larger audience. Having been raised in a Whig culture that prized patience and self-mastery, she was willing to defer entirely the prominence that might otherwise have been hers. She banked on fame, but only the notoriety that would come to her after death. "Lay this Laurel on the One/Too intrinsic for Renown," she wrote of her father several years after his death. In life, fame brought only distractions and the prying gaze of the public; after death, it could grant something much more satisfying:

> The first We knew of Him was Death —
> The second — was — Renown —
> Except the first had justified
> The second had not been. [#1006]

This "renown" fit neatly into her "strategy of immortality":

> A Spider sewed at Night
> Without a Light
> Upon an Arc of White.
>
> If Ruff it was of Dame
> Or Shroud of Gnome
> Himself himself inform.
>
> Of Immortality
> His Strategy
> Was Physiognomy. [#1138]

2

In saying that Dickinson's poetry was an "art of belief," I intend the phrase in several ways. Her poetry is in large measure about belief — about the objects of belief and its comforts, as well as belief's great uncertainties. With daring tenacity, she explored the full range of human experience in her reflections upon such subjects as God, the Bible, suffering, and immortality. "On subjects of which we know nothing, or should I say *Beings*," she wrote a few years before she died, "we both believe, and disbelieve a hundred times an Hour, which keeps Believing nimble."

To keep the "Believing nimble" one needed skill, and in this sense, too, Dickinson realized that belief is an art that demands trial and practice. A product of the romantic age and a prophet of modernity, she comprehended more fully than most people in her day how much the human mind contributes to the process of belief. Art, after all, is about the making of things; and in matters of belief, the history of the modern world is the story of our increasing awareness of the extent to which we participate in the making of truth as well as in the finding of it. However hard it was to fashion and sustain, belief was essential to Dickinson:

> So much of Heaven has gone from Earth
> That there must be a Heaven
> If only to enclose the Saints
> To Affidavit given.
>
> The Missionary to the Mole
> Must prove there is a Sky
> Location doubtless would he plead
> But what excuse have I?
>
> Too much of Proof affronts Belief
> The Turtle will not try
> Unless you leave him — then return
> And he has hauled away. [#1228]

From our vantage point more than a century later, Emily Dickinson stands as one of the major religious thinkers of her age. She knew the Christian tradition, and especially its scriptures and hymns, in depth; on several occasions, in adolescence and young adulthood, she

3

agonizingly approached the threshold of conversion but never passed over it; and throughout her adult life, in her poems and letters, she brilliantly meditated upon the great perennial questions of God, suffering, the problem of evil, death, and her "Flood subject," immortality. Though she never joined the church — and quit attending it at all around the age of thirty — she wrestled with God all her life. Only months before she died, she called herself "Pugilist and Poet." Like Jacob, who told the angel, "I will not let you go, unless you bless me," Dickinson would not let go of God.

For Dickinson the struggle with God had a great deal to do with the considerable challenges that arose to Christian belief in her lifetime. When she was born, the argument from design was securely in place on a six-thousand-year-old earth; at about the time that she began to write poetry regularly, Darwin published *The Origin of Species* and the earth had grown suddenly older. Like Fyodor Dostoevsky and Friedrich Nietzsche — contemporaries with whom she merits comparison — Dickinson was one of the first to trace the trajectory of God's decline. As she wrote in a brilliant poem about the ebbing of belief, God's "Hand is amputated now/And God cannot be found — ." Unlike Nietzsche, she was not gleeful about the possible loss of God but profoundly sad about it, because "The abdication of Belief/Makes the Behavior small — " [#1551].

At the same time that she wrestled with God the Father — questioning not his existence as much as his presence and justice — Dickinson was drawn irresistibly to Jesus the Son. It was the humanity of this one who was "acquainted with Grief" that drew her to him. "I like a look of Agony,/Because I know it's true," she observed in a poem, and in the suffering of Jesus she detected a truth that she could believe without a doubt [#241]. To the end of her life, Dickinson rarely wavered in her expressions of affection for this "Tender Pioneer."

In dwelling so exclusively on the humanity of Jesus, however, Dickinson also exposed the limits of the romantic turn in theology and culture. To a significant extent, she followed the lead of Ralph Waldo Emerson and others as they sought to feed the life of the spirit by drawing from the fathomless depths of the self. In her most expansive moods, she saw those inner resources as more than sufficient to nourish the soul. But when suffering scorched her life and parched her spirit, Dickinson learned the true poverty of human divinity:

4

It is easy to work when the soul is at play —
But when the soul is in pain —
The hearing him put his playthings up
Makes work difficult — then — [#244]

When theology turns into anthropology, Jesus becomes merely a pioneer in the endless process of bearing pain. A full half century before Karl Barth thundered against the bankruptcy of liberal theology, Emily Dickinson had already intuited the limits of romantic optimism. A Christ who is only a prophetic representative of our own humanity is trapped with us in our finitude. What to do with that finitude was a question that consumed her to the end of her life.

Emily Dickinson is unique among the major figures of modern culture. No other person in American history has become so famous in death after having been so anonymous in life. All comparable persons of greatness in the modern world have led lives that have been, to some degree, public. For the politicians, statesmen, religious leaders, and leaders of business whom we remember, it is a given that the interest they have generated after death has only intensified the importance they had established in life. The same is true even of those artists and intellectuals in whom we take an ever keener interest today. Those painters, poets, and composers may have had only slight influence over the course of world affairs, but as they labored at their crafts, they were known for what they did.

Matters were entirely different, however, for Emily Dickinson. All but alone among the major figures of the modern world, she had no audience for the public performance of her life or work. In the manner in which she lived and wrote her poetry, as well as in her views of God and the self, Dickinson developed the full implications of the modern move to what philosopher Charles Taylor has called the "inexhaustible inner domain." She pushed to the limit the Protestant tendency to shift the center of God's activity from the world outside the self to the spiritual world within it. This woman who loved letters because they gave her "the mind alone without corporeal friend" lived the most intensely focused inward life of any major figure in American history. In doing so, she discovered what Blaise Pascal once memorably termed the "greatness and wretchedness" of humanity. And in living her extraordinary life as she did, Dickinson was able to practice an art of belief that eventually made her the greatest of all American poets and one of the most brilliantly enigmatic religious thinkers this country has ever known.

1 The Props Assist the House

The Props assist the House
Until the House is built
And then the Props withdraw
And adequate, erect,
The House support itself
And cease to recollect
The Auger and the Carpenter — [#1142]

Memory is a strange Bell — Jubilee, and Knell.

REMEMBRANCE OFTEN OVERPOWERED Emily Dickinson. It ran like a fault line beneath the surface of her life, frequently shifting and disrupting the normal course of affairs. As the poet wrote shortly after her mother died in November 1882, memory was to her "a strange Bell — Jubilee, and Knell." It was "Jubilee" because it brought the dead to life and lodged them securely in the mansion of the mind. "My Hazel Eye/Has periods of shutting — /But, no lid has Memory," Dickinson claimed, for "Memory like Melody/Is pink Eternally" [#939, #1578]. Yet at the same time, memory also sounded the death "Knell," tolling the loss of ones she had loved. "Remorse — is Memory — awake," and the mind that raises the dead must also acknowledge that "The Grave — was finished — but the Spade/Remained in Memory" [#744, #784].

Because of Emily Dickinson's passion for memory and commemoration, it seems curious that there is but a single reference to her ancestry in all of her poems and letters. Her grandfather was a founder of Amherst College and a major public figure in his day; her forebears on the Dickinson side were among the first settlers of the Massachusetts Bay Colony and played vital roles in the life of the colony and the early republic. Yet all we hear of them in the writings of Emily Dickinson is one brief mention, in the form of a promise she made to send her aunt the family's copy of her grandfather's Bible.

Dickinson neglected her ancestral past because she had a remarkably concrete understanding of remembrance and cared little for history in the abstract. Neither the traditions of the church nor the legacies of her ancestors interested her greatly. Because she had not known them directly, she had no memory of them. For her, memory meant the recollection of intense experiences or encounters rather than rituals of general commemoration. It usually involved the revival of a sensory impress — the cadences of a voice or the sight of riveting eyes — that Dickinson carried in her mind and that brought back to life one who had been snatched from her grasp by death. To borrow one of her metaphors, she was intrigued only by the memory of what went on within the dwelling of her conscious life; in the props that had assisted in building that house she had little interest.

MILLENNIALISM AND MORALISM

It was indeed a rich family history to which Dickinson could have turned her attention, if she had chosen to do so. Her ancestry can be traced to the founding of the Massachusetts Bay Colony, when Nathaniel Dickinson was among the four hundred or so settlers who accompanied John Winthrop in the migration that began in 1630. Nathaniel and his wife Anna were doubtless present on the voyage when Winthrop preached his famous sermon, "A Model of Christian Charity," offering a prophetic vision of New England. In language that continues to resonate in the American experience, Winthrop reminded his fellow sojourners to the New World: "we are entered into covenant with Him for this work" and "we shall be as a City upon a Hill. The eyes of all people are upon us."

The New England Puritans were in the main postmillennialists. They believed, that is, that the thousand-year reign of Christ prophesied in Revelation, the final book of the Bible, would come as a result of their ardent efforts to purify the church. The Puritans with whom Anna and Nathaniel Dickinson came to the New World believed themselves to have been sent by God on a divine "errand into the wilderness." If they were successful, Christ would dwell in their midst and establish his rule over the earth.

The pursuit of godliness and opportunity sent Nathaniel Dickinson first from Boston to Wethersfield, Connecticut, and several decades later to the new plantation of Hadley, Massachusetts. Once planted in the Connecticut River Valley of Massachusetts, the descendants of Nathaniel Dickinson took root in the area and, for several generations, took charge of the town of Amherst. In a biography of her aunt, Martha Dickinson Bianchi wrote of the original Nathaniel Dickinson that "he appears to have dominated to a large extent the organization of his own world in his own time." Nathaniel had ten children, and families of nine or ten children became common among his descendants. So many of his heirs stayed in the Amherst area that by the 1880s a family historian could write that in central Massachusetts the Dickinsons "threatened to choke out all other forms of vegetation." In reporting on a Dickinson reunion held in Amherst in August 1883, the *Boston Journal* observed that "we may well doubt whether the Dickinsons belonged to Amherst or Amherst to the Dickinsons." At a Dickinson family reunion in 1933, Bianchi noted, "Our names outnumber even those of Smith in the telephone book, without counting those of us who have married into another family, and are a perplexity to strangers."

For many generations the Dickinsons farmed the land, remaining active in civic affairs and committed to the covenantal faith of their Puritan ancestors. Only in the generation of Emily Dickinson's grandfather, Samuel Fowler Dickinson, did some members of the Dickinson family begin to forsake farming for the professions. Following the lead of his older brother Timothy, Samuel entered college and eventually graduated second in his class from Dartmouth in 1795.

In selecting Dartmouth, Samuel Fowler Dickinson and his family chose to align themselves with the heritage of the colonial revival known as the Great Awakening. While the older Congregational colleges, Harvard and Yale, were skeptical of the emotions of revivalism, Dartmouth and other institutions had risen up to champion the Awakening. When he graduated from Dartmouth, Samuel Fowler Dickinson decided to follow his older brother into the ministry. Within a year, however, he gave up training for the pastorate and turned his attention to the law, thus setting the course for his family in Amherst for the next century. His son, Edward, and grandson, Austin, would follow his lead, both in their devoted service to Amherst College and in their legal careers that placed them at the center of Amherst's life. The stage for Emily Dickinson's life was set, then, when her grandfather left the ministry and entered the law in Amherst at the beginning of the nineteenth century.

Emily's grandfather was a brilliant man who struggled with conflicting impulses and demands throughout his life. Samuel Fowler Dickinson's ambition initially found a satisfactory outlet in the practice of law and political affairs in Amherst. After his marriage to Lucretia Gunn in 1802, Dickinson quickly rose to the top of his profession in the town. It was not long before his became one of the wealthiest Amherst families. By 1813, when Emily's father Edward was only ten, her grandfather had achieved such success that he was able to build the impressive Dickinson Homestead on Main Street several hundred yards east of the center of the town. This imposing structure was the first brick house in Amherst and was to be Emily Dickinson's home for all but fifteen years of her life.

Yet even as his legal career flourished, Samuel Fowler Dickinson felt driven to pursue loftier aims. There was in him a quality of restlessness that was passed down directly to Emily's father, brother, and herself. As a college graduate who had trained for the ministry and the law, Dickinson sought to advance both the Kingdom of God and the American republic through the establishment of a college in the Connecticut River valley. His tireless labors upon behalf of Amherst College were motivated in good measure by the postmillennial heritage that he shared with other New England Congregationalists of his day. Dickinson, Noah Webster, and others interpreted the moral, political, and economic prosperity of the new republic as a sign that God was about to establish the Kingdom foretold by John Winthrop two centuries earlier. In the words of the first historian of Amherst College, "the conversion of the world often pressed heavily on [Samuel Fowler Dickinson's] mind." He viewed Amherst as "one of the agencies that would surely hasten that promised event."

The realities of Emily Dickinson's evangelical Protestant inheritance run counter to many established conceptions about her religious life. It has become commonplace to claim that she was the product of a harsh Puritan environment that stifled her spirit and inspired her poetic rebellion. In her home, church, and school, young Emily supposedly had a rigid Calvinism drummed into her. With its visions of a terrifying hell and a dour heaven, this dire Puritanism oppressed the gifted young woman. Only through heroic resistance, the argument goes, did Dickinson manage to define herself in contradiction to it. Her eventual choice of a poetic career, her embrace of solitude, and her alleged lesbian practices, among other things, have been attributed to her revolt against the tyranny of an overbearing creed.

To be sure, the Puritan legacy was still strong in the Connecticut River valley in Emily Dickinson's day, and many of the poet's personal traits and poetic practices show the imprint of that heritage. Her poetry, as we shall see, was shaped in complex ways by the Trinitarian theology that had been preached from the pulpits for two centuries before her in the Connecticut River valley. Her complex understandings of God, self, nature, and human destiny were all influenced in manifold ways by the Reformation tradition that permeated life in the towns of western Massachusetts. Like many significant literary figures in nineteenth-century England and America, Dickinson adapted and transformed that inherited faith in her art, where its imprint remains clear and unmistakable.

To understand Emily Dickinson's life, however, it is crucial to note that by the time she was born in 1830, the transformation from the austere Calvinism of Jonathan Edwards to a more genteel Christian profession was well under way in the Amherst area. Edwards, who died in 1758, had promoted a majestic vision of God's economy; in the scheme of things as he envisioned it, the human will stood naked and vulnerable before the throne of God. "Natural men are held in the hand of God over the pit of hell," his most famous sermon asserted. "They have no refuge, nothing to take hold of, all that preserves them every moment is the mere arbitrary will, and uncovenanted unobliged

11

forbearance of an incensed God." Edwardsean Calvinism offered a bracing theological vision that demanded a great deal of the wounded rebel and promised even more to the repentant sinner. With its stringent diagnosis of sin, it labored to expose the gaping wound of the human will and applied the crucified and risen Christ as the only salve for that wound.

Gradually by the end of the eighteenth century and more rapidly in the first decades of the nineteenth, Edwards's descendants had begun to blunt the edge of the scalpel he had used to cut into the New England soul. Edwards's incisive depiction of the will in bondage to sin seemed poorly suited to the needs of the church in a nascent republic; instead, what the new nation needed was a clear vision of the social usefulness of Christian faith. "How does religion make a man useful to his fellow?" asked Edwards's grandson, Timothy Dwight, in "Farmer Johnson's Political Catechism." The answer: "By rendering him just, sincere, faithful, kind and public-spirited, from principle. It induces him voluntarily, and always, to perform faithfully in the several duties of social life."

Over the course of the first several decades of the nineteenth century, the transformation of the Edwardsean legacy continued across New England. Following the lead of Dwight and others, evangelical Christians sought increasingly to link church and society by stressing the moral improvement of the self rather than the inscrutable will and character of God. By promoting moral reform, ministers thought they could both strengthen the tie between a distant God and everyday life and bolster the waning influence of the church in a democratic culture. Gradually, "with passing decades," writes historian James Turner, "Evangelical millennialism merged imperceptibly into a more secular idea of progress. . . . At times, they [Evangelicals] almost identified growing prosperity, increasing knowledge, and improving social organization with the perfecting of the earth supposed to presage the millennium."

Emily Dickinson's immediate ancestors found little to object to in the theological changes taking place around them; indeed, especially in the case of her grandfather, they eagerly supported efforts to have their Calvinist heritage recast to bear the imprint of newly minted republican ideals. In the first several decades of the nineteenth century, the Dickinsons were, like many well-situated families in Congregational New England, Whiggish in their politics and New School Calvinist in their theology. The Whig ideal provided for these antebellum New Englanders a means of securing the social order for divinely appointed ends without emphasizing the more abstruse or embarrassing elements of the Puritan theological tradition. In the words of historian Louise Stevenson, "Whiggery stood for the triumph of the cosmopolitan and national over the provincial and local, of rational order over irrational spontaneity, of school-based learning over traditional folkways and custom, and of self-control over self-expression." It was the ideal faith for men of the rising professional class in the early nineteenth-century New England village, and it would prove to be a superb foil for Emily Dickinson, the greatest poet of the age.

For southern New England in general and the Dickinson family in particular, Yale College led the way in uniting Whiggery and New School Calvinism. Edward Dickinson graduated from Yale in 1823, and from 1840 to 1878 — virtually the whole of Emily Dickinson's adolescence and adulthood — the pulpit of the First Church of Amherst was filled by Yale graduates. It was at Yale, under the leadership of Timothy Dwight and Nathaniel Taylor, that the heirs of Edwards attempted to sustain his influence by modifying his teachings. Called New School Calvinists, these Yale theologians and their supporters had it as their objective "to blend the activist, voluntarist ambitions, fluid attitudes of nineteenth-century America, with the religious doctrines of the Reformation," argues Daniel Walker Howe. "Broadly stated, this meant formulating into a religious ideology the culture associated with Whiggery."

The theological milieu in which Emily Dickinson was raised, then, was dramatically different from the Calvinist world of William Bradford, Anne Bradstreet, or Jonathan Edwards. A curious mix of Whig republicanism and evangelical moralism framed the religious debate in her home, church, and village. If Dickinson was reacting against anything in her adult struggles with the church, it was against this alloy of elements rather than against the undiluted Calvinism of an earlier age.

The speech delivered by the famed lexicographer Noah Webster at the dedication of Amherst College in 1820 displays a perfect blend of Whig goals and evangelical principles. Webster was a close associate of Samuel Fowler Dickinson, and his granddaughter was to be one of Emily Dickinson's closest childhood friends. In his dedicatory speech,

13

Webster set forth the task of Amherst College as "that of educating for the gospel ministry young men in indigent circumstances, but of hopeful piety and promising talents"; he described that mission as "one of the noblest which can occupy the attention and claim the contributions of the Christian public." With deliberate echoes of the millennial and imperial imagery of his Puritan forebears, Webster depicted the college's efforts as seconding those of "the apostles themselves, in extending and establishing the Redeemer's empire — the empire of truth."

The truth to be discovered and propagated by Amherst College was to be not a body of doctrine but a way of life. Webster defined the mission of the college as a work of social improvement: "It is to aid in the important work of raising the human race from ignorance and debasement; to enlighten their minds; to exalt their character; and to teach them the way to happiness and glory." The benefits of an Amherst education were to spread throughout society; eventually the college would even help to "dispeople the state prison and the penitentiary!"

The goals of Amherst College's founders were impossibly ambitious, and Samuel Fowler Dickinson came close to ruining himself and his family in pursuing them. For several years Emily's grandfather was embroiled in disputes concerning the manner in which he and others had solicited funds for the new college. A special committee of the Massachusetts legislature was formed to investigate the charges, and though Dickinson was eventually exonerated, his reputation had been badly sullied by the affair. In addition, to help finish the necessary work to open the college, Dickinson had put up his own property as collateral for loans, had provided his own horses and laborers for the construction project, and had taken a number of the workmen on as boarders at no charge. "His large-heartedness and desire to help those in need sometimes overtaxed his judgment," one of his descendants wrote of him in August 1883, "and his name was often endorsed on notes to a large amount, which he was obliged to furnish the money for, while several men thus helped lived in affluence on his bounty, without recognizing the source."

Not surprisingly, Samuel Fowler Dickinson's difficulties caused problems for his eldest son, Edward. While the latter was enrolled at Yale in the early 1820s, his father sent him letters filled with complaints about money. Repeatedly, Samuel prodded Edward to find cheaper ways to travel home and to cut his expenses at school. At one point, he warned Edward that he might have to withdraw from Yale: "What may be my determination respecting your continuance at N[ew] H[aven] I do not know — this must be left till we see how things shall be at Amherst — One reason seems, however, almost unanswerable — necessity — inability to supply the money necessary at N[ew] H[aven]."

Reckless in the expenditure of his energy and funds on behalf of Amherst College, Samuel Fowler Dickinson was forced in 1833 to leave Amherst, at the age of 57. He, his wife, and their youngest children moved to Cincinnati, Ohio, where he served as the superintendent of labor and building at the new Lane Theological Seminary under its first president, Lyman Beecher. Within several years, he left Lane and traveled north to become the treasurer of Western Reserve College. He fared no better there than he had at Amherst College and Lane Seminary. Of Samuel Dickinson's tenure, the official historian of Western Reserve was to write that "his experience was insufficient for the position and his health was poor. He died in the second year of service leaving his accounts in a sorry mess."

While Samuel Fowler Dickinson was floundering in Ohio, his son Edward was doing what he could to restore the family name back home. Born in 1803, Edward was the only one of the nine children of Samuel and Lucretia Gunn Dickinson to make Amherst his permanent home. When he graduated from Yale in 1823, he returned to the village to study law, beginning a practice there in 1826. Though he never admitted it to be the case, Edward Dickinson may have returned to Amherst to restore the family's reputation, which had been so badly damaged by his father's failure. If that was his goal, he met and exceeded it impressively. He established himself as a highly successful lawyer, served as treasurer of Amherst College for almost four decades, and attained political prominence at the state and national levels.

On May 6, 1828, not long after he had begun his law practice in Amherst, Edward Dickinson married Emily Norcross of nearby Monson after a two-year courtship. The letters they wrote to each other during that courtship reveal two young adults well versed in the Whig virtues of prudence and self-restraint. In the history of Emily Dickinson criticism, the complaints against her parents run deep, with Edward in particular being singled out for his "harsh," "tyrannical," or "Puritanical" attitudes. His letters to Emily Norcross during their engagement, however, show a different man. They rarely mention God or anything that might be construed as Calvinist doctrine but contain countless references to "piety," "virtue," "universal benevolence," and "rational happiness." If Edward Dickinson was austere to the point of severity, his courtship letters indicate that his cramped personality and sober Whiggish views, rather than a rigid orthodoxy, made him so.

As a case in point, early in their relationship, Edward sent to Emily Norcross a letter containing an extended discourse on the beauty of "a virtuous life, correct deportment, & an universal benevolence." In naming the "object [for] which men were sent into the world," he cited "devot[ing] our lives to the improvement of our species" and "attempting to lead them into the paths of happiness." Less than two months before their wedding, he wrote of marriage as "the most interesting of all earthly relations — Let us prepare for a life of rational happiness. I do not expect, neither do I desire a life of *pleasure.*" Instead, he outlined his plan to engage "my whole soul in my business" and to pass whatever time might be spared from that "in the enjoyment which arises from an unreserved interchange of sentiment with My dearest friend — May we be happy & useful and successful, and each be an ornament in society — ." This is not the stark language of Puritan self-scrutiny but the polite discourse of Whig self-restraint.

Once Edward Dickinson and Emily Norcross were married in the spring of 1828, children followed in quick order — a son, William Austin, in 1829, and daughters, Emily Elizabeth, in 1830, and Lavinia Norcross, in 1833. By the age of thirty, with three healthy children, a thriving law practice, and excellent political prospects, Edward Dickinson seemed to have done a great deal to rebuild his family's name and fortunes. A man of probity and caution, he conducted himself throughout his adult life with a scrupulosity that would ensure that no one would write of him, as they had of his father, that he left his "accounts in a sorry mess." He would have been pleased with the judgment passed upon him by the first historian of Amherst College: "as Treasurer of Amherst College, he has never lost a dollar."

For virtually the entire nineteenth century, Dickinson men served as lawyers of stature in Amherst and vital figures in the early history of Amherst College. They and their families remained rooted to that rural spot, while the nation around them underwent enormous changes. "No Dickinson, at least in this branch of the family, flourished outside beloved Amherst," explains Richard Sewall. When the men did travel, their letters recorded their homesick displeasure. When Emily's brother Austin took a long trip through the South and Midwest in 1887, his letters were filled with loathing for the places he visited and with longing for home. "I am lost to be off in this way, without a connecting link with any usual experience," he complained only a few days out from Amherst. "No boy let out of school was ever more glad than I shall be to get the whole trip behind me." To this child of Amherst, the whole of the Midwest was "just a great, nasty, horrid human hoggery," and the deep South seemed populated by human creatures "which one's respect for his creator forbids him to believe God ever made, but are the result of some evolution, or the device of the Devil."

The realities of the lives of Emily Dickinson's grandfather, father, and brother put into perspective both the poet's own disdain for travel and her love of home. In outline form, the story of Dickinson's reclusiveness is familiar to many: except for one academic year at the Mount Holyoke Female Seminary and two extended visits to Boston for eye care in the mid-1860s, Emily Dickinson lived at home with her family for her entire life. In her thirties, she secluded herself so completely within her parents' home that few outside her family were ever to see her again. Her retreat became so total that she left the grounds of her home only once in her last twenty years.

In choosing seclusion, Emily appropriated and intensified a family tendency and developed it to the fullest possible extent. Like her brother and father, Emily had little good to say about travel and preferred the security of home. When Thomas Wentworth Higginson met the poet for the first time in 1870, he asked "if she never felt want of employment, never going off the place & never seeing any visitor." No, she said, " 'I never thought of conceiving that I could ever have the slightest approach to such a want in all future time' (& added) 'I feel that I have not expressed myself strongly enough.' " A few months later, she wrote to one of her closest friends that she had no need of travel, for "to shut our eyes is Travel. The seasons understand this."

"I do not go away, but the Grounds are ample — almost travel — to me, and the few that I knew — came — since my Father died," Emily explained in 1881. Her family and a select circle of friends, most of whom she knew chiefly through correspondence, were to comprise Emily Dickinson's world in adulthood. To understand and explore the world, she felt she needed to have nothing more than what her ordinary experience and her imaginative powers provided her. She had no desire to travel back in time through history or across vast stretches of the nation expanding around her. "I like travelling," Edward Dickinson wrote to his pregnant wife in May of 1830, "but *home* has charms for me, which I do not find abroad." What was true for the father would be infinitely more the case for the daughter about to be born into the Dickinson family.

2 The Child's Faith Is New

The Child's faith is new —
Whole — like His Principle —
Wide — like the Sunrise
On fresh Eyes —
Never had a Doubt —
Laughs — at a Scruple —
Believes all sham
But Paradise — [#637]

THOUGH NESTLED AMONG the beautiful hills of the Connecticut
River valley, the village of Amherst was not an attractive place
when Edward and Emily Norcross Dickinson settled down to raise a
family there in the late 1820s. The town was hardly a thriving center
of commercial activity, and it was decidedly not the tidy village of
popular New England lore.

In 1830, the year in which Emily Dickinson was born, some 2,600
people lived in Amherst, which consisted of a bare, unkempt common,
a small commercial center, a few churches, assorted buildings attached
to the struggling college, dirt roads, footpaths, and a number of isolated

homes and farmhouses. Amherst had no rail service until 1853, no telegraph office until 1861, and no permanent bank until 1864. In every way, it was set apart from the manufacturing and mercantile centers of the eastern seaboard. Only one hundred miles to the east, Salem and Boston had developed into centers of international trade and transport, while Amherst remained an outpost on the agricultural frontier. In the words of a noted later resident of the town, in the middle decades of the nineteenth century "Amherst was hardly more than a cluster of farms, each with its woodshed, barn and outhouses."

The best description we have of Amherst as it was in Emily Dickinson's childhood is contained in *Mercy Philbrick's Choice,* a novel by Helen Hunt Jackson, an Amherst native. In the novel, we see Amherst through the eyes of Mercy Philbrick on her first visit to the town. She steps out onto the piazza of the hotel after breakfast and begins "scanning with a keen and eager glance every feature of the scene. To her eyes, accustomed to the broad, open, leisurely streets of the Cape Cod hamlet, its isolated little houses with their trim flower-beds in front and their punctiliously kept fences and gates," Amherst looks positively "unattractive."

Everywhere that Mercy peers, she witnesses a world in disarray. Straight in front of her is "a poorly kept, oblong-shaped 'common,' some few acres in extent." Two cows blithely roam the grounds unimpeded by "fences [that] were sadly out of repair." Near the broken-down fences, "a few shabby old farm-wagons stood here and there," their horses being "tethered in some mysterious way to the hinder part of the wagons." The local court is in session, and these weary horses and decrepit wagons belong both to the lawyers trying the cases and to their clients, "alike humble in their style of equipage."

Running away from the hotel, down the eastern slope of the hill, is "an irregular block of brick buildings, no two of a height or size." After fires had decimated portions of this row of buildings, "each owner had rebuilt as much or as little as he chose." The result is "as incoherent a bit of architecture as is often seen . . . , so that the block itself seemed to be sliding down hill." And "to add to the queerness of this 'Brick Row,'" signs of every kind — "alphabetical, allegorical, and symbolic" — had been plastered on the facades of the sloping buildings, thus making the "whole front of the Row look at a little distance like a wall of advertisements of some traveling menagerie."

On the other side of the common, opposite the hotel, was a row of dwelling-houses, which owing to the steep descent had a sunken look, as if they were slipping into their own cellars. The grass was too green in their yards, and the thick, matted plantain-leaves grew on both edges of the sodden sidewalk. . . .

To the south, there was again a slight depression; and the houses, although of a better order than those on the eastern side of the common, had somewhat of the same sunken air.

"MEMORY DRAPES HER LIPS"

A few hundred yards to the east of this center of Amherst, Emily Elizabeth Dickinson was born at 5 a.m. on Friday, December 10, 1830. She came into the world only months after her father, mother, and older brother had moved into one half of Samuel Fowler Dickinson's home on Main Street. When Emily was born, her father owned the western half, while her grandfather and grandmother lived on the other side with their youngest children. In little more than two years, the Dickinsons, father and son, would be forced to sell the home. Emily and her family would remain in the home as tenants until she was almost ten.

As one might expect with a second child born to a family struggling to repair damages to its fortunes, Emily's early years were largely unremarkable. There are only a few isolated references to her in the surviving correspondence from her relatives and immediate family. The first recorded words of hers are in letters written by her aunt Lavinia Norcross, who had taken Emily to live with her when Mrs. Dickinson had trouble recovering from the birth of her third child, Lavinia, in 1833. On their way to nearby Monson, aunt and niece were caught in a thunderstorm. Two-year-old "[Emily] Elizabeth called it *the fire*" and "felt inclined to be frightened some — she said 'Do take me to my mother.'" Days later, Aunt Lavinia reported that Emily "has learned to play on the piano — she calls it the *moosic*." In every way, she seemed to be "a very good child & but little trouble — . . . She has a fine appetite & sleeps well & I take satisfaction in taking care of her." (It is worth noting that even at this early date, family members were worried about the emotional balance of Mrs. Dickinson; while caring for Emily, Lavinia Norcross admonished her sister, "You must not

21

worry your-self more than you can help — for there is nothing so wearing as anxiety — .")

Dickinson's adult recollections of her own childhood point to nothing more than the customary terrors and delights of early life. For example, Dickinson wrote years later to her cousins that when she was a baby, "father used to take me to mill for my health. I was then in consumption! While he obtained the 'grist,' the horse looked round at me, as if to say "'eye hath not seen or ear heard the things that' I would do to you if I weren't tied!'" In some cases in her memory, fear is traced to its religious source: "When a few years old — I was taken to a Funeral which I now know was of peculiar distress, and the Clergyman asked 'Is the Arm of the Lord shortened that it cannot save?'" A similar incident is recorded in a fragment the poet left behind at death:

> We said she said Lord Jesus — receive my Spirit — We were put in separate rooms to expiate our temerity and thought how hateful Jesus must be to get us into trouble when we had done nothing but Crucify him and that before we were born.

A final fragment sums up the mystery of childhood and memory for the adult poet:

> Two things I have lost with Childhood — the rapture of losing my shoe in the Mud and going Home barefoot, wading for Cardinal flowers and the mothers reproof which was more for my sake than her weary own for she frowned with a smile [now Mother and Cardinal flower are parts of a closed world —] But is that all I have lost — memory drapes her Lips.

The imagery Dickinson employs here to describe her adult memory of a lost childhood is revealing. Her phrase "memory drapes her Lips" calls to mind similar language from her poems and letters, for she frequently employed images of dumb silence to depict God, nature, and the dead. Just as her own childhood was muffled in memory, the great divine and natural forces arrayed against her often seemed mute. "I know that He exists/Somewhere — in Silence — /He has hid his rare life," one poem reports of God [#338]; another asks of the "Bees," "In those dim countries where they go,/What word had they, for me?"

[#348]; and from the dead person, whose mouth is "the awful rivet" and whose lips are "hasps of steel," one can expect no answer to one's questions: "How many times these low feet staggered — /Only the soldered mouth can tell" [#187]. For the dead about to go to heaven and meet God, Dickinson has many questions:

> That could I snatch Their Faces
> That could Their lips reply
> Not till the last was answered
> Should They start for the Sky. [#900]

But those lips, of course, would make no reply.

Dickinson refused to sentimentalize the silence by putting words into the mouths of the mute realities she questioned. That refusal put her at odds with the romantic poetic tradition and with the sentimental culture of the mid-nineteenth century. Where she detected silence, they heard voices everywhere. While Dickinson could never get past the "awful rivet" of "the soldered mouth," William Wordsworth, for instance, had a robust romantic confidence that the living could commune with the dead. In the words of critic Gerald Bruns, Wordsworth was "a connoisseur of epitaphs" who felt that an epitaph could both "resurrect the mind of the person whose remains lie a few feet below" and allow the "writers of epitaphs [to] speak in their own voices." To the "cottage girl" of Wordsworth's "We Are Seven," there is no distinction between her dead siblings and her living ones. She knits her stockings, eats her supper, and plays her games in the churchyard where her brother and sister are buried, and stubbornly considers the deceased to be active members of the family:

> "But they are dead; those two are dead!
> Their spirits are in heaven!"
> 'Twas throwing words away; for still
> The little Maid would have her will,
> And said, "Nay, we are seven!"

To Dickinson, the problem with the romantic view of childhood was its naiveté. It was not possible, she held as an adult, to recapture the winsome innocence of those early years. If childhood spoke at all to the adult, it did so in a language that he or she could no longer take refuge in:

> The Child's faith is new —
> Whole — like His Principle —
> Wide — like the Sunrise
> On fresh Eyes —
> Never had a Doubt —
> Laughs — at a Scruple —
> Believes all sham
> But Paradise —
>
> Credits the World —
> Deems His Dominion
> Broadest of Sovereignties —
> And Caesar — mean —
> In the Comparison —
> Baseless Emperor —
> Ruler of Nought,
> Yet swaying all —
>
> Grown bye and bye
> To hold mistaken
> His pretty estimates
> Of Prickly Things
> He gains the skill
> Sorrowful — as certain —
> Men — to anticipate
> Instead of Kings — [#637]

Illuminated by unassuming faith, the child of this poem looks upon the world with "fresh Eyes," which shed an aura of enchantment about them. The "Sovereign" world projected by childish sight makes Caesar look "mean" by comparison and everything else seem "sham but Paradise." But with the coming of consciousness, the light dims and the world grows dark, for the "grown" child finally apprehends the creative, distorting power of sight. The child's vision had been "mistaken" in taking "pretty estimates/Of Prickly Things." In acquiring the "skill" that is as "Sorrowful — as certain — " the adult at last sees things as they are.

Dickinson's treatment of childhood, of her own in particular and of the phenomenon in general, is but one of many signs of her uneasiness with romantic assumptions about the innocent power of the self. For the whole of her adult life, she was torn between her romantic aspirations and her realistic apprehensions. She yearned to share the faith that Wordsworth, Emerson, and Thoreau had in the unaided human consciousness, but her sense of human limitation would not let her do so. As literary critic Albert Gelpi argues, Dickinson's "peculiar burden was to be a Romantic poet with a Calvinist's sense of things; to know transitory ecstasy in a world tragically fallen and doomed."

Like the romantic poets and philosophers, Dickinson considered the central human dilemma to be a problem of knowledge rather than a matter of the will. That is, she came to regard ignorance as a greater problem than sin and held out more hope for the change of perception than for the transformation of the will. But at the same time, Dickinson could not accept the romantics' optimism about the self. Apprehending the limits of memory and death, she knew that though it was a joy to "anticipate kings," those kings never arrived. By the time she became a young adult, she had learned too well the lessons of the "skill sorrowful." "But it is my nature always to anticipate more than I realize," she wrote of herself at fifteen. As she matured, young Emily Dickinson would learn repeatedly how bitingly true this self-assessment was.

LEARNING THE WAYS OF DISENCHANTMENT

Death was to serve as one of Emily Dickinson's earliest and most effective teachers, drilling its lessons home even in her adolescence. In the mid-nineteenth century, the life expectancy of a newborn child was little more than half what it is today. In that era before antibiotics and modern surgical procedures, young children were especially vulnerable, and it was a rare young adult who had not lost at least several beloved friends or family members. And when death struck, it did not visit in the distant sterility of a hospital but invaded the intimacy of the home. For a young girl coming of age in mid-nineteenth-century New

25

England, there were many opportunities to be trained in "The Science of the Grave" that "No Man can understand" [#539].

In the nineteenth century, it was the custom for family members or friends to keep a "watch" at the bedside of a gravely ill person. New Englanders had long been schooled in the *ars moriendi,* the "art of dying" from which the living were meant to draw lasting lessons of faith. One of Emily Dickinson's closest friends (and future sister-in-law), Susan Gilbert, kept two such vigils and later referred to them as "the two most terrifying nights of her life." When she was thirteen, Emily herself watched as the health of her friend Sophia Holland failed. "I visited her often in sickness & watched over her bed," she recalled two years later. When Sophia lost consciousness — "at length Reason fled" — her doctor would not let anyone enter her room. Emily was determined, however, to see her friend again, and eventually was permitted "to look at her a moment through the open door. I took off my shoes and stole softly to the sick room."

"There she lay mild & beautiful. . . . I looked as long as friends would permit," Dickinson explained. She did not shed a tear when Sophia died, "for my heart was too full to weep, but after she was laid in her coffin & I felt I could not call her back again I gave way to a fixed melancholy." Emily "told no one the cause of my grief, though it was gnawing at my very heart strings." Having kept the secret of her sadness from her family, she suffered in solitude. Her melancholy eventually proved so strong that her parents sent her to stay with her aunt Lavinia Norcross in Boston for the better part of a month.

Death had been something of a regular presence for young Emily since 1840, when her family moved from the Homestead on Main Street to a newly purchased dwelling less than a mile away. This house bordered on the Amherst cemetery, and from its windows the adolescent Emily watched a steady stream of funeral processions. "I have just seen a funeral procession go by," she wrote at fifteen to her friend Abiah Root, ". . . so if my ideas are rather dark you need not marvel." The darkness of the mood quickly gave way to playfulness, as the cemetery procession made Emily dream of deathlessness: "I have lately come to the conclusion that I am Eve, alias Mrs. Adam. You know there is no account of her death in the Bible, and why am not I Eve?" Yet only weeks later, Emily was back at it again, writing Abiah another long letter whose major theme was death. As she mused on death and everlasting life, she told Abiah that "yesterday as I sat by the north window the funeral train entered the open gate of the church yard, following the remains of Judge Dickinson's wife to her long home."

In fixing her attention upon death as she did, the adolescent Emily Dickinson was following the ghoulish fashion of her day. What critic Ann Douglas has called "the domestication of death" progressed at a rapid pace in the decades leading up to the Civil War. Instead of the stoic, sober acceptance of death that had been the norm in the Puritan past, there was in mid-nineteenth-century America a concerted effort to drain it of its terror by denying its power. Puritan attitudes toward death had been driven by the fear of hell and the hope of heaven; death was accepted as a hard reality to be overcome only through the power of God to raise the dead. In Dickinson's lifetime, efforts focused instead on smothering the sting of death with sentimental pieties. In the years that she was growing to maturity, there developed an elaborate body of the literature of consolation as well as a new set of therapeutic attitudes toward death, burial, and the afterlife. Emily Dickinson grew up in a culture in which, in the words of one observer, "dying was a way of being 'born to the purple,' a coronation as much as a crucifixion."

Dickinson appropriated the new sentimental customs of her day up to a point. When she was fifteen, she made a pilgrimage to Mt. Auburn cemetery in Cambridge, Massachusetts, while visiting her aunt and uncle. Officially opened in 1831, Mt. Auburn was the first of many rural cemeteries in America. Up to that time, the local churchyard had served as the burial ground for each community, but the opening of Mt. Auburn marked a dramatic shift in burial practices and mourning rituals. The purpose of the rural cemetery was to blur distinctions between death and life. The bucolic settings of these cemeteries, complete with winding paths, gentle slopes, and the profusion of graveside flowers, were meant to reassure the living about the sweet comforts of the dead. Theodore Cuyler, a prominent New York minister, wrote of visiting the grave of his son in Greenwood cemetery: "The air was as silent as the unnumbered sleepers around me; and turning toward the sacred spot where my precious dead was lying, I bade him, as of old, *Goodnight!*" It was as though his son had simply gone to a summer camp or boarding school, for the cemetery was "simply a vast and exquisitely beautiful dormitory."

Having visited Mt. Auburn in the summer of 1846, Dickinson wrote enthusiastically to Abiah Root about the experience. She called Mt. Auburn the "City of the Dead" and was struck by the fitting beauty of the place. "It seems as if Nature had formed the spot with a distinct idea in view of its being a resting place for her children," she explained, making curious use of the argument from design to explain the comfort she derived from the cemetery. In this garden, the "wearied and disappointed" dead can "stretch themselves beneath the spreading cypress & close their eyes 'calmly as to a nights repose or flowers at set of sun.'" Death as a painless slumber or the setting sun — these are standard images of the literature of consolation and domesticated death.

Yet in the same letter, Dickinson showed how she had already gone beyond the sentimental limits of her day. Near the letter's close, her thoughts about the passing of the seasons led Dickinson to paraphrase several lines from *Night Thoughts*, by the eighteenth-century English poet Edward Young. "We take no note of Time but from its loss," she wrote to Abiah Root. "Pay no moment but in just purchase of it's worth & what it's worth, ask death beds. They can tell. Part with it as with life reluctantly." But at this point, instead of resigning herself to mortality and giving up all for Christ, Dickinson stood her ground and told Abiah, "I have not yet made my peace with God. . . . I feel that the world holds a predominant place in my affections. I do not feel that I could give up all for Christ, were I called to die." While her culture was increasingly striving to make death seem enchanting, Dickinson found her sense of disenchantment deepening, as she weighed the delights of this world and considered the grave cost of their loss:

> Love can do all but raise the Dead
> I doubt if even that
> From such a giant were withheld
> Were flesh equivalent
>
> But love is tired and must sleep,
> And hungry and must Graze
> And so abets the shining Fleet
> Till it is out of gaze. [#1731]

Dickinson's adolescent responses to death — alternating between melancholy disenchantment and angry disbelief — would remain throughout her adulthood. Those early encounters with death contributed to the sense she shared with her Enlightenment and romantic predecessors that finitude rather than sin was the fundamental human dilemma. For the adult Dickinson, it was not the perversity of the will but the inevitability of death that could make life unbearable and heaven necessary. Without death, earth would have been enough, she thought. "If roses had not faded, and frosts had never come, and one had not fallen here and there whom I could not waken, there were no need of other Heaven than the one below," Dickinson wrote to a friend in 1856, "and if God had been here this summer, and seen the things that *I* have seen — I guess that He would think His Paradise superfluous." Were it not for death, the world might remain enchanted and God himself become a relic.

Like her views on childhood, Dickinson's understanding of death marked her as a true product of modernity. In *The Nature and Destiny of Man*, Reinhold Niebuhr notes that with the Renaissance, first, and then the Enlightenment, the revival of ancient Greek ideas led to a significant change in Western beliefs about evil and death. At their center, both Enlightenment rationalism and romantic intuitionism represented modern variations upon ancient Greek beliefs that "consider man's involvement in nature as the very cause of evil, and define the ultimate redemption of life as emancipation from finiteness." As theologian Emil Brunner explains, the Christian faith historically has consistently posited "a clear relation between sin and death. 'The wages of sin is death'" (Romans 6:23). Dickinson never accepted that connection. It simply did not make sense to her: "'Whom he loveth, he punisheth,' is a doubtful solace finding tart response in the lower Mind." And because she rejected the tie between sin and death, Dickinson was to find it difficult to see the connection between suffering and truth. The fact of suffering she knew all too well; the truth to which it pointed, however, remained hidden:

> Of God we ask one favor,
> That we may be forgiven —
> For what, he is presumed to know —
> The Crime, from us, is hidden —

29

> Immured the whole of Life
> Within a magic Prison
> We reprimand the Happiness
> That too competes with Heaven. [#1601]

It was not only a preoccupation with mortality and the fading of life's splendor that led to the disenchantment of the young Emily Dickinson; her formal education also played a crucial role in teaching her "Men — to anticipate/Instead of Kings — ." From that education she acquired a keen sensitivity to science and a deep interest in languages and literature. In her eight years of formal schooling at the Amherst Academy and Mount Holyoke Female Seminary, Dickinson developed her extraordinary intellectual powers and sharpened her awareness of the limits set to those powers by nature and the social order she inhabited. The formal training ended when Emily was only seventeen, after her first year at Mount Holyoke, but its influence can be traced throughout her poetic career.

Dickinson was nine when she entered the Amherst Academy, and in her years there she studied a broad curriculum that included Latin, Greek, geography, ancient history, botany, physiology, and English grammar. She thrived in this environment, where the teachers were excellent, many of them being recent graduates of Amherst College. The course work was challenging and sufficiently interesting for someone of Dickinson's abilities. In one of her earliest letters, eleven-year-old Emily told her friend Jane Humphrey, "I am in the class that you used to be in in Latin — besides Latin I study History and Botany I like the school very much indeed — ."

This same letter to Jane Humphrey also gives evidence of the critical playfulness already developing in the precocious Emily Dickinson. She told her friend that in that afternoon's "Speaking and Composition" section, one "young man" read a "Composition the Subject was think twice before you speak — ." The boy spoke of a young gentleman who "knows a young lady who he thinks nature has formed to perfection let him remember that roses conceal thorns." Emily would not accept this slight without her own retort. "He is the sillyest creature that ever lived I think," she explained to Jane. "I told him that I thought he had better think twice before he spoke — ." Even at an early age, Dickinson was never at a loss for words.

By all accounts, Dickinson was an outstanding student. Shortly after her death in 1886, one of her early principals at the Amherst Academy, Daniel Taggart Fiske, set down his "very distinct and pleasant impressions" of the young Emily Dickinson. "I remember her as a very bright, but rather delicate and frail looking girl," he wrote, "an excellent scholar, of exemplary deportment, faithful in all school duties; but somewhat shy and nervous. Her compositions were strikingly original; and in both thought and style seemed beyond her years, and always attracted much attention in the school and, I am afraid, excited not a little envy."

Emily enjoyed her studies and impressed her peers and teachers, but her education was to equip her in ways her father and grandfather may not have anticipated. The Dickinson men were fervent supporters of women's education at a time when the practice had many detractors, but they did not envision it producing spinster skeptics of the kind Emily became. Instead, they saw the education of women as a key link in the chain of virtue in the republic. Through education, the perfection of women's domestic roles could be made complete, Samuel Fowler Dickinson and his son believed.

In a speech delivered less than a year after his granddaughter Emily had been born, Samuel Dickinson vigorously promoted women's education as a means of furthering the glorious work of God in the American republic. "*The whole earth is to be subdued, and made habitable and productive; and its whole population, civilized,*" he exhorted his audience. "Let every one, therefore, gird on his strength; putting forth his first efforts, *on his own farm making Eden his pattern.*" He called for the training of daughters in the "useful sciences," including the study of language, geography, history, mathematics, and moral philosophy. The purpose of that education was clear to him: "the business and cares of a family . . . are among *the first objects* of woman's creation; they ought to be among *the first branches* of her education. *She was made for a mother.*" The irony, of course, is that instead of equipping Emily Dickinson for marriage, formal education deepened her suspicions about the very institutions for which it was intended to fit her.

Of all the subjects that Dickinson studied formally, the natural sciences were to have the most lasting influence in developing her skeptical turn of mind. For nature she had from early childhood a fascination that emerged readily as she grew up in a region of abundant

31

beauty and variety. Dickinson's education, however, trained her to move beyond the simple observation of nature to the complex analysis of it. One of her early biographers, George Whicher, noted that the formal study of science "taught her to look closely at the object before her, to record her observations unchanged, to respect facts."

Throughout her life, Dickinson would remain a close reader of nature's text and a keen chronicler of its activities. Her poetry is replete with observations of natural processes as minute as a spider "sewing at night" and as vast as the "firmaments rowing" their way across the heavens. Of the more than seven hundred words from special sources that Dickinson employed in her poetry, the largest body came from contemporary technology and science. And as the understanding of nature changed radically in her lifetime — particularly in the fields of geology and biology — Dickinson continually gauged the sometimes shocking theological and ethical implications of these changes.

The most important figure in Dickinson's scientific training was Edward Hitchcock, a professor of natural theology and geology at Amherst College for more than three decades and its president from 1845 to 1854. One of the last great pre-Darwinian defenders of the argument from design, Hitchcock had influence far beyond Amherst College. He spent his life building bridges between the Christian faith and science, only to have them swept away in his final years by the Darwinian flood.

In the two decades before Darwin — the years when Dickinson came under Hitchcock's influence — efforts at reconciling science and religion centered upon not biology but geology. Long before the publication of *The Origin of Species* in 1859, geological studies had already undercut the biblical chronology of a six-day creation and belief in a six-thousand-year-old earth. In Sir Charles Lyell's "uniformitarian" understanding of geological processes, wind and water replaced the will of God as the primary agents of change in nature. In Lyell's own words, "all former changes of the organic and inorganic creation are referrible [sic] to one uninterrupted succession of physical events, governed by the laws now in operation." Seen through uniformitarian eyes, the creation of the world was not a miraculous event but an excruciatingly slow process.

Hitchcock sought to reconcile orthodoxy and the new geology by arguing that the long history of the earth was merely one more evidence of the constancy and glory of God. The problems posed by the new geology were only matters of perception and interpretation. "If geology," Hitchcock explained in the opening chapter of his most important book, "or any other science, proves to us that we have not fairly understood the meaning of any passage of Scripture, it merely illustrates, but does not oppose, revelation." According to historian Sydney Ahlstrom, for a brief time in the two decades before the Civil War, the "Hitchcock compromise opened the way to more constructive thought on the relations of science and religion."

To effect the reconciliation he sought, Hitchcock relied upon the argument from design and his own poetic ability to divine the spiritual meanings hidden within the text of nature. In 1850, for example, he published *Religious Lectures on Peculiar Phenomena in the Four Seasons.* Its premise was that each season is laden with theological significance and that spring, with its reality of new life, is the supreme season. The frontispiece of the book had a color engraving by Hitchcock's wife, entitled "Emblems of the Resurrection." It showed a pond in spring with life breaking forth in and around it. A butterfly flutters beneath cocoons attached to a branch, while a frog emerges from the pond, in which tadpoles are swimming. The message is clear — death gives way to life, and in the divine order of things higher life always emerges from lower forms. As a young adult, Dickinson took comfort in Hitchcock's message. Later in life, she confided to a friend that "when Flowers annually died and I was a child, I used to read Dr Hitchcock's Book on the Flowers of North America. This comforted their Absence — assuring me they lived."

Hitchcock's method mattered more to Dickinson than his conclusions. He reinforced her inclination to read nature as a text possessing an abundance of spiritual meanings; he also encouraged her to think of the broad contexts of scientific discoveries. What Hitchcock and the Amherst Academy did for the future poet, explains biographer Richard Sewall, "was to open her eyes, give her a discipline, and set her studies in the largest possible frame of reference."

Soon after Dickinson left the Academy, however, that frame of reference grew incomprehensibly larger than Hitchcock could ever have imagined. Because he died less than five years after the publication of Darwin's *The Origin of Species,* the Amherst geologist was spared the task of trying to harmonize his spiritualizing interpretations of natural

33

phenomena with Darwin's bleak reading of the book of nature. By removing the necessity of a supernatural design and agent, Darwin attacked the very heart of Hitchcock's argument. In an introduction to a modern reprint of Hitchcock's *Religion of Geology,* Conrad Wright points out that it was precisely the "purposive adaptation by God between organisms and their environments . . . that Darwinism cast into question, giving encouragement in the long run to a purely naturalistic world-view."

It was the generation after Hitchcock that had to come to terms with the stark naturalism of the Darwinian universe. It was probably Darwin's vision of reality, for example, that Dickinson had in mind in 1882, when she wrote of the impossibility of tracing any kind of path from nature to the creator: "God's Right Hand . . ./is amputated now/And God cannot be found —" [#1551]. And it was Darwin whom Dickinson cited in that same year, when she described a troubled visit to the Homestead by the widow of a former Amherst College president. "Mrs Dr Stearns called to know if we didnt think it very shocking for [Benjamin F.] Butler to 'liken himself to his Redeemer,'" Dickinson explained, "but we thought Darwin had thrown 'the Redeemer' away." Hitchcock and his generation had taught the adolescent Emily Dickinson the value of reading nature closely; Darwin and others then gave the adult poet a dramatically different code with which to decipher the text.

At many different levels and in many different ways, then, young Emily Dickinson learned "To hold mistaken/[Her] pretty estimates/Of Prickly Things." Through her personal experiences, as well as her immersion in contemporary culture, she acquired an intense fascination with death, as well as a keen awareness of the evanescence of delight, while through her formal education she gained a critical knowledge of the great transformations in nineteenth-century thought. Her sense of loss in these matters was palpable:

> A loss of something ever felt I —
> The first that I could recollect
> Bereft I was — of what I knew not
> Too young that any should suspect
>
> A Mourner walked among the children
> I notwithstanding went about

As one bemoaning a Dominion
Itself the only Prince cast out —

After allowing for hyperbole, we can recognize the underlying melancholy of Dickinson's adolescence in this poem. Even though she is now "Elder . . . wiser/And fainter," she still finds herself "softly searching/For my Delinquent Palaces — " [#959]. Though "Bereft," this "Mourner among the children" is still "searching" for the mystery that will enchant the world once again.

Dickinson was developing in these years a form of what philosopher Hans-Georg Gadamer has called "tragic pensiveness." This quality, Gadamer explains, is what the spectator of a tragic drama learns when he "recognizes himself and his own finiteness in the face of the power of fate" and "emerges with new insight from the illusions in which he, like everyone else, lives." Gadamer calls this insight "religious" and sees it as an essential prerequisite to the proper understanding of nature, texts, and life. Without this insight, one is blind to the undeniable limits that God has placed upon the order of human things. This tragic pensiveness that Gadamer considers foundational to human understanding was an undeniable aspect of Emily Dickinson's ethical and poetic education in mid-nineteenth-century Amherst.

The melancholy that emerged in Emily Dickinson's adolescence was not an uncommon thing, of course, and it should not obscure the fact that her seven years at the Amherst Academy were largely a time of happiness and growth. She blossomed socially and intellectually in the Academy's stimulating academic environment; she acquired there many of her lifelong habits of mind and enduring intellectual interests. The letters she wrote in adolescence were filled with exuberance and displayed an impressive, playful brilliance. Much later, Emily Dickinson was remembered with fondness by those who had known her as a student at the Academy, and her own memories of those years were happy ones.

At the same time, however, it was during this period that young Emily Dickinson began to develop her "skill" of disenchanted understanding. She was losing her "child's faith" and acquiring "through suffering" what Gadamer calls "insight into the limitations of humanity . . . — the kind of insight that gave birth to Greek tragedy." To be certain, it would be many years before such insights would fully ger-

35

minate, but the seeds for the later flowering were planted in her years at the Amherst Academy.

MOUNT HOLYOKE AND MARY LYON

Dickinson finished her final term at the Amherst Academy on August 10, 1847. To mark the end of the year, the school staged an "Exhibition," featuring orations by all members of the graduating class, including sixteen-year-old Emily Dickinson. An Amherst College sophomore recorded the events of the graduation in his diary and expressed special appreciation for the "choir of young girls and several youths" that performed in place of the customary band. In all likelihood, Emily, who already played the piano and sang quite well, was a member of that choir. "They sang most *beautifully*," the Amherst student remarked, "and I thought the music far better adapted to a literary exhibition than the loud noises of martial music."

Her academy exams and graduation ceremonies behind her, Dickinson enjoyed a brief vacation before entering the Mount Holyoke Female Seminary in nearby South Hadley, Massachusetts. When Emily began her term at Mount Holyoke on September 30, 1847, the school was still under the direction of its founder, Mary Lyon, a woman who had enormous intellectual ability and impressive theological acumen. Before she founded Mount Holyoke in 1837, Lyon already had an outstanding record of educational accomplishments. She had been trained at the Amherst Academy (in 1818) and had studied under Edward Hitchcock during his years as a minister in the 1820s. She had taught at the Ipswich Female Seminary, and in 1835 she had established the Wheaton Female Seminary.

Lyon's school at Mount Holyoke resembled the Amherst Academy in many regards, with its emphasis upon rhetoric, classical studies, the sciences, and theology; yet it differed from the academy in the degree to which Mary Lyon emphasized spiritual discipline and the missionary enterprise. One of her associates wrote after her death that Mary Lyon "sought not merely [the students'] conversion, but their enlistment in the great work of saving a lost world. It was the end and aim of all her efforts to make the seminary a nursery to the church."

Like Edward and Samuel Fowler Dickinson, Mary Lyon avidly supported women's education, but she differed from them in seeing it as more than a mere means of training wives and mothers for the republic. In an address commemorating the fifth anniversary of Mount Holyoke in 1842, Lyon outlined her view of education — of women as well as men — as a right "infinitely more precious than personal liberty: the right and the power of cultivating the faculties by which alone they are distinguished from the brutes that perish." She announced at the beginning of the address that her theme was to be "the slavery of the immortal mind, of its subjection, whether voluntary or involuntary, to any of the thousand petty tyrants, that from the beginning, have lorded it over the human soul, and made merchandize of its lofty powers, and crushed its expanding energies."

According to Lyon, one of the greatest threats to that "immortal mind" in women was "the responsibility of culinary manipulations." Skill in this area "is generally thought to be the perfection of her education," as Samuel Fowler Dickinson had indicated. While giving her days and hours "to the preparation of delicacies for the table," Lyon complained, a woman has "only the shreds and patches of life" that remain to "devote to the cultivation of her mind." A woman should instead simplify the life of home and table to free herself to "store her mind with a richer fund of knowledge." She was kept from doing so, however, by "tyrannical custom and tyrannical man, [which] bind her down in hopeless servitude."

In the second half of her anniversary address, Lyon offered her sweeping vision of what educated women might accomplish working in tandem with men. She foresaw a time when people would "act according to the principles of reason and religion" and "all that now goes into the war channel, will then be consecrated to the service of knowledge and benevolence." Lyon based her confidence upon the fact that the "Bible predicts unequivocally a period of universal peace. . . . Assuredly this vision is not imagination; and it looms up in the future, and I would fondly hope not in the distant future."

Among the impediments standing in the way of this glorious future were the "prodigious waste of time in . . . party politics," "the strong passion for accumulating property," and the lust for "works of fiction . . . devoured with epicurean greediness by almost all classes, especially the young." Though these forces of evil were tenacious, Lyon

37

was hopeful for the future, because "a beautiful bow of promise already spans the horizon. For when Christianity prevails in all lands, and fully controls all hearts, then those powerful causes of intellectual waste and perversion . . . shall pass away." The purpose of Mount Holyoke was to train "daughters [who] shall go forth . . . burning with a desire to bless mankind." Working through these "daughters," Lyon declared, Mount Holyoke "shall add new power to that lever, which benevolence has placed beneath the regions of ignorance and sin, and which is fast heaving them up into the day light of Christianity and Science." The female seminary will form one of the "radiant points" from which "the blended rays of knowledge and religion will go forth" and aid in "forming that halo of light which shall at length encircle the whole earth, and make it noon day among all the nations."

Mary Lyon's address exuded a spirit of confidence in the benevolent power of the God she worshiped and the religious training she promoted. As the talk made evident, the religious environment in which Emily Dickinson was trained and to which she responded little resembled the stereotypes of the Dickinson legend. In reality, the Christian faith promoted by Edward Hitchcock, Mary Lyon, and Edward Dickinson was a blend of historic Calvinist orthodoxy and American cultural Christianity. Though it was Calvinist at its core, the belief system that Dickinson encountered in her home, school, and church represented a clear compromise between the Puritan past and the progressive present. Like Hitchcock and the Dickinson men, Lyon believed that orthodox Christianity was in essential harmony with American culture and scientific advancement. The Christianity promoted by Lyon at Mount Holyoke was not a severe, otherworldly faith. Instead, it set forth an elaborate vision of individual and cultural development; through strenuous moral effort, educated Christians could liberate oppressed peoples "in every quarter of the globe." Like Hitchcock and Dickinson's father and grandfather, Lyon promoted a postmillennial version of evangelical Christianity. She undoubtedly believed in the resurrection of the body and eternal life, but her primary hope "looms up in the future, and I would fondly hope not in the distant future."

As one might expect at an institution whose founder looked for great things from her charges, life at Mount Holyoke was strictly regimented. Drawing upon Jonathan Edwards's teachings about the virtue of "disinterested benevolence," Lyon labored to create at Mount

Holyoke "a communal alternative to the commercial order that [she] saw emerging around her." As market forces fragmented towns, institutions, and families, Lyon sought to uphold the ideal of benevolence at her seminary. In contrast to the selfishness of the market, the women at Mount Holyoke were to demonstrate benevolence as Edwards had defined it: "Love of *benevolence* is that affection or propensity of the heart to any being, which causes it to incline to its well-being, or disposes it to desire and take pleasure in its happiness."

To achieve that ideal of benevolence, all aspects of life at Mount Holyoke were intended to build a community marked by selfless giving, self-discipline, and self-restraint. Instead of employing servants, the seminary required students to assume responsibility for the daily domestic affairs of the school. More than seventy rules governed life at the institution, and they covered everything from the requirement that students not speak above a whisper in the laundry room to the prohibition of informal meetings in student rooms. Daily life at Mount Holyoke was ordered to a higher end, and every moment in the day was filled with assigned tasks.

One of Dickinson's letters from Mount Holyoke conveys the spirit of the place and the rigors of its routines:

At 6. oclock, we all rise. We breakfast at 7. Our study hours begin at 8. At 9. we all meet in Seminary Hall, for devotions. At 10¼. I recite a review of Ancient History, in connection with which we read Goldsmith & Grimshaw. At .11. I recite a lesson in 'Pope's Essay on Man' which is merely transposition. At .12. I practice Calisthenics & at 12¼ read until dinner, which is at 12½ & after dinner, from 1½ until 2 I sing in Seminary Hall. From 2¾ until 3¾. I practice upon the Piano. At 3¾ I go to Sections, where we give in all our accounts for the day, including, Absence — Tardiness — Communications — Breaking Silent Study hours — Receiving Company in our rooms & ten thousand other things, which I will not take time or place to mention. At 4½, we go into Seminary Hall, & receive advice from Miss. Lyon in the form of a lecture. We have Supper at 6. & silent-study hours from then until the retiring bell, which rings at 8¾, but the tardy bell does not ring until 9¾, so that we dont often obey the first warning to retire.

. . . My domestic work is not difficult & consists in carrying the Knives from the 1st tier of tables at morning & noon & at night washing & wiping the same quantity of Knives.

Spiritual life at Mount Holyoke revolved around the ministry of Mary Lyon, who sought to bring each student to a confession of faith in Christ. As she worked for the conversion of every young woman under her charge, Lyon was laboring in the tradition of the New England Puritans, who had revolutionized church history and set the course for American Protestantism by requiring a confession of faith from all who would join the church. According to historian Edmund Morgan, the demand of a "demonstration of saving grace was a distinct addition" to the procedures of the church in England and Europe. In the European model, one was born into the church and received membership as a gift and expectation prior to conscious choice. Puritan practice, on the other hand, required evidence that one had been "born again" and had deliberately appropriated the gift of grace. In the words of one observer in early New England, candidates for conversion and membership in the church had to show "that they have beene wounded in their hearts for their originall sinne, and actuall transgressions, and can pitch upon some promise of free grace in the Scripture, for the ground of their faith."

To be sure, the standards for conversion were not as rigorous in Emily Dickinson's lifetime as they had been in seventeenth-century New England. But the principle remained the same. In New England history, the Puritan tradition was following to its logical end the Reformation belief in "free consent as the basis of both state and church." More than anything else, this belief — that the individual must make a free, publicized decision to submit to Christ and the church — served as the stumbling block that kept Dickinson from joining the church through profession of her faith in Christ.

In working toward the conversion of her students at Mount Holyoke, Lyon divided them each year into three groups: the "No-Hopers," the "Hopers," and the "Christians." The latter group was the largest of the three and was made up of women who could testify to the certainty of their salvation; at the beginning of Emily's year at the seminary, 150 of the 230 Mount Holyoke students were counted among the "Christians." About fifty of the remaining students were

"Hopers" — that is, young women who believed themselves on the verge of conversion. That left a group of about thirty students, including Dickinson, who were "without hope" and could not attest to faith in Christ. The members of this final group were the subject of Lyon's most fervent attention.

.The spiritual trials that Emily Dickinson passed through at Mount Holyoke shaped her later life, poetry, and letters, but it is hard to separate fact from legend in accounts of her year at the school. For instance, not long after Emily's death, her first editor, Mabel Loomis Todd, talked with Lavinia Dickinson about Emily's experiences at the seminary. In her journal entry concerning their conversation, Todd contemptuously dismissed Mount Holyoke with Victorian self-satisfaction: "There were real ogres at South Hadley then." In like manner, Martha Dickinson Bianchi complained that Mount Holyoke "cramped, curbed, repressed . . . every natural desire or impulse" in her Aunt Emily, and that it was in good measure "responsible for her later almost wilful love of solitude and the habit of repression."

In the end, such statements tell us more about the antipathy of Victorian commentators toward antebellum evangelical piety than about Emily Dickinson's actual experience at Mount Holyoke. It is possible to compare, for example, what Bianchi calls the "legend of Emily's insurrection . . . in the family archives" with accounts from primary sources written at the time of the events. According to Bianchi, when Mary Lyon announced that Christmas 1847 would be a fast day at the seminary, she asked all of the women in the assembly to "rise in token of responsive observation." Supposedly, every one of the school members stood, with the exception of Emily and her cousin and roommate, Emily Norcross. Lyon then demanded that any who did not wish to fast on Christmas should "stand that the whole school might observe them. And be it said to her eternal glory, of the two terrified objects of her anathema Emily stood alone."

In the records from this period, however, there is no mention at all of the Christmas "fasting incident," and the few references to Emily's condition portray her as ambivalent rather than defiant. Early in 1848, there was a flurry of activity and a small revival at the school. Emily Norcross wrote to a woman back home: "I attended another meeting of Miss Lyons this eve. . . . She spoke of Eternity as being unchangeable and asked why we should not be unchangeable in our preparation for eternity." Among those who remained unmoved by Mary Lyon's discourse, reported Emily Norcross, was the cousin from Amherst: "Emily Dickinson appears no different. I hoped I might have good news to write with regard to her. She says she has no particular objection to becoming a Christian and she says she feels bad when she hears of one and another of her friends who are expressing a hope but still she feels no more interest." Only days after this, a classmate reported in a letter that Emily Dickinson "still *appears* unconcerned" about the call of Christ.

In spite of her apparent lack of interest, Dickinson attended a Sabbath evening meeting on January 16 in Mary Lyon's room. It was intended for "all who had decided that they would to day to serve the Lord, and those who had to day felt an uncommon anxiety to decide." This meeting of "all who are particularly anxious" included seventeen students, and according to one of those students "Emily Dickinson was among the number." The very next day, January 17, Dickinson wrote to her friend Abiah Root that "there is a great deal of religious interest here and many are flocking to the ark of safety. I have not yet given up to the claims of Christ, but trust I am not entirely thoughtless on so important & serious a subject." Dickinson's tone in this letter was sober and reserved. It betrayed uncertainty about the deepest subjects of the spirit, rather than the flippancy highlighted by those who have portrayed her as defiantly embittered during her time at Mary Lyon's school.

Evidence for Dickinson's ambivalence can be found in other letters from that year. Even early in 1848, when she was questioning whether she should "give up to the claims of Christ," Emily wrote to Austin to tell him how much she had appreciated sermons she had heard the previous Sunday, February 13, 1848. They had been preached by Henry Boynton Smith, then a member of the Amherst faculty and later a distinguished professor at New York's Union Theological Seminary. Smith was a convert from Unitarianism to Trinitarian orthodoxy, and both his preaching and writing stressed the uniqueness of the historic Christian faith. Dickinson was hardly put off by his orthodoxy. "Such sermons I never heard in my life," she told Austin. "We were all charmed with him & dreaded to have him close."

By the end of the year, many of Dickinson's classmates at Mount Holyoke had "found hope," but she had not. To the end, she resisted the "converting influences" of the Spirit and felt guilty about it. Her final letter to Abiah Root from Mount Holyoke was filled with self-recrimination about the opportunities she had missed. In the letter, she "trembles" at the thought that, because she has wasted her days, her "fate will be sealed, perhaps. I have neglected the *one thing needful* when all were obtaining it." She told Abiah that she would be justified in being suspicious of such talk, because Emily had claimed to be uninterested in this "all-important subject" of salvation. "But I am not happy," Emily reported, "and I regret that . . . I did not give up and become a Christian. It is not now too late . . . , but it is hard for me to give up the world." With their mutual friend Abby Wood ready to "cast her burden on Christ," Emily wished she "could say that with sincerity" but had to report, "I fear I never can."

In this letter, Emily also told Abiah of her father's decision not to send her back to Mount Holyoke in the fall. Having received reports of Emily's illness during the spring term, her parents had dispatched Austin to bring his sister home. Emily obeyed, but did so against her will, "not because I do not love home — far from it. But I could not bear to leave teachers and companions before the close of term and go home to be dosed and receive the physician daily." She stayed out of school for more than a month, and though her parents allowed her to return to complete the academic term, they ruled out a second year at the seminary. So it was that at the close of the 1847-48 school year, Dickinson's formal academic training came to an end. As she left Mount Holyoke, seventeen-year-old Emily also seemed to be leaving behind the friendships and frames of reference that had been hers in childhood. Her education had changed her irrevocably. How fully it had changed her would only become apparent when she began to write poetry a decade later.

"A LOSS OF SOMETHING"

During her years of schooling, like countless other young women and men in the modern world, Emily Dickinson had lost that cast of mind that the French philosopher Paul Ricoeur has termed the first or "primitive naiveté." ("A loss of something ever felt I — /The first that I could recollect/Bereft I was — .") The "first naiveté" is Ricoeur's term for the uncritical "immediacy of belief" that had been commonplace to men and women in the ancient and medieval worlds but that has become "irremediably lost" in modern experience. Ricoeur attributes this loss to modernity's "forgetfulness of the signs of the sacred," and he takes that "forgetfulness" to have been a consequence of technology and "the great task of nourishing men, of satisfying their needs by mastering nature through a planetary technique." Early modern philosophy and science transformed the world into a mechanism to be manipulated for human ends. The critical detachment called for by this manipulative approach also detached the human subject from a direct apprehension of God and the sacred order of things.

In a memorable phrase, the German sociologist Max Weber once described this modern detachment from the sacred as "the disenchanting of the world." For Weber, such "disenchanting" was a product of the Protestant denigration of the sacraments and the modern scientific attack upon magic. By stressing what he labeled "the absolute transcendality of God" and "the inner isolation of the individual," Protestantism, according to Weber, set the modern self adrift in a soulless world. As a result, we find in the modern world a vast gulf separating the lively inner world of the creative individual and the spiritless forms of social and natural life.

For Dickinson and other nineteenth-century poets, the "disenchanting of the world" did indeed point to a sharp dichotomy between the self and all that lay outside it. Over the course of that century, nature came to seem increasingly mute and dark to the heirs of the romantic tradition, while the human mind appeared ever more expressive and illuminating. Among the poets of the age, there was a good deal of worry about the loneliness of the vibrant imagination in a lifeless world. Samuel Taylor Coleridge, for instance, wrote of his despondent awareness that "I may not hope from outward form to win/ The passion and the life, whose fountains are within." Or, as Dickinson's contemporary Ralph Waldo Emerson tellingly put it: "Once we lived in what we saw; now, the rapaciousness of this new power, which threatens to absorb all things, engages us. . . . Nature and literature are subjective phenomena; every evil and every good thing is a shadow which we cast."

The contemporary American philosopher Richard Rorty has cogently summarized the complex intellectual backdrop against which Dickinson's life played itself out. "About two hundred years ago, the idea that truth was made rather than found began to take hold of the imagination of Europe," he observes. In his telescoped history, the nineteenth century appears as the period when men and women realized for the first time that the world outside ourselves had nothing to say. "The suggestion that truth, as well as the world, is out there is a legacy of an age in which the world was seen as the creation of a being who had a language of his own," says Rorty. But since we no longer believe in such a being who is the source of language, it makes no sense to argue that the world has anything to tell us: "The world does not speak. Only we do. The world can, once we have programmed ourselves with a language, cause us to hold beliefs. But it cannot propose a language for us to speak. Only other human beings can do that." This is a fully disenchanted world.

This experience of "disenchantment" was to become an intellectual commonplace and a widespread cultural phenomenon in the twentieth century. But in Dickinson's day to possess the "disenchanting" sense as acutely as she did was to go against the prevailing wisdom of the era. The disenchanted person is one who has been, unlike most people, undeceived:

> Whoever disenchants
> A single Human soul
> By failure of irreverence
> Is guilty of the whole.
>
> As guileless as a Bird
> As graphic as a star
> Till the suggestion sinister
> Things are not what they are — [#1451]

As Dickinson came to understand it, the disenchantment of the "Human soul" was inevitable in an age when scientific and philosophical discoveries were making innumerable "suggestions sinister" that "Things are not what they are — ."

What did this disenchantment have to do with Emily Dickinson's becoming a great modern poet? One way to answer that crucial question is to consider that in an *enchanted* world, every reality is understood in terms of another reality, often a transcendent one; to see any one

45

thing for what it is, one must see it as it is and in relationship to something else. To view the world in a disenchanted manner, however, is to find the connections between separate realities or experiences to be missing or unconvincing; it is to suspect that there may be no deeper principle holding together the disparate elements of the world. Albert Gelpi notes that in the nineteenth century in general and in Dickinson's poetry in particular, there are certain questions about ultimate reality that surface repeatedly: "Do I know myself only in connection with, even in submission to, something beyond self? Or must I make my own meaning in a murky universe?" In poetic terms, "the question is whether Nature is type or trope."

If nature is a *type*, it is grounded in a reality higher than itself, and every one of its elements points to that ultimate reality. This was the Puritan view of nature in the New World, just as it had been, in modified form, the dominant understanding of reality in medieval Catholic Europe. By the early nineteenth century, however, Puritanism had all but disappeared as a vital intellectual force, and at the same time, German philosophy and English and American romanticism had begun to trumpet the newly discovered powers of the imaginative self. From the start, romanticism had the tendency to consider reality as a *trope* anchored in the human mind and its creative powers, rather than as a *type* of a transcendent reality. In Rorty's categories, *types* are truths as they are supposedly found; *tropes* are truths as they are actually made.

Dickinson chose poetry in part because she took its metaphorical — or *tropic* — activity to be the most viable means of *enchanting* the world once more. In Paul Ricoeur's terms, having cultivated the "critical function" in an age still caught up in the "first naiveté," Dickinson longed for the "second naiveté" by means of which she might believe again. Whether its metaphors proved to be types of another world or tropes of human desire, poetry provided a means of achieving that goal. Ricoeur argues that "beyond the desert of criticism" those possessed by the modern spirit of disenchantment desire "to be called again." He suggests that the disenchanting power of criticism can be overcome only by that "second naïveté," which, through the interpretation of sacred symbols, enables us to hear "being still speak" to us.

The metaphor of the "speech of being" calls to mind Dickinson's image of "memory draping her lips," a phrase that the poet used as a "critical" adult to describe what she had "lost with childhood" and its "first naiveté." The silence of the world outside her self vexed Dickinson. Did nature say anything to her?

> I could not bear the Bees should come,
> I wished they'd stay away
> In those dim countries where they go,
> What word had they for me? [#348]

In the solitude of pain, could "being still speak" to her? "I felt a Funeral, in my Brain," begins one Dickinson poem, "And Mourners to and fro/Kept treading — treading — " until, finally,

> Then Space — began to toll,
> As all the Heavens were a Bell,
> And Being, but an Ear,
> And I, and Silence, some strange Race
> Wrecked, solitary, here — [#280]

Would "being still speak" to her, or were silence and solitude the fate of the "strange [human] Race/Wrecked, solitary, here — "? About this question, the disenchanted Dickinson would never cease to wonder.

By the time that she had finished her formal schooling at Mount Holyoke in 1848, Dickinson had already begun to move toward the seclusion of her adult life. Having acquired the "skill sorrowful — as certain — " she sensed that her critical consciousness had shut her out from the innocence of childhood and had somehow made the assurances of Christian belief unavailable to her in a conventional form. Having met silence on every side — in God, nature, and memory — she sought, through seclusion, to marshal her resources and summon her speech to break the silence. Though her seclusion would not become complete for more than a decade, even by the age of seventeen Dickinson was beginning to assume toward the outside world the curious, confounded stance that would mark her maturity. At a significant human price, she was fashioning a life that would eventually enable her to pursue the poetic craft that was to be her calling.

3 I've Stopped Being Theirs

I'm ceded — I've stopped being Theirs —
The name They dropped upon my face
With water, in the country church
Is finished using, now,
And They can put it with my Dolls,
My childhood, and the string of spools,
I've finished threading — too — [#508]

THE ESTRANGEMENT FROM her world that Emily Dickinson began to sense during adolescence surfaced most dramatically in her struggles over whether to join the church. Her difficulties began to crystallize when she was fifteen and reached a point of crisis a few years after she left Mary Lyon's seminary. Less than two years before she enrolled at Mount Holyoke, Dickinson had told Abiah Root that she "was almost persuaded to be a christian. I thought I never again could be thoughtless and worldly — and I can say that I never enjoyed such perfect peace and happiness as the short time in which I felt I had found my savior." But other concerns quickly crowded Christ out of her life, "and I cared less for religion than ever." In spite of feeling "that I shall never be happy without I love Christ," she reported that she could not decide in his favor. "Last winter there was a revival here," she told Abiah, ". . . but I attended none of the meetings. . . . I felt that I was so easily excited that I might again be deceived and I dared not trust myself." In the closing sentence of the letter, Dickinson let her friend know that "although I am not a christian still I feel deeply the importance of attending to the subject before it is too late."

BEYOND MOUNT HOLYOKE: THE REVIVAL OF 1850

The "Articles of Faith and Government" in force at the First Church of Amherst in Emily's youth provide a good picture of what it meant to "become a Christian" in an antebellum New England village. The question of "coming to Christ" was never separated from joining the church in the New England Congregational tradition; in claiming Christ, one also claimed membership in the fellowship of believers by making public testimony to the grace of God. At the First Church of Amherst, when Emily Dickinson was a young woman, this involved a candidate for membership being examined by the pastor and deacons "as to his knowledge of the Gospel and experiential acquaintance with the grace of God."

The requirement of a testimony was meant to secure the distinct identity of the church within the larger culture. With its doctrine of election and emphasis upon individual responsibility, Puritan Calvinism rejected the medieval model of the universal church in which an individual was simply born into the church. It replaced the biological model of membership with a psychological one. The public testimony was meant to provide compelling evidence of this supernatural second birth in the believer's life.

In the seventeenth century, Puritan leaders had required lengthy narrative accounts of the soul's struggles and the Spirit's blessings as evidence of the applicant's "acquaintance with the grace of God." These narratives often scaled the bright peaks of spiritual bliss and traversed the darkened valleys of sin and despair. They were elaborate, dramatic tales of the special providences of God. What was at stake here was the eternal destiny of the individual soul as well as the future of God's covenanted people in the New World.

By the nineteenth century, the mountains had been leveled and the dark places flooded with the light of love. With heaven increasingly sentimentalized and hell only spoken of in whispers, there was no need for prospective church members to give harrowing accounts of their wrenching conversions. Instead, as the history of the First Church in Dickinson's own lifetime indicates, church leaders of that period did all they could to remove the last sources of torment or embarrassment from the process. To "become a Christian" and join the church in Amherst at mid-century, a person needed only to subscribe to the articles of faith and offer the briefest assurance of belief in Christ. This was hardly a demanding standard, but even such a minimal requirement proved too great an obstacle for young Emily Dickinson.

The subject of "becoming a Christian" was much on Dickinson's mind two years after her departure from Mount Holyoke, as she watched the revival of 1850 roll through her town, her church, and her family. This particular revival swept into the very heart of the Dickinson home, with her father, sister, and future sister-in-law all confessing Christ and joining the church as a result of it. Pressured by their example, Emily pondered again this option. About to turn twenty and with her education finished, she was at a crucial point in her development when the Spirit descended upon Amherst in 1850. As she confronted the choice of marriage and church membership, the revival served to crystallize her thinking about the future.

It is easy to assume, as many have, that Dickinson turned against the revivals because she saw them as carnivals of irrational behavior and craven capitulation. In this view, the revivals were the frenzied consequence of divisive theological disputes and manipulative emotional practices. They marked interludes of irrational excess in the otherwise sober progress of secular ideals. In point of fact, they were the exact opposite. As the revival of 1850 was described years later by key participants and apologists, it seems to have been more an exercise in Whiggish control than an effort to duplicate the potent passions of the Great Awakening or the religious excitements of the American frontier.

In Amherst, the revival of 1850 began quietly. Aaron Colton, the pastor of the Dickinsons' church at the time, later told how early in January the regular prayer meetings of his church became "notably fuller and more solemn. A cloud of mercy seemed to hang over us, and ready to drop down fatness. Days and weeks passed, but no conversions. What was the hindrance?" At length, the pastor and others came to realize that "the *trouble* . . . was in the rum places in the village, with fires of hell in full blast. What could be done?" Colton's spiritual counselors advised a course of "prudence," because it was well known that "the rum men were desperate." Yet "kind words" had done nothing to alleviate the problem, and it was obvious that a more bracing course of action was called for.

Colton and his allies came up with the solution of holding a town meeting on the subject, to be capped with a special plea from Edward Hitchcock. When the Amherst College president concluded with a challenge — "But it were better that the college should go down, than that young men should come here to be ruined by drink places among us" — the crowd demanded action. "Four hundred hands shot up for abating the nuisance," and the following morning the selectmen went around town shutting down the rum shops. "Then the heavens gave rain — blessed showers, and there was a great refreshing."

In classic Whig fashion, the 1850 revival worked men and women into a state of emotional crisis for the express purpose of making them more self-controlled and disciplined. It was a frenzy for the ordered life, a drunken quest for spiritual sobriety. The temperance movement fit neatly within the Whig view of the world, for as historian Daniel Walker Howe observes, "the Whig personality ideal emphasized self-development but not self-indulgence, and it encouraged striving to shape the self according to an approved plan." There were sinners' benches at tent meetings in Ohio at this time, and revival fervor in Kentucky struck some as bearing the signs of a spiking fever, but Amherst experienced nothing of the kind. Like virtually everything else in Emily Dickinson's early environment, the revival of 1850 conformed to Whig standards. Whatever fervor there was, the Amherst authorities were not about to let a revival, or anything else, get out of hand.

The historical record of the revival of 1850 calls into question the standard assessment of Dickinson's response to revivals in particular and the Christian faith in general. For instance, Paula Bennett claims that "reared in an era when theological points were the subject of vituperative debate in the popular press, and surrounded by religious

51

revivalism and sectarian controversy, Dickinson . . . chose not to 'listen.'" Or in the words of Dickinson biographer Richard Sewall, writing about the poet's reluctance to be converted during an earlier revival: "It seems clear that her absence from the revival meetings was not because she was unmoved, or alienated, or bitter. She was afraid of being too much moved and her imagination overstimulated."

Dickinson's own accounts show that she did indeed "listen" to the pleas of the revival and that the circumstances surrounding it never threatened to overwhelm her. Only weeks after the closing of the rum shops, Dickinson wrote to Jane Humphrey: "How lonely this world is growing. . . . Christ is calling everyone here . . . , and I am standing alone in rebellion, and growing very careless." Of the number who had found Christ, including Emily's sister Lavinia, she said, "I cant tell you *what* they have found, but *they* think it is something precious." The sanctification undergone by the converts Dickinson called "strange." It did not issue in passion, ecstatic gestures, or frenzied outbursts, but in calm, measured actions exhibiting self-control. "They seem so very tranquil, and their voices are kind, and gentle, and the tears fill their eyes so often, I really think I envy them." In a letter written a month later to Abiah Root, Dickinson spoke of a mutual friend's face as being "calmer, but full of radiance, holy, yet very joyful." It was the quiet tranquility of Amherst and the church that she noted, for "the place is very solemn, and sacred."

Without question, Dickinson felt that she had failed somehow in refusing conversion. Later in life she would take a bemused approach to revivals, but as a young woman she worried that in resisting conversion she had spurned a priceless offer of divine love. Just as she had learned earlier in life to scrutinize the faces of the dead for signs that they had been "willing to die," so did she now scan the countenances of the living. She detected on many faces evidence of something "precious" that she could not name but envied others for possessing. Like many of her friends, Dickinson felt beset by the vague fears and aching longings that were a vital element of the romantic sentimentalism of the day. Here in conversion and revival, many of those friends had found a peace that passed all understanding and that left them exuding a "radiance, holy, yet very joyful."

And yet Emily Dickinson did not know this joy. Even as others found themselves blissfully transformed, she continued to set herself apart, "standing alone in rebellion." At this point in her life, Dickinson believed that the glory the revivals claimed to disclose was genuine but that it had been denied to her: "It *certainly* comes from God — and I think to receive it is blessed — not that I know it from *me*, but from those on whom change has passed," she wrote to Jane Humphrey in April of 1850. Dickinson feared that her rebellion had cut her off from bliss. If she did not experience "radiant, holy joy," it was because she did not deserve it.

If in late adolescence Dickinson yearned for the "glories" delivered through the revivals, why did she not convert and join the church? Undoubtedly one factor was her reluctance to make a public profession of any kind. Even a brief testimony before the church leaders and a public assent to articles of faith seemed to demand too much of her. As much as she longed to experience the joy others had known, she cherished the shelter of her solitude even more. Though she was eager to be known, addressed, and loved, she was even more fearful of being violated. An observer who did not wish to be observed, Dickinson would have found it painful to hazard the gaze of congregation and community.

In addition to her fear of exposure, Dickinson's failure to detect the fruits of grace in her experience also kept her from professing the faith as her own. A person saved by Christ was called to recognize dramatic changes in his or her life, as Emily's brother Austin did when he gave his confession of faith. "I tell each of you," he testified, "the full abounding happiness of the last two weeks has been more than all I have ever know[n] before, that never has life seemed half so bright, my friends half so dear, nor the future half so glorious." But as Emily examined her own experience, she could not detect a similar joy or tranquility. Whenever she came to the brink of conversion, Emily stepped back because she found her attention wavering and her heart curiously empty. At fifteen, she had been "almost persuaded to be a christian," but her mind strayed from the object of faith and soon "I cared less for religion than ever." Unable to taste the fruits of the Spirit in her life, she refused to claim that she had been grafted onto the vine that was said to be their source.

Larger cultural forces also worked upon Dickinson to keep her from joining the church. One of the most powerful was the conception of the self that she had already begun to cultivate in adolescence. From the books she read and culture she inhabited, Dickinson acquired a highly romantic view of the person in her years after Mount Holyoke. That understanding of selfhood placed an inordinate emphasis upon the role of volition in the formation of beliefs and the practice of virtues. In effect, it took to an extreme the Reformation's stress upon the necessity of the individual appropriation of beliefs. As John Dillenberger and Claude Welch explain, for Martin Luther, John Calvin, and the other major Reformers, the preached and written word "became the Word of God" only "when they became alive in the heart and mind of man through the Spirit." For the Reformers, "one of the prerequisites of a proper sacrament was the faith of the believer." In Protestantism, faith became the subjective appropriation of the objective reality of God's activity; in romanticism, the subjective powers of choice came to eclipse even the object of that choice. "It is not this or that political, philosophical, religious or even aesthetic commitment that marks the romanticist," argues literary historian Robert Langbaum. "It is the subjective ground of his commitment, the fact that he never forgets his commitment has been chosen."

This was how Emily Dickinson knew the self; for her in adulthood, the substance of belief remained secondary to the fact that that belief had been chosen. In the mid-twentieth century, the poet W. H. Auden wrote of his adopted land that America had come to stand "for the principle . . . that liberty is prior to virtue, i.e., liberty cannot be distinguished from license, for freedom of choice is neither good nor bad but the human prerequisite without which virtue and vice have no meaning. Virtue is, of course, preferable to vice, but to choose vice is preferable to having virtue chosen for one." As she wrestled with decisions about faith, marriage, and life in public, Dickinson was hammering out an understanding of the self that was unique to her but also reflected crucial changes in American culture.

As a young adult, Dickinson wrote a poem that clarified her stance toward the Christian faith. It connected her refusal to join the church to her need to define her own identity:

> I'm ceded — I've stopped being Theirs —
> The name They dropped upon my face
> With water, in the country church
> Is finished using, now,

And They can put it with my Dolls,
My childhood, and the string of spools,
I've finished threading — too —

Baptized, before, without the choice,
But this time, consciously, of Grace —
Unto supremest name —
Called to my Full — The Crescent dropped —
Existence's whole Arc, filled up,
With one small Diadem.

My second Rank — too small the first —
Crowned — Crowing — on my Father's breast —
A half unconscious Queen —
But this time — Adequate — Erect,
With Will to choose, or to reject,
And I choose, just a Crown — [#508]

The poem opens with a reference to Emily's baptism as an infant in 1831. That first baptism had made her "Theirs" — her parents' and her community's — "without the choice," but this second baptism she has chosen "consciously, of Grace." Her received identity she has stored away "with my Dolls,/My childhood, and the string of spools." As an adult, the poet is now the "half unconscious Queen" who is able to stand on her own, "Adequate — Erect,/With Will to choose, or to reject." As the product of a consciously free choice, the second baptism has an authenticity utterly lacking in the first.

"THE REVERY ALONE WILL DO"

The disestablishment of the New England church, first in Connecticut in 1818 and then in Massachusetts in 1833, only served to reinforce the voluntarist tendencies incipient in New England Protestantism. Deprived of state support and sanction, the Congregational churches turned to revivalism and moral suasion to replenish their ranks. In virtually every New England village, voluntary societies sprang up to supplement the work of local congregations. Some of these "societies," such as Amherst College and Mount Holyoke Female Seminary, furthered the kingdom of God by training moral agents and missionaries to serve in neighboring villages and foreign lands. Other "societies" drew together people of like mind on a particular subject for a concerted moral effort; there were Sabbatarian societies, temperance societies, and even "cent" societies that raised funds by the penny to support young people training for ministry or missions.

In Amherst and across the land in 1850, revivalism and moralism worked hand in hand to perfect the disciplined self and redeem the culture. Increasingly in the decades before the Civil War, the New England church saw itself not as a holy body called out *from* the world but as an earnest organization cast *into* the world. Having lost through disestablishment their power to shape directly the course of public life, ministers under the new dispensation scrambled to find ways to influence what they could no longer control.

Dickinson shrank from the voluntary societies as much as she did from the revivals. As the revival of 1850 was about to begin, Emily wrote to a friend in late January that the "Sewing Society has commenced again — and held its first meeting last week — ." If Emily is to be trusted in her hyperbole, this society was typical in the daunting scope of its mission: "Now all the poor will be helped — the cold warmed — the warm cooled — the hungry fed — the thirsty attended to — the ragged clothed — and this suffering — tumbled down world will be helped to it's feet again — which will be quite pleasant to all." While all of this was going on, Emily had made herself conspicuous by her absence. "I dont attend — notwithstanding my high approbation — " she wrote. "I am already set down as one of those brands almost consumed — and my hardheartedness gets me many prayers."

If Dickinson was listening for a counterpoint to the boring melody of moralism at this time of revival, she did not have to wait long to hear it. Later that same year, a new novel struck a responsive chord in Emily, Lavinia (or Vinnie, as her family called her), Austin, and countless other young adults. In the fall of 1850, *Reveries of a Bachelor* by Ik Marvel (Donald G. Mitchell) appeared. The book consisted of a set of fantasies and ruminations about subjects as vast as life and death and as petty as the passing fancies of a young man. It quickly made the rounds of the Dickinson children and their friends, even though many parents, Edward Dickinson included, did not approve of it. More than two years after *Reveries* appeared, Emily wrote to Austin that their father had given her "quite a trimming about . . . these 'modern Literati' who he says are *nothing*, compared to past generations, who flourished when *he was a boy*. Then he said there were 'somebody's *rev-e-ries*,' he did'nt know whose they were, that he thought were very ridiculous."

"Can we understand reverie as an historical phenomenon?" asks historian Richard Rabinowitz, and his question is pertinent to the life of Dickinson in the decade before the Civil War. Mid-nineteenth-century diaries show that young people spent much more of their time in daydreams and "reveries" than their parents and grandparents had ever done. The generation emerging into maturity at mid-century found encouragement for their "reveries" in contemporary devotional literature as well as in sensational novels. The Christian devotionalists urged believers to cultivate their unfettered imaginations, for they were thought to afford unique access to truth and the presence of God. For a group saturated in romantic poetry and sentimental fiction, as Emily's circle was, "reverie became the perfect antidote for those long boring meetings of the local self-improvement league and the perfect medicine for a hundred other social disappointments." While conventional society mumbled in a monotone, those who experienced reverie overheard a resonant harmony in their inner selves.

An 1851 letter from Emily to her friend and future sister-in-law Susan Gilbert illustrates the place of this newly discovered "reverie" in her life. When Emily wrote to her, Sue was hundreds of miles away, teaching school in Baltimore. In the letter, after having mused upon the "'sweet silver moon'" that was shining on both of them that night, Emily told her friend: "It is such an evening Susie, as you and I would walk and have such pleasant musings, if you were only here — perhaps we would have a 'Reverie' after the form of 'Ik Marvel.'" But there would be a difference; "'Marvel' *only* marvelled, and you and I would *try* to make a little destiny to have for our own."

Emily then mentioned newspaper notices about the new Ik Marvel novel, *Dream Life*, which was to be published in two months. She asked Sue, "Dont you hope he will live as long as you and I do — and keep on having dreams and writing them to us." She followed that rhetorical question with a statement of devotion: "We will be willing to die Susie — when such as *he* have gone, for there will be none to

57

interpret these lives of our's." Those lives, Emily wrote, could not possibly be interpreted by the same texts and doctrines that made sense of the lives of ordinary people. Writers like Marvel and Longfellow were necessary, "for our sakes dear Susie, who please ourselves with the fancy that we are the only poets, and everyone else is *prose.*"

Dickinson's letters from this period show what cultural forces were touching the nerve of the generation before the Civil War. The fascination with "reveries" was only one of many signs pointing to significant developments in thinking about God, truth, and the self. By 1850, the year that Emily Dickinson turned twenty, English romantic poetry had been circulating for half a century; for more than two decades German Idealist philosophy had been making inroads into American culture; and in the 1830s and 1840s the novels of Dickens, the poetry of Longfellow, and the essays of Emerson had been spreading the message of sentiment and intuition among the educated public.

Mid-nineteenth-century evangelical religion was hardly immune to the powerful appeal of the romantic view of the self being trumpeted about in many quarters. New ideas promised to secure the unmoored faith in a time of intellectual storms. As the higher criticism of the Bible and scientific naturalism began to wear away at the pillars of belief, evangelical leaders scrambled to lash their faith to the moorings of the self and the innocent human heart. The children of these same evangelical leaders, who were reading Byron and the Brontës, rather than Goethe and Coleridge, were only too happy to endorse such efforts and to carry them even further than their parents had dared. When Lyman Beecher welcomed his son Charles into the ministry in 1844, he advised him, "Take heed to thy heart. . . . The power of the heart set on fire by love is the greatest created power in the universe — more powerful than electricity, for that can only rend and melt matter; but LOVE can, by God's appointment, carry the truth quick and powerful through the soul." Charles and his generation, which included Emily Dickinson, accepted the charge gladly.

By the time Dickinson turned her back on the church and her face toward poetry in the 1850s, New England theology had been struggling for almost a century with the issues laid out in Jonathan Edwards's monumental *Freedom of the Will*, in which he had attacked the Arminian idea of freedom. Their "notion of liberty," Edwards had written of the Arminians, is "that it consists in a self-determining power in the will, or a certain sovereignty the will has over itself, and its own acts, whereby it determines its own volitions; so as not to be dependent in its determinations, on any cause without itself, nor determined by anything prior to its own acts." Edwards's critique of Arminianism reads like a commentary on Dickinson's "second baptism":

> My second Rank — too small the first —
> Crowned — Crowing — on my Father's breast —
> A half unconscious Queen —
> But this time — Adequate — Erect,
> With Will to choose, or to reject,
> And I choose, just a Crown — [#508]

Poetry was to be the "Crown" that Dickinson chose. It would serve as her means of moving through the impasses of conventional religious faith as well as her way of establishing an identity that she had freely willed. For several centuries before Dickinson, of course, many devout Protestants had turned to poetry to explore their spiritual experience in ways unavailable in prose. So in one sense, in choosing poetry, Dickinson was merely following in a line of great Protestant devotional writers. Some, such as George Herbert, John Donne, and Edward Taylor, had been ministers who found in the poetic medium vital resources for their life of faith. They used poetry to clarify their convictions and purify their practices. Others, such as Christopher Smart and Samuel Taylor Coleridge, while not preachers or pastors, also found in lyric poetry an irreplaceable means of delving into sacred matters to deepen the faith they already held.

Like other key romantic poets, Emily Dickinson drew upon this devotional tradition of Christian poetry while leaving its specific commitments behind. That is not to say that in her maturity Dickinson definitively renounced the Christian faith; there is too much evidence of her continuing spiritual passion and intense religious devotion to prove any such assertion. Instead, it is to say that, unlike Herbert, Donne, and others of an earlier age, Dickinson chose poetry as a surrogate for traditional religion rather than as a support for an established belief or practice. For her willing self, the world of infinite aesthetic possibilities and inward reveries seemed more enchanting than the ordered world of orthodoxy and Whig moralism:

> I dwell in Possibility —
> A fairer House than Prose —
> More numerous of Windows —
> Superior — for Doors — [#657]

To remain viable, orthodox faith needed the support of history, science, and the suspension of critical disbelief, while poetry demanded only an unassailable belief in the unimpeachable self:

> On a Columnar Self —
> How ample to rely
> In Tumult — or Extremity —
> How good the Certainty
>
> That Lever cannot pry —
> And Wedge cannot divide
> Conviction — That Granitic Base —
> Though None be on our Side —
>
> Suffice Us — for a Crowd —
> Ourself — and Rectitude —
> And that Assembly — not far off
> From furthest Spirit — God — [#789]

The life of conventional faith and practice called for assent to a body of doctrine and active participation in the life of the church, but the poetic imagination demanded nothing more than a spirit of reverie:

> To make a prairie it takes a clover and one bee,
> One clover, and a bee,
> And revery.
> The revery alone will do,
> If bees are few. [#1755]

In choosing poetry, Dickinson thought she was opening herself to infinite possibilities. In this realm, she could "stop being theirs" and lean instead on the "Columnar Self" that she was coming to recognize as her greatest asset. If her choices meant that she might have to experience her "revery alone," that was sufficient, for "The revery alone will do,/If bees are few."

In the choices she made and refused as a young adult, Dickinson implacably set herself upon a course that would lead her away from marriage and church and into solitude. Whatever its costs, that solitude to her was worth its price. It granted her a freedom of self-definition unavailable in the obligating arrangements of marriage, family, and church. And it offered her a more fertile world than the sterile Whig culture she knew so well.

4 Homeless at Home

We deem we dream —
And that dissolves the days
Through which existence strays
Homeless at home. [#1573]

WHEN EMILY DICKINSON returned home from her year at Mount Holyoke Female Seminary in August 1848, she was a few months shy of her eighteenth birthday. She had completed her formal schooling and was ready to face a future in which, as a woman, she had precious few alternatives. She could become a teacher or a missionary, try to find her place as a writer in the burgeoning literary marketplace, or become a wife and mother. Beyond those limited choices, there were not many options for a woman of eighteen to weigh.

As much as Dickinson had admired Mary Lyon and in spite of the fact that a number of young women from Mount Holyoke became missionaries, that calling was out of the question. "What shall we do . . . , when trial grows more, and more . . . and we wander, and know not where, and cannot get out of the forest — ," she wrote to Abiah Root shortly after she had returned from Mount Holyoke,

62

"whose is the hand to help us, and to lead, and forever guide us, they talk of a 'Jesus of Nazareth,' will you tell me if it be he?" A person with such doubts did not make a good candidate for the mission field.

Nor can one imagine Emily Dickinson as a teacher, regardless of her family's devotion to education. Of all the members of her family, Emily was closest to Austin in temperament, and his teaching experience in a neighboring town in 1851 must have given her pause. He had trouble from the start. After only a week on the job, he wrote home about his frustrations. "I am glad you are *not* delighted [with teaching]," Emily responded. "Father remarks quite briefly that he 'thinks they have found their master,' mother bites her lips, and fears you 'will be *rash* with them' and Vinnie and I say masses for poor Irish boys souls." Austin painted a bleak picture of teaching, as he complained of having "a dozen compositions a week to decipher and correct . . . of the time occupied with scholars and others, who call at my room to interrogate me on literary and scientific points — . . . Just think of these and a thousand nameless little things which conspire to fill up the out-of-school hours."

The fact that she might be unsuited to these vocations did not relieve Emily of the burden of choosing a course of action after Mount Holyoke. She did have luxuries that many others, including her friend and future sister-in-law, Susan Gilbert, did not enjoy. Sue had been orphaned at an early age and had to rely upon her own initiative and the generosity of relatives to survive. Emily knew no such deprivation. Whatever spiritual and physical struggles she was to undergo as a result of having chosen to stay at home, once Dickinson returned there in 1848 she would be secure from destitution and want for the rest of her life.

Freed from concerns for her own sustenance, Dickinson embarked in her early twenties on a lifelong journey of self-definition, with her choice to remain at home serving as her first major stride down that path. For the rest of her life, "home" would serve for Dickinson as a metaphor of an ideal state of security. Her letters regularly idealized "home," portraying it as an unassailable place; there are no fewer than eighty-six references to "home" in her poems, making it one of the most frequently used words in her entire lexicon. It was for her a sacred place and became her inviolable space. "Home is a holy thing," she wrote to Austin in her twenty-first year. " — [N]othing of doubt or distrust can enter it's blessed portals. . . . [But] fairer it is and *brighter* than all the world beside."

Already by the age of twenty, Dickinson had begun to think of her home as a safe haven from which she could regulate her contact with the world. At first when she returned from Mount Holyoke, she balanced the secure pleasures of home with an active social life in Amherst. She paid regular visits to friends and neighbors around the village and received her own steady stream of guests at home. On several occasions during the 1850s she journeyed to other towns in Massachusetts and even traveled, in 1855, to Washington and Philadelphia with her sister. Only by the end of the decade, as she approached the age of thirty, did she begin to be reluctant to leave home at all.

Dickinson's gradual assumption of solitude coincided closely with the discovery of her poetic calling. The soul, she came to realize, does indeed "select its own society," and she set about fabricating one on her own terms, using the materials of her own letters and poems. In the last thirty years of her life, Dickinson accomplished the remarkable feat of becoming a major author without any access to the outside world, save that which her reading and correspondence provided. Through the medium of the written and printed word, she crafted a means of securing the sheltered stability of home while also enjoying the exquisite liberty of inner exploration. While others roamed the world in search of volcanoes "in Sicily and South America,"

> A Lava step at any time
> Am I inclined to climb —
> A Crater I may contemplate
> Vesuvius at Home. [#1705]

THE DICKINSON FAMILY

Yet even while Dickinson's home sheltered her from the demands of the outside world, that home did seem at times like an alien land and she a stranger in it. Emily loved the members of her immediate family, but gulfs separated her from each of them. Because of the intensity of her sense of solitude, even within the confines of her own home, she spent her entire adult life managing the commerce both between herself and the outside world and between herself and the separate members of the Dickinson family. "Home" may have been "a holy place" for Emily Dickinson, but even within its confines she often felt "homeless at home."

By 1850, Edward Dickinson had repaired the damage done to the family's reputation and fortunes by Samuel Fowler Dickinson's fiscal irresponsibility. His law practice had grown nicely during Emily's childhood years, and around Amherst he acquired a reputation for probity and dependability. His appointment as treasurer of Amherst College in 1835 was one sign of the high esteem in which he had already come to be held. By 1850, Edward Dickinson had also established himself as a significant political force in western Massachusetts, having served in various capacities in both state and local government; in 1852, he was even elected to a term in the U.S. House of Representatives. In these active years, Dickinson involved himself in virtually every civic project of note in Amherst and took particular pride in his role in spearheading the drive to bring the railroad to the town in 1853.

In a letter to Austin, Emily reported on their father's proud bearing on the day the rail line opened. As was often the case, the daughter was amused by her father's peculiar public persona. "The New London Day passed off grandly," Emily wrote. (The first train to Amherst had carried a contingent from New London, Connecticut.) She reported that "it was pretty hot and dusty, but nobody cared for that. Father was, as usual, Chief Marshal of the day, and went marching around the town with New London at his heels like some old Roman General, upon a Triumph Day." While her father led the parade, Emily took to the woods to watch the spectacle in seclusion. "They all said t'was fine. I spose it was — I sat in Prof Tyler's woods and saw the train move off, and then ran home again for fear somebody would see me, or ask me how I did." As was to be so often the case in their relationship, Edward provided the spectacle and Emily served as the spectator.

In every facet of his adult life — from his avid support of formal education to his view of marriage as "a life of rational happiness" — Edward Dickinson was captivated by Whig standards of balance, prudence, and sobriety. He exhibited a starchy restraint that many noted when they first met him. After Thomas Wentworth Higginson paid his initial visit to the Dickinson home in 1870, he summed up his impression memorably: "I saw Mr. Dickinson this morning a little — ," he

65

wrote his wife, "thin dry & speechless — I saw what her life has been." Higginson concluded his assessment with a perceptive distinction: "Her father was not severe I should think but remote."

Two decades later, after the first editions of Emily's poetry had appeared, the subtlety had disappeared from most accounts of Mr. Dickinson's character, as he became a convenient explanatory device for his daughter's unusual behavior. For instance, Mabel Loomis Todd turned Higginson's critical sketch into a damning portrait. "It must have been a stiff, Puritanical and trying home. . . . It made me indignant [to hear of Edward Dickinson's behavior]," she wrote in her journal several years after Emily's death. "The father was terrific[,] . . . an overbearing man. He kept the girls down in a little valley in his mind," Todd complained. Emily "was repressed, and had nothing to do with young men." The reason was simple: "The father and mother would not let young men come [to the house] for fear they would marry."

Emily Dickinson's own picture of her father — drawn in a number of letters from her adult life — is more subtly sketched and carefully shaded than this caricature. To be sure, her father does appear in her letters as a distant figure badly out of place in the world of sentiment and romantic ideas that appealed to his children. As such, he became over the years a natural subject for his daughter's satire. Yet while Emily gently mocked his foibles, she did so with a mixture of consternation and affection. Edward Dickinson may not have fathomed his daughter's character, but she gauged him with impressive accuracy. When she discussed him in her letters, her tone was neither reverential nor dismissive. And as much as he frustrated and occasionally frightened her, she accepted his peculiarities and encouraged others, especially Austin, to do the same.

While Austin was away from Amherst for several years in the early 1850s, teaching school and then attending Harvard Law School, Emily wrote him often and made their father a common subject. In one letter, she described the elaborate ritual Edward Dickinson went through each time a letter from Austin arrived. First, he took the letter to his law office and read it in privacy, regardless of whether it had been addressed to him or another family member. Then he went home, had Emily read the letter aloud to the whole family at supper, and, finally, "he cracks a few walnuts, puts his spectacles on, and with your last [letter] in his hand, sits down to enjoy the evening." All in all,

"Father says your letters are altogether before Shakespeare, and he will have them published to put in our library."

Austin often skirmished with his father, and Emily's letters to her brother during this period made frequent reference to their differences. "For all you differ, Austin — " Emily told her brother, "he cant get along without you, and he's been just as bleak as a November day, ever since you've been gone." Emily had to accept the fact that, as the only son, Austin was viewed with a special deference by the father he challenged so often. "I do think it's so funny — " she confessed to him, "you and father do nothing but 'fisticuff' all the while you're at home, and the minute you are separated, you become such devoted friends; but this is a checkered life."

Every bit as strong willed as her brother, and more witty than he, Emily herself crossed swords on occasion with her humorless father. One letter to Austin recounted an evening out in Amherst and the price she paid for it: "Tutor Howland was here as *usual*, during the afternoon — after tea I went to see Sue — had a nice little visit with her — then went to see Emily Fowler, and arrived home at 9 — found Father in great agitation at my protracted stay — and mother and Vinnie in tears, for fear that he would kill me." Yet Emily was hardly defenseless in such combat. If her father sternly disapproved of her actions, she could counter with impish resistance. One instance of the daughter's defiance became known as "the anecdote of the plate": "One day, sitting down at the dinner table, [Edward Dickinson] inquired whether a certain nicked plate must always be placed before him. Emily took the hint. She carried the plate to the garden and pulverized it on a stone, 'just to remind' her, she said, not to give it to her father again."

As she entered adulthood, Emily was particularly struck by her father's awkward earnestness. At times, his dour personality prompted her own mirth. On one occasion, she, her father, mother, and Lavinia traveled to hear the fabled Jenny Lind in concert in neighboring Northampton. "Father sat all the evening looking *mad*, and *silly*, and yet so much amused you would have *died* a laughing," she reported to Austin. When the performers took their bows at the end of the concert, "he said 'Good evening Sir' — and when they retired, 'very well — that will do,' it was'nt *sarcasm* exactly, nor it was'nt *disdain*, it was infinitely funnier than either of those virtues, as if old Abraham had come to see the show, and thought it was all very well, but a little excess of *Monkey!*"

Prudent and rational as he was, Edward Dickinson could not comprehend the passion for sentimental fiction that his children shared with their peers. "Father was very severe to me; he thought I'd been trifling with you," Emily reported to Austin on one occasion, "so he gave me quite a trimming about 'Uncle Tom' and 'Charles Dickens' and these 'modern Literati.'" Many years later she related how, in 1849 or 1850, Austin had smuggled into the home a copy of Longfellow's popular romance *Kavanagh*. Brother and sister hid it under the piano cover, where their father eventually came upon it and expressed his strong displeasure. As a Whig, Edward Dickinson sought to balance liberty with control, particularly in training his two daughters for the circumscribed roles he and his culture envisioned for them. For Emily, this meant that he wanted her to be well educated yet protected from any possible harmful effects of the ideas she encountered. As she explained in her first letter to Higginson: "[Father] buys me many Books — but begs me not to read them — because he fears they joggle the Mind."

On rare occasions, Edward Dickinson dropped his reserve. "My father seems to me often the oldest and the oddest sort of a foreigner," Emily wrote to a friend who had left Amherst. But at times, "Father says in fugitive moments when he forgets the barrister & lapses into the man, says that his life has been passed in a wilderness or on an island — of late he says on an island." His daughter reported that sometimes she heard his voice in the morning and it seemed to come "from afar & has a sea tone & there is a hum of hoarseness about [it] & a suggestion of remoteness as far as the isle of Juan Fernandez."

Like a number of his qualities, Edward Dickinson's stiffness worked its way into Emily's understanding of God. When Higginson asked about her family in 1862, Emily informed him that she had a "Father, too busy with his Briefs — to notice what we do — ." She went on to tell Higginson that her father worshiped a deity as remote from him as he, her father, was from her. "They are religious — except me — and address an Eclipse, every morning — whom they call their 'Father.'" Even in his leisure habits, her father could be chilly and stately. "My father only reads on Sunday — he reads *lonely* & *rigorous* books," she told Higginson, running together in her account God, her father, and their mutual lonely rigor.

Like her father, God often appeared to Emily to be remote and taciturn:

I know that He exists.
Somewhere — in Silence —
He has hid his rare life
From our gross eyes. [#338]

While God lives "Somewhere — in Silence," we are "Immured the whole of Life/Within a magic Prison" for a "Crime" which "from us, is hidden." Perhaps our ignorance is due to the fact that "Omnipotence — had not a Tongue" and speaks not directly but only through "Lightning — and the Sun — . . . [and] the Sea — " [#420]. These signs may hint of God, but he himself remains silent:

Aloud
Is nothing that is chief,
But still,
Divinity dwells under seal. [#662]

Like Edward Dickinson, "the Jehovahs — are no Babblers — " [#626].

When Dickinson decided not to join the church, she knew she was spurning a heavenly father who resembled her earthly one in his shrouded loneliness. While her family, led by her father, came to terms with the "Eclipse," she kept her distance and embraced a costly isolation. From a later vantage point, it is perhaps easy to celebrate as a triumphant gesture her dismissal of this distant God, but Emily's opinion at the time was not that settled. For whatever brave statements she made to the contrary, Emily would always have some misgivings about having swerved from the path her father had put down before her.

It took a long time for Emily to become comfortable with her rejection of an active life in the church. In 1854, when she was still attending weekly services with the family, she wrote to friends about a sermon that had agitated her. A visiting minister had "preached about death and judgment, and what would become of those, meaning Austin and me, who behaved improperly — and somehow the sermon scared me." While she had been troubled by the sobering message, she concealed her distress from her family, because "father and Vinnie looked very solemn as if the whole was true. . . . The subject of perdition seemed to please [the visiting minister], somehow. It seems very solemn to me."

Looked at one way, this incident appears to confirm the view that Emily Dickinson's father, her God, and her Puritan training formed an unholy alliance against which the enlightened Emily rebelled. One of her foremost biographers, for example, interprets the episode in this manner. Richard Sewall contrasts her response with a comment in a letter she wrote near the end of her life. When Josiah Holland died in 1881, Emily wrote to comfort his widow Elizabeth. She remembered a prayer offered by Josiah when she had visited the Holland home thirty years earlier. "*That* God must be a friend — *that* was a different God — and I almost felt warmer myself, in the midst of a tie so sunshiny," she assured Elizabeth Holland. Comparing this happy memory to the account of the "solemn . . . subject of perdition," Sewall concludes that the Hollands' "congeniality was . . . religious. Their God was her God." And the "sunshiny" Deity was infinitely preferable to "the God she left behind in Amherst."

In actuality, the fact that the sermon "scared" and "troubled" Emily without disturbing her father suggests that she may have been closer in temperament to the Puritans than were her church and family. One cannot imagine early Puritans like John Winthrop, Mary Rowlandson, or Jonathan Edwards being "pleased" by "the subject of perdition" in this way. Sermons about hell were meant to terrify their hearers, not to comfort them. Afflicted by that sermon, Emily was brought close to the point of what the Puritans would have called saving grace. Her father's equanimity, on the other hand, bears the marks of a self-satisfied cosmopolitan who is confident that his own rectitude will shield him from peril.

Edward Dickinson was as formal with God as he was with his family, friends, and associates. Years after the fact, Austin's college friend George Gould described Mr. Dickinson's conversion in 1850: "While Hon. E.D. of Amherst was converted — who had long been under conviction — His pastor said to him in his study — 'You want to come to Christ as a *lawyer* — but you must come to him as a *poor sinner* — get down on your knees & let me pray for you, & then pray for yourself." Edward Dickinson was "a grand type of a class now extinct — An Old-School-Gentleman-Whig!" wrote his niece years after his death, as she tried to put into perspective this taciturn man. "His bearing was almost stern in its dignity and nobility, but his nature was as beautiful, and sympathetic, and tender as a mother's."

If Edward Dickinson had both a bearing as stiff as "an Old-School-Gentleman-Whig" as well as a nature as "tender as a mother's," then one might wonder what traits were left for the poet's mother, Emily Norcross Dickinson. Of all those in Emily Dickinson's immediate family, she is the one least remarked upon in Emily's writings as well as in the remembrances of friends. Unlike her husband and three children, Mrs. Dickinson never gained prominence of any kind; she left behind a scanty record of letters, and she is the one member of the Dickinson family whose presence never looms large in Emily's own letters. The niece who called Edward a "Gentleman-Whig" described her aunt, Emily Norcross Dickinson, as "a quiet, sweet, practical, un-pretentiously-modest woman . . . to whom I think Emily was a great mystery and constant surprise." And while it may overstate the case, Mabel Loomis Todd's summary judgment has the ring of truth: "Their mother, quiet gentle little lady, died without causing a perceptible ripple on the surface of anyone's life or giving concern to any of her family."

Emily Norcross Dickinson's phlegmatic temperament made her unremarkable in a household of talented and volatile individuals. Her natural tendency to withdraw from affairs in and outside of the home was intensified around 1850, when she began to suffer a series of unspecified infirmities. For much of Emily Dickinson's adult life, her mother was a semi-invalid who required considerable care and whose share of the household duties increasingly fell to her daughters. After visiting Mrs. Dickinson in 1843, a neighbor, Ann Shepard, reported to her sister Mary that Mrs. Dickinson "was as usual full of plaintive talk." Two decades later, the Shepards were still taking note of Mrs. Dickinson's health and mental states. In 1860, Mary told relatives that "*Mrs. Edward Dickinson*" had paid a call and appeared "as well as 4 years ago — when she last was here." Mrs. Dickinson, it seems, was so often ill and incapacitated that her periods of health were news in Amherst. Mary Shepard wrote in 1863 that "Mrs. Edward Dickinson sent [Dr. Stearns, President of Amherst College] a most elegant Boquet — on Monday, — she . . . is now quite herself."

Emily's own references to her mother point to a relationship that was complex without being deep. While she treated her father with ironic defensiveness, Emily was at times openly dismissive of her mother. "I never had a mother," Dickinson told Higginson at their first meeting in 1870. "I suppose a mother is one to whom you hurry when you are troubled." The harshness of this claim spoke of the distance that separated mother and daughter. After he had paid a second visit four years later, Dickinson wrote to Higginson of her sadness after he had left. "I always ran Home to Awe when a child, if anything befell me," she explained. "He was an awful Mother, but I liked him better than none. There remained this shelter after you left me the other Day."

At times in Emily's letters Mrs. Dickinson became the subject of lighthearted laughter rather than sarcastic reproach. "Father and mother sit in state in the sitting room perusing such papers only, as they are well assured have nothing carnal in them," Emily wrote in one letter to Austin, gently mocking her mother's moralizing habits. "Mother feels quite troubled about those little boys," she told her brother, when he had written home about his problems with disciplining difficult students. "[She] fears you will kill one sometime when you are punishing him — for *her sake* be careful!" Mrs. Dickinson rarely swerved out of the orbit of family and friends, and when she did so she was lost. For example, when Mrs. Dickinson attended an Amherst lecture on the economic theory of Adam Smith, Emily had to report that "mother went out with Father, but thought the lecture too high for her unobtrusive faculties."

So too were Emily's poetic gifts and peculiar temperament apparently "too high" for her mother's "unobtrusive faculties." Mrs. Dickinson showed little interest in Emily's literary activities and had no idea of her daughter's phenomenal intellectual range. Edward Dickinson at least recognized Emily's intelligence and bought her books, even if he did fear that they might "joggle her mind." Emily Norcross Dickinson never even reached that point of insight in her understanding of her daughter.

Yet at the same time, with the exception of Vinnie, no one spent more time with Emily Dickinson as an adult than did her mother. For almost twenty years, they were together every day. While Edward and Austin Dickinson were absent from home much of the time, the Dickinson women were together, at work on domestic affairs, for as Millicent Todd Bingham explains, "in Emily's day domestic activity was still a full-time career for women." From the earliest days of Emily's life, when Emily Norcross Dickinson wrote to Edward, "I have retired to my chamber for a little space to converse with you, with my little companion on the bed asleep," to the last days of her mother's life, when Emily and Lavinia cared for their incapacitated parent, daughter and mother were united by propinquity and a reversal of roles. "We were never intimate Mother and Children while she was our Mother," Emily admitted to a friend soon after Mrs. Dickinson's death, "but Mines in the same Ground meet by tunneling and when she became our Child, the Affection came."

In early adulthood, Dickinson had begun the journey that would carry her ever deeper into herself. Limited as a woman to a narrow range of choices, she began in the years after Mount Holyoke to make a virtue of necessity by forsaking the social world and its allotted roles for the sake of the infinite possibilities of the inner life. However "homeless" she felt at home, Emily nonetheless found within her family's home a shelter of inestimable value, as she set out to map the uncharted territories of consciousness. Hers was to be a quintessentially modern life, one in which inner realities outweighed the whole of the outside world. Having chosen to move within herself, Emily Dickinson would demonstrate both the grand creative possibilities of modern inwardness and its sometimes frightening, self-consuming powers.

5 Laying Away the Phantoms

The Soul selects her own Society —
Then — shuts the Door —
To her divine Majority —
Present no more — [#303]

Ah John — *Gone?*

Then I lift the lid to my box of Phantoms, and lay another in, unto the Resurrection — Then will I gather in *Paradise,* the blossoms fallen here, and on the shores of the sea of Light, seek my missing sands.

ON A DECEMBER MORNING in the late 1840s, Austin Dickinson sat down to write to Joseph Lyman, his former roommate at the Williston Academy. He had much to tell his friend, because there had been great activity in the Dickinson household in recent weeks. "It is a beautiful, warm morning. I am seated at the kitchen table," began Austin. "The window is wide open. Within is no one, without is Mr. Godfrey, feeding his hens; a brisk fire crackles in the old stove. The

74

cocks, all about, are crowing, Emily has just come in with an old tin pail in her hand (what she has been, or is going to do with it I dont know), and, now, has gone out again. The college clock is striking 'seven.'" An hour earlier, as Austin was finishing tethering the family horse and buggy to the front steps, the "two mysterious forms" of his mother and father appeared and "immediately seated themselves in the wagon and drove off to Monson" to visit Mrs. Dickinson's family. Since they were to be gone until the following day, and Vinnie was away in Boston, Austin told Lyman "that Emily and I are left, lord and lady of the 'mansion', 'with none to molest or make us afraid'. We are anticipating a fine time in the absence of the ancient people. Wish you were here to help us laugh — I think there is a chance for our having some company tonight. — "

Austin's letter gives the impression of high spirits and constant activity in the Dickinson household and the Dickinson children's lives. When he wrote this letter, Austin was a twenty-year-old college student whose friends were always stopping by the Homestead to pay their respects to the family and flirt with his younger sisters. Vinnie was a high-spirited girl in her mid-teens, and Emily, two years older, was fresh out of school and active in Amherst social life. Never again would the Dickinson home be as lively as it was in the years between Emily's return from Mount Holyoke in 1848 and Austin's marriage in 1856.

"The last week has been a merry one in Amherst, & notes have flown around like, snowflakes," Emily wrote to a recent Amherst graduate on Valentine's Day in 1849. "Ancient gentlemen, & spinsters, . . . have doffed their wrinkles — in exchange for smiles — even this aged world of our's, has thrown away it's staff — and spectacles, & *now* declares it will be young again." A year later, she announced to her uncle that "Amherst is alive with fun this winter. . . . Parties cant find fun enough — because all the best ones are engaged to attend balls a week beforehand — beaus can be had for the taking — maids smile like the mornings in June — Oh a very great town this is!"

Almost half a century later, Emily Fowler Ford, an Amherst native and close childhood friend of Emily's, would recall these active years with fondness. "We had a Shakespeare Club — a rare thing in those days." When one of the men from Amherst College suggested that they mark out in their texts all the "questionable passages," Emily with a "lofty air . . . took her departure, saying, 'There's nothing wicked in

75

Shakespeare and if there is I don't want to know it.'" Emily Dickinson, Ford tells us, "mingled freely in all the companies and excursions of the moment and the evening frolics."

According to Ford, Emily Dickinson "was not beautiful yet she had great beauties. Her eyes were lovely auburn, soft and warm, and her hair lay in rings of the same color all over her head." (Dickinson was a little over five feet tall; we can only estimate her height, based upon the fact that her coffin was 5' 6" long. One who had seen her in adulthood remembered her as "a tiny figure in white . . . [with] a pair of great, dark eyes set in a small, pale, delicately chiseled face, and a little body.") Emily had a "demure manner which brightened easily into fun, where she felt at home." But even then, Emily had developed a tendency to withdraw within herself. When strangers came into her midst, she became "shy, silent and even deprecating." Already, it seems, Emily had begun to draw a small circle of intimates around herself and to close out the world.

"A GENTLE, YET GRAVE PRECEPTOR"

Of the many friendships Emily Dickinson formed in the years immediately after Mount Holyoke, none made as deep an impression as the one she had with Benjamin Franklin Newton. She met Newton in 1848, when he was training as a clerk in her father's law office. During the two years that he studied with Edward Dickinson, Newton was a frequent guest at the Dickinson home, where he spent many hours talking with the family's elder daughter about innumerable subjects, including poetry. When he finished his training, Newton returned to his native town of Worcester, Massachusetts. From Worcester, he often wrote to Emily, until his death from tuberculosis in 1853.

Several months after Newton's death, Dickinson contacted his pastor for reassurance about her friend's spiritual state and eternal destiny. The pastor was Edward Everett Hale, a Unitarian minister who was later to become an author and public figure of some renown. She turned to him in desperation for news about her deceased friend, because she had nowhere else to go to learn about his last days. "I have never met [his wife]," she told Hale in January of 1854, "nor have I a friend in Worcester who could satisfy my inquiries."

She was especially eager to learn whether Newton's "last hours were cheerful, and if he was willing to die." That phrase — "if he was willing to die" — had deep roots in Puritan tradition and nineteenth-century New England practice and was connected to the practice of the deathbed vigil. If a dying person's "behavior was characterized by calm acceptance and Christian composure, the chances were good that the soul could be sure of its election," explains Barton Levi St. Armand. Thus Dickinson informed Hale that Ben Newton "often talked of God, but I do not know certainly if he was his Father in Heaven — Please, Sir, to tell me if he was willing to die, and . . . I should love so much to know certainly, that he was today in Heaven."

Newton had been to her "a gentle, yet grave Preceptor, teaching me what to read, what authors to admire, . . . and that sublimer lesson, a faith in things unseen," Dickinson told Hale. During his time in Amherst, the law student had encouraged Dickinson to hone her poetic skills. When she was nineteen, he had given her an edition of Ralph Waldo Emerson's *Poems* — "a beautiful copy," she called it — and before he left Amherst, Newton inscribed her autograph book: "All can write autographs, but few paragraphs; for we are mostly no more than *names*. B. F. Newton August 1849."

Newton was the first to recognize Dickinson's remarkable verbal dexterity, and he encouraged her to dream of a poetic career. "My dying Tutor told me that he would like to live till I had been a poet," she told Higginson many years later. Newton, she explained to Higginson, had opened poetry to her: "When a little Girl, I had a friend, who taught me Immortality — but venturing too near, himself — he never returned." In mourning Ben Newton, Dickinson was lamenting the untimely death of a brilliant young man, but she was also grieving the loss of one of the most encouraging critics she would ever have.

In calling Newton her "Preceptor," Dickinson gave him a name that she prized but used sparingly. She thought of a "Preceptor" as one who had traveled before into an unknown land and could, as a result, tutor her about all that he learned. She granted this title to only a few people in her lifetime. At the beginning of her correspondence with Higginson, she asked, "but, will you be my Preceptor, Mr Higginson?" With his experience as a published author and widely recognized man of letters, Higginson could help her make her way through uncharted waters. And in a letter written to console her sister-in-law Susan over the sudden death of her eight-year-old son, Gilbert, Emily was to write, "Now my ascended Playmate must instruct *me*. Show us, prattling Preceptor, but the way to thee!"

As she turned to her "Preceptors," Dickinson saw them as one of several supports for bearing the pressures of the autonomy she treasured. She was, in effect, seeking guidance for her solitary journey, looking for assistance on how to live without aid. While cherishing the soul's power to "select her own Society," she knew how isolating it was to close the "Valves of her Attention — /Like Stone" [#303]:

> Adventure most unto itself
> The Soul condemned to be —
> Attended by a single Hound
> Its own identity. [#822]

As she chose not to have intimate, immediate contact beyond her family, Dickinson increasingly came to speak in terms of communion with the printed page, of conversation with disembodied thoughts, and of inner dialogue with her own consciousness. Even relatively early in her life, when "Tutor [Newton] died," she wrote years after the fact, "for several years, my Lexicon — was my only companion — ."

In times of strength, Dickinson could lean confidently upon her "Columnar Self," but in times of sorrow, grief, or fear, she often stumbled and cast about for support. In her poems, the lost guide and vanished path became potent images of her need. "Those — dying then,/Knew where they went," she wrote in one poem. They went to "God's Right Hand," but since "That Hand is amputated now," God "cannot be found" [#1551]. In search of evidence of the kind that Dickinson had sought concerning Ben Newton — information about the destiny of loved ones and the nature of the next world — we anxiously watch "a Dying Eye/Run round and round a room" and desperately seek to find "what it be/'Twere blessed to have seen" [#547]. Lost in our confusion, we "pluck" at any "twig of Evidence" and ask of "a Vane, the way" to God [#501]; and yet it is left to each of us alone to "slowly ford the Mystery" that the dead have already "leaped across!" [#1564].

Ben Newton's death was the first of many that would make her passionately protective of those she loved and jealous of the God who stole them from her. "Perhaps Death — gave me awe for friends,"

Emily explained to Higginson in 1863, at the height of the Civil War, "— striking sharp and early, for I held them since — in a brittle love — of more alarm, than peace." In 1885, after death had robbed her of many friends and family members in only a few short years, Emily asked: "Why should we censure Othello, when the Criterion Lover says, 'Thou shalt have no other Gods before Me'?"

When Dickinson told Higginson that "for several years" after Newton's death, her "Lexicon — was my only companion," she was being only mildly hyperbolic. In these years of early adulthood, Dickinson was fashioning a manner of living that would enable her to endure the pain of dying. She was learning how to do so largely by sharpening, and deepening, her use of language. "I never lost as much but twice,/And that was in the sod," she explained in one of her earliest poems, written only a few years after Newton's death:

> Twice have I stood a beggar
> Before the door of God!
>
> Angels — twice descending
> Reimbursed my store —
> Burglar! Banker — Father!
> I am poor once more! [#49]

Here, at the outset of her poetic career and the start of her seclusion, Dickinson sounded like Job, who responded to shocking loss and suffering with worshipful resignation and prayerful supplication: " 'Naked I came from my mother's womb, and naked shall I return there; the Lord gave, and the Lord has taken away; blessed be the name of the Lord'" (Job 1:21). As she came to doubt the character of God, however, Dickinson grew ever more protective of her loved ones and her intimate feelings. The more God stole from her, the more she tried to hoard.

Like Herman Melville's Captain Ahab, over the years Dickinson came to think of God as a jealous God. Ahab confronted the jealousy of God with a jealousy of his own: "I'd strike the sun if it insulted me. For could the sun do that, then could I do the other; since there is ever a sort of fair play herein, jealousy presiding over all creations." But rather than strike out at God, Dickinson secluded herself. By withdrawing from the world, she could husband her emotional resources by keeping others from intruding into her grief, and she could steel herself against disappointment by guarding her most cherished memories and experiences.

"ONLY A HAPPEN"

While Dickinson's seclusion would not become complete until her early thirties, then, her retreat had begun a decade earlier. Initially, the withdrawal took the form of a self-conscious distancing from events in which she participated and from certain people she wished to avoid. Only later did it become the complete isolation so readily associated with the poet in the popular mind. Because it unfolded gradually, Dickinson's seclusion did not strike her family as exceptional, nor did they or anyone else at the time attribute it to an emotional trauma or romantic disappointment. Her slow assumption of isolation was, Vinnie remarked years later, "only a happen."

To a significant extent, Dickinson learned the virtues of emotional seclusion from the sentimental fiction of her day and from the romantic tradition she had inherited. Even in adolescence, she had begun to acquire that habit of "thinking" which may leave us "beside ourselves in a sane sense," as Henry David Thoreau describes it in *Walden*. Thoreau's point is that "by a conscious effort of the mind we can stand aloof from actions and their consequences; and all things, good and bad, go by us like a torrent. We are not wholly involved in Nature." Explaining that he knows himself only "as a human entity," Thoreau says that he is "sensible of a certain doubleness by which I can stand as remote from myself as from another."

According to Thoreau, this doubleness can alienate us from our own experience as well as from neighbors, family, and friends. "However intense my experience, I am conscious of the presence and criticism of a part of me, which, as it were, is not a part of me, but spectator, sharing no experience, but taking note of it. . . . When the play, it may be the tragedy, of life is over, the spectator goes his way. It was a kind of fiction, a work of the imagination only, so far as he was concerned. This doubleness may easily make us poor neighbors and friends sometimes."

Dickinson's letters from this period offer a clear picture of the "doubleness" that made her a "poor neighbor and friend sometimes." In early 1854, she wrote to Austin about a dull night she had spent talking with George Howland, an Amherst classmate of her brother's. Vinnie was visiting Austin in Cambridge at the time, and Emily wrote that while her brother and sister were no doubt having "nice times, . . . sitting and talking together," Emily was "lonely here," forced to endure the company of Howland while her mind drifted to imagined scenes one hundred miles to the east of her: "I *wanted* to sit and think of you, and fancy what you were saying, all the evening long, but — ordained otherwise." In like manner, a year later she reported from Washington to Susan Gilbert that while she and Vinnie were outwardly busy in the nation's capital, "my thoughts are far from idle, concerning e'en the *trifles* of the world at home, but all is jostle, here — scramble and confusion."

For the first several years after her return from Mount Holyoke, life at home for Dickinson did indeed seem "all jostle . . . scramble and confusion." Her social calendar was often packed with visits from friends and outings around Amherst. Only a week after Ben Newton's death, for example, Emily wrote to Austin about the hectic pace of life in the Dickinson home. She explained to him that Susan Gilbert "comes down here most every day," that their friend Emily Ford had spent the previous afternoon at the house, that one "Dr. Brewster was in town yesterday, and took tea here," that "the girls 'Musical'" met at the Dickinson home on Tuesday evening, that Rufus Cowles paid a call the previous evening, and, finally, that the children of their new neighbors seemed to "spend most of their time in our door yard."

Vinnie documented the hectic pace of life at the Dickinsons' home in a diary that she kept in 1851, Emily's twenty-first year. Her entries tell of ceaseless activity in the Dickinson household, showing that over the course of the year she and Emily made and received "social calls to be numbered in the hundreds." For Vinnie, two of the callers that year prompted serious thoughts of marriage, and one actually proposed to her.

One of those men was Joseph Lyman, Austin's friend. A frequent visitor at the Homestead, Lyman took liberties with seventeen-year-old Vinnie and relished recounting them in detail years later: "She sat in my lap and pulled the pins from her long soft chestnut hair and tied the long silken mass around my neck and kissed me again & again. She

81

was always at my side clinging to my arm and used to have a little red ottoman that she brought & placed close by my chair and laid her book across my lap when she read. Her skin was very soft. Her arms were fat & white and I was very, very happy with her."

Thoughts of marriage were on the minds of Vinnie and Joseph on what turned out to be the last day they spent together, March 25, 1851. On that day Emily, Vinnie, Joseph Lyman, and "a large company" went on a sugaring expedition to neighboring Montague. Lyman was scheduled to depart the following day for an indefinite stay in the South. "A gay party of us went up from Amherst to Montague on a Sugar Excursion. I was with the Dickinson family," Lyman wrote several years after the fact. "Vinnies Love was shed around me softer than the balmy air," he explained. "We spent all the afternoon in the woods there rambling about, laughing, talking. I had been with Emily a good deal & with Jane Hitchcock and Mary Warner."

Pondering the loss of "Vinnies Love, & what I could do with it during all the years," Lyman slipped away from Emily and her friends. "Then Vinnie came unto me & took my hand & said — 'O Joseph I havn't seen much of you today.'" Lyman defended himself by explaining that he had stayed away from Vinnie because he thought it best not to "pay you very marked attention before all these people. I would avoid everything like gossip." Vinnie overpowered him by insisting that he come with her: "I love you, and I am proud of you and I am proud of you and of your love — I want people to know that you love me — come, Joseph, they are all going to the carriages. Let me take your arm and we will sit together in the carriage. — O Joseph *must* you go tomorrow!'" When they returned to the Dickinsons', "*a storm arose* in the house," apparently over Vinnie's flirtation with Lyman. He came to the Dickinson house the next day for a final walk with Vinnie and then left Amherst for good.

Several years later, Lyman explained to his fiancée, Laura Baker, the differences between the Dickinson sisters. "If Vinnie had been fit to be the wife of a self-made man I would have married her some time ago. But she is only a 'milk white fawn' — But her kisses — those kisses!" According to Lyman, Vinnie's problem was that her "kisses & caresses" were of the kind "that make us naughty handsome men fawn upon & flatter beauty and then pass her bye." Solid and substantial, Vinnie was rooted in the earth. "If she had not thought so much of that fine house & carriage & roses her student lover would have 'come back' long ago."

Emily, on the other hand, was a creature too fine for earthly passions. "Emily you see is platonic," Lyman wrote. Unlike Vinnie, "She never stood 'tranced in long Embraces mixed with kisses sweeter, sweeter than anything on Earth.'" Instead, Emily shared with Joseph "a consciousness of what the whole of Life is — . . . . I regard even small acts as segments of one Grand Circle of Life" and "the spiritual world — the sphere of sainted souls & angelic intelligences never seems very far from my memory & conceptions." For Lyman, Emily was at the center of this "Sphere": "It is the blending of these gleams of the highest spirituality with the common details of human life that gives a quaintness & originality that used to amuse & please Em Dickinson greatly — Emily understood it perfectly — She was inside the ring — but Vinnie only admired & loved — .''

Lyman understood Emily Dickinson better than some of her relatives and early biographers did. His image of being "inside the ring" gives a clue to one of Dickinson's own favorite words, "circumference." Lyman told Laura Baker that Emily was one of the very few people who had, in regard to himself, "closed the circle of knowledge"; she had "understood."

This image fit with the sense of inwardness that Emily's generation was cultivating so assiduously. In matters of aesthetic taste and sentiment, Austin, Vinnie, Joseph, and Ben Newton were in the ring, while her parents were decidedly outside. And so it was in any number of areas for the educated young adults in general in that generation and for Emily in particular. But on the question of Emily's decision not to marry, who was "inside the ring"? Who knew her heart on these matters? Here, as elsewhere, Emily was guarded and secretive, keeping her reasons to herself or expressing them so elliptically that few could decipher her intentions. What she once wrote about immortality seems apropos of certain of her own life's secrets: "Secrets are interesting, but they are also solemn — and speculate with all our might, we cannot ascertain." In some of the most intimate matters of her life, Emily left little evidence for later interpreters, and in the history of speculation about that life, the lack of evidence has provided a rich soil for rumors to grow in.

The story of Dickinson's early romantic life was to be further complicated by a history of bitter division within her own family. Less than three years before Emily died, her brother began a twelve-year affair with Mabel Loomis Todd. She was the wife of an Amherst professor and was to become the first editor of Emily Dickinson's poems and letters. In addition to embittering relations within his immediate family, Austin's affair with Mabel Todd divided the town of Amherst and distorted both the early editions of Emily's poetry and the first accounts of her life.

Following a series of personal and legal battles in the years immediately after Austin's death in 1895, Emily's poetic manuscripts were almost evenly divided between his widow and his mistress. One partisan in the ongoing dispute between Susan Dickinson and Mabel Loomis Todd called it the "War between the Houses." Alfred Stearns, who had been raised in Amherst at the end of the nineteenth century, wrote decades later that "this strange feud . . . refused to die, and for many years continued to rear its ugly head. Even hostesses had to plan their parties and dinners with meticulous care lest inadvertently they should invite representatives of enemy camps."

The animosities aroused by the Todd-Dickinson affair were quickly projected back upon Emily Dickinson's life, once her poetry had found an appreciative audience. She had appeared, as it were, out of nowhere, and her readers were insatiably curious about the life behind the poems. Advocates of both sides in the dispute fabricated stories about Emily's failures at love, creating competing accounts of rejected suitors and varying tales of doomed affairs. When Emily died, her life became, in effect, a blank slate upon which partisans in a bitter family feud drafted their separate versions of her story.

There were, of course, understandable reasons for the speculation about Dickinson's refusal of marriage and her seclusion. Why would a young woman of enormous energy and ability begin a retreat into a forbidding solitude? In her twentieth year, Emily was writing about how "the last week has been a merry one in Amherst," celebrating the fact that "Amherst is alive with fun this winter," and declaring, "Oh a very great town this is!" She was a vibrant woman on the go in Amherst and the Connecticut River valley. Yet by her thirtieth year, she had retreated within her home, rarely entertaining visitors and hardly ever emerging again. What happened?

For many observers, the only explanation could be that Emily was a forsaken woman who had been frustrated in love. This view was furthered by her niece, Martha Dickinson Bianchi, a fierce partisan in the protracted war between Austin and Sue. In her account of her aunt's life, Bianchi fabricated a sensational story out of precious few facts. To explain her aunt's seclusion, she focused on the trip that Emily made to Washington in 1855. Having visited their father there at the end of his single term in the House of Representatives, Emily and Vinnie stopped in Philadelphia for several weeks. While staying with friends in that city, Emily may have heard the famed Presbyterian preacher, Charles Wadsworth. The two became somehow acquainted around this time, and he later paid two brief visits to the Dickinson home, in 1860 and 1880.

Working with nothing but this bare outline and a "confidence [told by Emily] to her Sister Sue, sacredly guarded under all provocation," Bianchi concocted a version of her aunt's life as a gothic story of doomed spinsterhood. Alluding to Wadsworth, Bianchi wrote that in Philadelphia "Emily met the fate she had instinctively shunned." Without warning, love struck her, and she could not resist: "Emily was overtaken — doomed once and forever by her own heart. It was instantaneous, overwhelming, impossible." Emily and Wadsworth were "two predestined souls kept apart only by high sense of duty." That sense of duty kept Emily from doing something that would have led to "the inevitable destruction of another woman's life."

"Without stopping to look back, she fled to her own home for refuge — as a wild thing running from whatever it may be that pursues." Within days, Wadsworth followed her to Amherst, "but the one word he implored, Emily would not say." Having been wounded and rebuffed, Wadsworth did the only honorable thing; he "silently withdrew [from Philadelphia] with his wife and an only child to a remote city, a continent's width remote." Undeterred by an utter lack of evidence, Bianchi, and many who followed her interpretive lead, read Wadsworth's decision to assume a San Francisco pastorate in 1862 as proof of his embarrassed retreat in the aftermath of Emily's rejection of him.

According to the poet's niece, Wadsworth moved a continent away in disgrace, and "Emily went on alone in the old house under the pines. . . . From this time on she clung more intensely to the tender shadows of her father's house. She still saw her friends and neighbors from time to time, but even then her life had begun to go on in hidden ways." Only her sister-in-law Susan was to know that "love had been home to [Emily] for an instant." The despondent Emily dwelt only within the memory of that love, while "her little form flitted tranquil through the sunny small industries of her day, until night gave her the right to watch with her flowers and liberated fancies." For the rest of her life, Emily chose the solitude of "her father's house," because "she was as truly a nun as any vowed celibate, but the altar she served was veiled from every eye save that of God."

Those who sided with Mabel Loomis Todd and against Susan Dickinson offered their own versions of this love story. The most elaborate of the opposing accounts appeared in an early biography of Dickinson by the American poet Genevieve Taggard. Her account came complete with a sworn affidavit from a person designated as "X." According to "X," at the age of nineteen, Emily fell in love with George Gould, one of Austin's Amherst classmates and a frequent visitor at the Dickinson home. Shortly before Gould was to graduate, claims Taggard, "Emily sent word to her lover to meet her at a certain hour." She arrayed herself all in white, "and when her lover appeared she told him that her father had forbidden her to see him" or to write to him anymore. While submitting to her father's will, she nevertheless "promised to love him [George Gould] as long as she lived, . . . [and] told him she would dress in white, fall, winter, spring, and summer, and never again would go outside the gate, but live the life of a recluse — for his sake."

Though they were on opposing sides of the Todd-Dickinson dispute, Martha Dickinson Bianchi and Genevieve Taggard were each convinced that their separate disclosures would solve the riddle of Emily's seclusion. Bianchi boasted that she had finally made sense "of that chapter" in her aunt's "life which has been so universally misunderstood, so stupidly if not wantonly misrepresented." And Taggard claimed that the "revelation [of George Gould as Emily's lover] . . . is the single fact we have so much needed to know in order to simplify Emily Dickinson's life, cluttered as it now is with absurd and unnatural suppositions."

Common to each of these claims is the belief that only the renunciation of a man's love could explain Emily Dickinson's refusal to marry and her retreat from society. These accounts turned her seclusion into a heroic gesture chosen for the noblest of middle-class ends, the sacrifice of marriage. In making Dickinson's solitude a story of renunciation, Bianchi, Taggard, and others take their place in a long history of the romantic praise of women's suffering on behalf of men. More recent accounts that trace Dickinson's seclusion to her alleged lesbianism are essentially following the lead of the earlier versions of her life. They attribute her actions to a different sexual principle but retain the standard heroic reading of her renunciation of a public life.

In contrast, it is striking that for all the antagonisms that divided Austin, Vinnie, and Sue from one another after Emily's death in 1886, these family intimates offered similar interpretations of her reclusiveness. Unified in their reading of her retreat from outward life, they were neither alarmed nor mystified by Emily's seclusion. They took it as a matter of course and offered no dramatic explanations for what they considered a perfectly plausible choice.

Of the three, Austin sympathized most readily with Emily's decision to withdraw from the world. Like her, he loved solitude and was subject to attacks of melancholy anxiety. Grandfather Samuel Fowler Dickinson had sought leadership in the Connecticut River valley; father Edward Dickinson had worn the mantle of responsibility with stoic pride; Austin, the last of the Dickinson men to lead a public life, squirmed under the burdens of duty. He might well have longed for the isolation that became his sister's lot. To Austin, Emily's "curious leaving of outer life never seemed unnatural," according to Mabel Loomis Todd. "He told me about her girlhood and her normal blossoming and gradual retirement, and her few love affairs. Her life was perfectly natural. All the village gossip merely amused him."

The gossip did not amuse Vinnie. When a reviewer of the first edition of the *Letters* repeated a rumor already circulating widely about Emily — less than a decade after her death — Vinnie responded tartly. The reviewer claimed that a Dickinson relative had come to see her and had told her "'it was in Washington . . . that Emily met her fate. Her father absolutely refused his consent to her marriage for no reason that was ever given.'" Denied this man's love, Emily lived off the resources of her own spirit. She "needed no sustenance, so immortal was her love, so elastic her spirit. . . . In a few years her friend passed out of sight. I think from various indications that she never knew where his body lay."

Vinnie, ever protective of her family's legacy and her sister's reputation, dismissed this lachrymose account. "Emily never had any love disaster," she wrote. "She had the choicest friendships among the rarest men and women all her life, and was cut to the heart when death robbed her again and again." Emily chose seclusion gradually and naturally. "Emily's so called 'withdrawal from general society', for which she never cared, was only a happen. Our mother had a period of invalidism, and one of her daughters must be constantly at home; Emily chose this part and, finding the life with her books and nature so congenial, continued to live it, always seeing her chosen friends and doing her part for the happiness of the home." Vinnie complained that this was not the first time she had been forced to respond to lies about her sister's life. As she put it, "there has been an endeavor to invent and enforce a reason for Emily's peculiar and wonderful genius."

After Emily died, Vinnie and her sister-in-law Sue were often bitterly at odds on family matters. But on the subject of Emily's choice of seclusion, they were in almost complete agreement. In an unsigned obituary that appeared in the *Springfield Republican* three days after Emily's death, Sue wrote of her sister-in-law and neighbor that "as she passed on in life, her sensitive nature shrank from much personal contact with the world, and more and more turned to her own large wealth of individual resources for companionship, sitting thenceforth, as some one said of her, 'in the light of her own fire.'" Emily was "not disappointed with the world, [and was] not an invalid." Nor did she lack sympathy for the world; she could well have had a flourishing "social career — her endowments being so exceptional — but the 'mesh of her soul,' as Browning calls the body, was too rare, and the sacred quiet of her own home proved the fit atmosphere for her worth and work."

"SISTER SUE"

When the editors of the *Republican* turned to Sue for an obituary of Emily, they chose a person especially well suited to document the course of the secluded poet's life. Sue had been Emily's closest friend for a number of years in late adolescence and early adulthood, she had married into the Dickinson family in 1856, and she had lived in the house next door to Emily for the last three decades of the poet's life. Over the course of almost forty years, Emily had sent Sue more than one hundred letters and close to three hundred poems. Aside from the members of Emily's immediate family, no one had known Emily as intimately as Susan Gilbert Dickinson had.

The friendship began around 1850, when the two of them were emerging into adulthood from dramatically different backgrounds. Emily had grown up in a stable home headed by a father whose professional reputation was impeccable; Susan, on the other hand, had been an orphan for almost a decade when she met Emily and was struggling to overcome her tavern-keeping father's legacy of poverty and shame. As a child, Sue had to live at times off the charity of neighbors, for the Gilbert family was "'so poor that the neighbors had to take things in to make them comfortable.'" When their mother died in 1836, Sue and her three sisters went to live with an aunt and uncle in Geneva, New York; when Thomas Gilbert died in 1841, records listed him as an "insolvent debtor." Sue moved back to Amherst several years later. She soon met the Dickinsons, and in 1856, ten years after her return, she married Austin and settled next door to Emily and her family.

Emily had a number of close women friends and correspondents throughout her life, but her intimacy with Sue was unique. In the words of Lillian Federman, Emily's early letters to Sue are unmistakably different from those she wrote to women "with whom she was merely good friends." They daringly develop themes only hinted at in Emily's early letters to Jane Humphrey and Abiah Root; and they express passions that appear only "in a significantly attenuated form" in certain of Emily's later letters to such women as Kate Scott Anthon and Elizabeth Holland. When she wrote to Sue, Emily indulged fantasies about the sharing of secret affections and perceptions, including the furtive exchange of "hurried kisses and whispered good-byes," and spoke repeatedly of her desire to join with her friend in a league against parents and the adult world.

In many of the letters written before the marriage of Austin and Sue in 1856 — and especially those from the year that Sue spent teaching in Baltimore (1851-52) — Emily freely mixed romantic passion and religious devotion. "The dishes may wait dear Susie — " she wrote in one, "*them* I have always with me, but you, I have 'not always' — *why*

Susie, Christ hath saints *manie* — and I have *few*, but thee — ." Parted
from Sue against her will, Emily could do nothing but "take up my
little cross again of sad — *sad* separation." Several letters spoke of
Emily's urge to yield to Sue's care: "Oh Susie, I would nestle close to
your warm heart. . . . Is there any room there for me, or shall I wander
away all homeless and alone?" She needed the love of Sue, because
"nobody loves me here [at home]." Her refuge was "here in dear Susie's
bosom," where she could "hide away from them all" and find the "love
and rest" she so ardently sought. Once safely caught up in Sue's love,
"I never would go away, did not the big world call me, and beat me
for not working."

In another letter, written on a Sunday morning in February of
1852, Emily urged Sue not to follow "the people who love God, [and]
are expecting to go to meeting." Instead, she pleaded, "come with me
this morning to the church within our hearts, where . . . the preacher
whose name is Love — shall intercede there for us!" In the sanctuary
of their intimacy, Emily spoke a language of erotic devotion. "When I
was gone to meeting," she told Sue in another Sunday letter, the
thought of "one kiss" from Sue "filled my mind so full, I could not find
a *chink* to put the worthy pastor; when he said 'Our Heavenly Father,'
I said 'Oh Darling Sue.'" As the pastor read Psalm 100, Emily recited
to herself a recent letter from Sue, and as the choir sang, Emily "made
up words and kept singing how I loved you, and you had gone, while
all the rest of the choir were singing Hallelujahs." And in a final Sunday
letter, written only a week before Sue was to return to Amherst from
Baltimore, Emily explained that, while the minister that morning was
giving some "startling" facts about "the Roman Catholic system,"
Emily found herself "trying to make up my mind wh' of the two was
prettiest to go and welcome *you* in, my fawn colored dress, or my blue
dress." Just as she decided to wear the blue dress, "down came the
minister's fist with a terrible rap on the counter, and Susie, it scared
me so."

Her friendship with Sue fit into a pattern that had already begun
to take shape in Emily's childhood relationships with Austin and
Vinnie. They were the first to have joined Emily "inside the ring,"
where the secrets of private experience were more highly prized than
the truths of common life. In the solitude of her reflections and the
privacy of her intense experiences, Dickinson was reaching the conclu-

sion, as one observer has put it, that "real life is private life, the events happening in the grand theater of the mind." She seized upon the nineteenth century's unprecedented emphasis upon inwardness and developed it in her own highly individual manner.

Others were invited "into the ring" in Emily's adolescence, as she formed her circle of female friends, and then in early adulthood, as Ben Newton, Susan Gilbert, and a few others became members of her "select society." By the time this pattern had become fixed in Emily's late twenties, she had grown thoroughly accustomed to making sharp distinctions between an intimate group of friends and family and all her other contacts with the world outside her door. Like many romantic poets and nineteenth-century novelists, Dickinson considered the illicit pleasures of secrecy and inwardness superior to the dull demands of public life. What distinguished her from the other major writers of her day was the degree to which she lived out the distinctions established in romantic theories of society and the self. She embodied what they imagined.

In her lived understanding of intimacy and "the grand theater of the mind" Dickinson was once again playing out some of the extreme possibilities latent in New England Puritanism. Where they had the inscrutable mysteries of the doctrine of election, she had secrecy and selection; where they had the gathered church, she had her own coterie of friends "inside the ring"; and where the Puritans had confession as a prerequisite for admission to the intimacies of the Lord's Supper, Dickinson set rigorous standards of emotional and aesthetic intensity for her closest friendships.

The Puritan inwardness of Dickinson's theological past fed into the romantic inwardness of her cultural present. As Harold Bloom explains, for more than a millennium in Western history before the Enlightenment and romanticism, the movement of Christian narratives had been "from nature to redeemed nature, the sanction of redemption being the gift of some external spiritual authority, sometimes magical." Redemption came to the fallen self as a gift from outside and beyond that self. But with its stress upon volition and inwardness, Protestantism began the slow shift toward the modern view of the solitary self as a vast source of spiritual power. Romanticism dramatically accelerated that turn inward by transferring the center of redemptive activity from external sources — be they nature, church, or God — to the inner domain of the ever-expanding self. In Bloom's words, the romantics moved "from nature to the imagination's freedom, and the imagination's freedom is frequently purgatorial, redemptive but destructive of the social self." Neither Emily Dickinson's particular form of seclusion nor her poetic vision of the self would have been conceivable without the Puritan past and romantic present that shaped her understanding.

While welcoming what Bloom calls the "destruction of the social self," Emily's letters to Susan reveal some of the costs of "imagination's freedom." In appropriating for the self powers and prerogatives formerly assigned to God, romanticism exposed the self to a heightened risk of disillusionment. It did so by placing the burden of unlimited expectations upon very limited human realities. Simply put, the ability of the human mind to imagine perfection is infinite, while the capacity to achieve it is not. In the Christian tradition, this difficulty is related to the distinction that St. Augustine outlined in *On Christian Doctrine.* "Some things are to be enjoyed, others to be used," he noted. Those "things which are to be enjoyed are the Father, the Son, and the Holy Spirit," and if we "seek to enjoy those things which should be used, our course will be impeded and sometimes deflected, so that we are . . . shackled by an inferior love." Viewed in light of Augustine's categories, the romantic impulse that swept through northwestern Europe and America in the early nineteenth century involved an attempt to transform objects of use — self, other, nature — into objects of enjoyment.

At one level, of course, Emily was merely being playful when she told her friend that she had substituted "Oh Darling Sue" for the pastor's "Our Heavenly Father." But at another level, she was absolutely serious about such substitutions, and her disappointment could be deep when her subjects failed. As many romantics did, Dickinson regretted that her objects of devotion never lived up to her expectations. Her difficulties were a specific instance of what Erich Heller has identified as a negative consequence of the romantic stress upon infinite human desire. Disappointed at every turn by the meager response it receives to its ardor and affections, the romantic temperament is tempted to conclude that the world is "an unfit partner for receiving the confidences of spirit and passion." Having placed in Sue nothing short of a religious trust, Emily was inevitably going to conclude that this friend was somehow "an unfit partner" for her spirit and passion.

The relationship between the two began to be troubled a few years before Sue married Austin. In a letter written sometime in the early 1850s, Austin told Sue that he was surprised to have learned of her "deprivation of 'Spiritual converse' with my sister." He was concerned that Sue's and Emily's "correspondence was at an end." Always protective of his sister and the family bond, Austin told Sue that she should not "suspect" him "of having interfered with [her] epistolary intercourse" with Emily. He could neither be blamed for his Emily's obstinacy nor expected to dictate her choices, for his sister had always exercised liberty in creating the society she desired: "Her choice of friends and correspondents is a matter over which I have never exerted any control — ."

In November of 1853, Emily heard a sermon on disappointment at the First Church. It was preached by Edwards Amasa Park, the distinguished theologian from Andover Seminary, and its subject was Judas. In Emily's words, Park's theme was "the disappointment of Jesus in Judas." Twenty years later, she still referred to it as "the loveliest sermon I ever heard." What fascinated her about this "mortal story of intimate young men" was its focus upon betrayal and disenchantment. Judas was hardly the man that the human Jesus had taken him to be: "I suppose no surprise we can ever have will be so sick as that." The sermon no doubt spoke to Emily's own "surprise" at what she was learning about Sue, and about herself, as their friendship failed to meet her matchless expectations.

In a letter written in the summer of 1854, Emily complained of Sue's failure to write to her. Sue had been away from Amherst for some time, visiting relatives in New York and Michigan. Emily admitted, "I've not written to you," but gave as her reason the fact that "I was foolish eno' to be vexed at a little thing." That "little thing" was that Sue had not written once to Emily during her entire time away from Amherst. Emily had received her only news of Sue "thro' Austin." Though hurt by her friend's failure to write, Emily nevertheless had told "nobody in this world except Vinnie and Austin, . . . I have not heard from you."

Such notes of discord served as a prelude to a decisive letter Emily wrote later that year. In some unexplained way, Sue had grievously disappointed her friend. "Sue — you can go or stay — " begins the letter. "There is but one alternative — We differ often lately, and this must be the last." Emily anticipated and mocked the concern that Sue might claim to have for her, for she, Emily, was beginning to understand the comforts of retreat and seclusion. "You need not fear to leave me lest I should be alone, for I often part with things I fancy I have loved, — sometimes to the grave, and sometimes to an oblivion rather bitterer than death — ." Here, as elsewhere, the letters of the young woman anticipated the imagery of the mature poet, for less than a decade after this painful breech with Sue, Emily was to write of a "Quartz contentment, like a stone — " and of closing "the Valves of her attention — /Like Stone — ." Disappointment, she was learning, can wither and harden the heart:

> Such incidents would grieve me when I was but a child, and perhaps I could have wept when little feet hard by mine, stood still in the coffin, but eyes grow dry sometimes, and hearts get crisp and cinder.

In this letter, Emily identified her affection for Sue as a form of idolatry, drawing a link between the pain of disillusionment and the prohibition against idols in monotheistic religion. Dickinson was, after all, a descendant of Calvinism as well as a child of romanticism, and she retained enough Protestant skepticism to censure her own idolatry of persons. "Few have been given me, and if I love them so," she concluded to Sue, "that for *idolatry*, they are removed from me — I simply murmur *gone*, and the billow dies away into the boundless blue, and no one knows but me, that one went down today." With a melodramatic flourish, Emily told her friend that even if "the Jesus Christ you love, remark he does not know me — " she, Emily, could be content to "remain alone," for "there is a darker spirit will not disown it's child."

Like others before and after it, this tempest subsided and gave way to a period of calm with Emily's and Sue's friendship damaged but renewed. Not surprisingly, after the mid-1850s that friendship would never again have the intensity of its initial years. But it did endure in altered form until the end of Emily's life, as Sue served a number of crucial roles for her, including sister, neighbor, confidant, and critic. She would never again, however, be the object of enchantment she had been for Emily for a few brief years.

Her father had tried to teach her the mastery of her passions, but lessons in stoic acceptance did not come easily for the Amherst poet. She never grew accustomed to loss, but felt each new incident like the rawest of wounds, and she was forced to relearn the healing power of self-control with each new grief. "After great pain, a formal feeling comes — " she wrote in one of her best-known poems. "The Nerves sit ceremonious, like Tombs — ."

> This is the Hour of Lead —
> Remembered, if outlived,
> As freezing persons, recollect the Snow —
> First — Chill — then Stupor — then the letting go — [#341]

Dickinson was letting go of a great deal in the 1850s. In those years — the period immediately before she began to write poetry on a regular basis — she was giving up any thought of a vocation, any prospect of marriage, and any sustained direct contact with the world beyond her "Father's house." At least twice in the mid-1850s, Emily used an image of phantoms to speak of her losses while justifying the withdrawal of her affections and her retreat from the world. Early in 1855, she wrote to Sue in Michigan, complaining again about her friend's failure to write. "Not one word comes back to me from that silent West," she wrote. "If it is finished, tell me, and I will raise the lid to my box of Phantoms, and lay one more love in." A year later she wrote a final letter to her cousin John Graves, a favorite of hers who had spent a great deal of time at the Dickinson home during his senior year at Amherst College. When she wrote to Graves in 1856, he was about to enter the ministry in another state:

> Ah John — *Gone?*
> Then I lift the lid to my box of Phantoms, and lay another in, unto the Resurrection — Then will I gather in *Paradise*, the blossoms fallen here, and on the shores of the sea of Light, seek my missing sands.

In the decade after she had finished her schooling, Emily was developing the "piercing virtue" of renunciation. The exercise of that virtue entailed far more than a simple distaste for the world or a fear of human contact. It had to do with the mastery of the self, its appetites and expectations. As a product of Whig culture, Dickinson was always scouting out the most effective means of self-development and self-mastery. By her late twenties, she had realized that she could best control her complex apprehensions and longings through closely managed solitude. "To put this World down, like a Bundle — / And walk steady, away," she wrote in 1862, "Requires Energy — possibly Agony — " [#527].

In adulthood, Dickinson came to accept as a paradox the fact that the very limits that thwarted her desires also prompted her to develop her imaginative powers. By accepting restraints and imposing them upon herself through renunciation, she defined her adult vocational choice. By the age of thirty, she was ready to enter the theater for her career. She had chosen, that is, to train her formidable attention on the "Human Heart," the "Only Theatre recorded Owner cannot shut." For the remainder of her life, Dickinson's primary work was to be that of acting and interpreting the drama played out in "the grand theater of the mind." As far as she was concerned, there was never an end to this work, for "To live is so startling, it leaves but little room for other occupations."

"As for Emily," Lavinia perceptively observed after her sister's death, "she was not withdrawn or exclusive really. She was always watching for the rewarding person to come, but she was a very busy person herself. She had to think — she was the only one of us who had that to do. Father believed; and mother loved; and Austin had Amherst; and I had the family to keep track of." During the decade following her return home from school, Emily learned to think in the exceptional manner that was to manifest itself in her poetry and letters so distinctly. She was about to become a poet.

6 A Soul at the White Heat

Dare you see a Soul *at the White Heat?*
Then crouch within the door —
Red — is the Fire's common tint —
But when the vivid Ore
Has vanquished Flame's conditions,
It quivers from the Forge
Without a color, but the light
Of unanointed Blaze. [#365]

A S SHE APPROACHED the age of thirty, having laid one after another of her intense relationships into her "box of Phantoms . . . unto the Resurrection," Emily Dickinson slowly retreated to the confines of the Homestead and the precincts of her own consciousness. From there she would continue to sally forth until the end of her life, but only in the manner she chose, through her letters and poems.

Dickinson began to write poetry in earnest in her mid-twenties and reached a peak of productivity in her early thirties, when she wrote more than 350 poems in a single year, 1862. During the same years that she began her steady production of poetry, Dickinson stopped visiting at the homes of Amherst neighbors and gave up going to church. She would make two more trips to Boston in 1864 and 1865, but these were for the sole purpose of receiving special care for her eyes. For all practical purposes, Emily Dickinson had become a recluse by 1860, when the Civil War was about to begin.

Dickinson's drive to seclude herself was aided by a subtle yet distinct shift in Amherst social life. Soon after Austin and Sue were married in 1856, their home, the Evergreens, replaced the Edward Dickinson household as a social center in the village. Increasingly, family, friends, and notable visitors came to Austin's and Sue's home, rather than to the Homestead next door.

Emily maintained close contact with events at the Evergreens and remained for several years a participant in its social life. In an 1858 letter to Samuel and Mary Bowles, she wrote that "Jerusalem must be like Sue's Drawing Room, when we are talking and laughing there, and you and Mrs. Bowles are by." Half a century later, Emily's and Sue's friend, Kate Anthon, would recall with pleasure evenings at the Evergreens: "The golden days you & I have spent together — Oh! dear Sue how vividly I recall them! Those happy visits at your house! Those celestial evenings in the Library — the blazing wood fire! Emily — Austin — the music — the rampant fun — the inextinguishable laughter." Within a few years, even these visits would end.

For Dickinson, the period from 1858 to 1862 proved as trying to her personally as it was to be for the nation politically. Her letters from this period make repeated reference to pain. "Much has occurred, dear Uncle, since my writing you," she wrote to Joseph Sweetser in the summer of 1858, " — so much — that I stagger as I write, in its sharp remembrance. . . . Today has been so glad without, and yet so grieved within." In this letter, for Emily the particular source of pain was "this hand upon our fireside," the vague but persistent infirmity of her mother. Later in the same year, the death of a servant's daughter prompted her to write: "Good-night! I can't stay any longer in a world of death!" And less than two years later, Aunt Lavinia Norcross's death overwhelmed her yet again with the pain of life. Emily wrote to Vinnie, who had gone to Boston to nurse their dying aunt: "Blessed Aunt Lavinia now; all the world goes out, and I see nothing but her room. . . . Then I sob and cry till I can hardly see my way 'round the house again."

Whatever its sources, sorrow staggered Dickinson repeatedly in these years. The weight of that sorrow can be felt in one of the first letters she wrote to Thomas Wentworth Higginson in 1862: "I had a terror — since September — I could tell to none — and so I sing, as the Boy does by the Burying Ground — because I am afraid — ." Dickinson told Higginson nothing more specific about this "terror," but years later it was still on her mind. In 1869, a year before Higginson was to pay his first visit to his Amherst correspondent, she wrote to him about the sorrow she had suffered in 1861 and 1862: "You were not aware that you saved my Life. To thank you in person has been since then one of my few requests."

"TITLE DIVINE — IS MINE"

The letters that Dickinson wrote are our best source of information about her life during her most prolific years. From the period of her greatest poetic productivity — 1858 to 1865 — more than 125 letters have survived. Among them are three sets of correspondence that reveal with clarity the tensions Dickinson felt keenly about love, solitude, and poetry in this period of inner turmoil and national conflict. Each set of letters to a different correspondent evidences its own unique concerns; yet, taken together, they provide a surprisingly coherent picture of Dickinson's passion and pain at this harried time.

The smallest and most cryptic set of letters consists of three drafts written to an unknown recipient between 1858 and 1861 and found among the poet's papers at her death. There is no proof that they were ever sent, but as Ralph Franklin suggests, "Dickinson did not write letters as a fictional genre, and these were surely part of a much larger correspondence yet unknown to us." We may never know the identity of the man, or woman, to whom these letters were written, but their subject was undeniably an object of Dickinson's deep affection at the time that she wrote them.

The first of the three letters, written in 1858, is addressed "Dear Master." It begins with the statement "I am ill," and then proceeds to sympathize with "Master's" own illness, which may have brought him close to death. "I thought perhaps you were in Heaven, and when you spoke again, it seemed quite sweet, and wonderful, and surprised me so — " Dickinson writes. "I wish that you were well." Compared to the two later "Master" letters, this first is positively subdued. It concludes with Dickinson's hope of seeing her "Master" again and with wishes for his complete recovery. "Each Sabbath on the Sea, makes me count the Sabbaths, till we meet on shore — . . . Will you tell me, please to tell me, soon as you are well."

The two "Master" letters written in early and mid-1861 sound a note that is markedly more passionate. These drafts are filled with enough clues and ambiguities to have kept several generations of readers guessing at the identity of the "Master." The first of the two opens with an apology for an unspecified offense: "Oh, did I offend it — [Did'nt it want me to tell the truth]." Dickinson's offense may have been that she had declared her love, "a love so big it scares her, rushing among her small heart — pushing aside the blood and leaving her faint." Calling herself "Daisy," an image of gentle beauty and perhaps "Master's" pet name for her, she confesses that although she "never flinched thro' that awful parting," she "held her life so tight he should not see the wound." She worries that perhaps she did "grieve her Lord" and pictured herself "low at the knee that bore her once into [royal] wordless rest." Some have argued that such references point to Otis Phillips Lord as "Master." Lord was a friend of her father, he could have dandled young Emily on his knee, and she did write a series of passionate love letters to him twenty years after the "Master" letters had been composed.

"You send the water over the Dam in my brown eyes — " Dickinson tells "Master" in her second letter. She has "a Tomahawk in my side but that dont hurt me much. Her master stabs her more — ." More than anything, this letter concludes, she craves rest from her "Master" and a mooring for her weary spirit. She closes with a plea: "Master — open your life wide, and take me in forever, I will never be tired — ."

The final of the three letters begins with a protest over "Master's" refusal to believe what Dickinson has confided to him. "Master," she implores, "If you saw a bullet hit a Bird — and he told you he was'nt shot — you might weep at his courtesy, but you would certainly doubt his word." What would it take to make him believe her? "One more drop from the gash that stains your Daisy's bosom — then would you *believe?*" The erotic undertone in this letter is clear. "Daisy" only wished that "it had been God's will that I might breathe where you breathed — and find the place — myself — at night — ." She longs "with a might

I cannot repress — that mine were the Queen's place — . . . To come nearer than presbyteries — and nearer than the new Coat — that the Tailor made — ." What would have been his response had their roles been reversed? "If I had the Beard on my cheek — like you — and you — had Daisy's petals — and you cared so for me — what would become of you?"

Dickinson represents herself as desperate to see "Master." "What would you do with me if I came 'in white?'" she asks. "I want to see you more — Sir — than all I wish for in this world — . . . Could you come to New England — [this summer — could] would you come to Amherst — Would you like to come — Master?" She has been faithful to him and honest with him. She can "wait more — wait till my hazel hair is dappled — " but would rather have him by her side: "It were comfort forever — just to look in your face, while you looked in mine — then I could play in the woods till Dark — till you take me where Sundown cannot find us — ."

This final letter contains enough clues to lead one to believe that "Master" might have been the Presbyterian pastor from Philadelphia, Charles Wadsworth. Dickinson wanted to "come nearer [to him] than Presbyteries," spoke of having asked him for one kind of " 'Redemption' — which rested men and women" and of having received another kind ("you gave me something else"), and begged him to "come to New England, to Amherst" as soon as possible. Wadsworth left his Philadelphia pulpit to assume a San Francisco pastorate in 1862. Though there is no evidence to this effect, some have speculated that his departure was the "crisis" that marked Dickinson's life at the start of the Civil War.

But on the other hand, "Master" might have been Samuel Bowles, the Dickinson family friend and editor of the *Springfield Republican*. Bowles was the only one of the candidates who had a "Beard on [his] cheek"; he was seriously ill during the period when the letters were written; and some of the "Master" letters' symbolic terms — "Daisy," "Chillon," and others — found their way into letters that Dickinson wrote to him at roughly this same time.

To know the identity of the Master would solve some of the riddles about Emily Dickinson's life. But until new evidence surfaces, perhaps the most that one can say with certainty is to agree with Vivian Pollak that "while in all probability not a figure of pure fantasy,

101

['Master'] is best understood as an idealized masculine alter ego." Some "Master" no doubt existed and was the object of Dickinson's complex, frustrated affections at this difficult point in her life. Yet to interpret her life, it may be less important to know who the "Master" was than to understand the considerable role he played in her imagination.

Austin scoffed at attempts to identify a single lover as the source of Emily's emotional afflictions and her withdrawal from public life. "He said that at different times Emily had been devoted to several men. He even went so far as to maintain that she had been several times in love, in her own way," Millicent Todd Bingham explains. "But he denied that because of her devotion to any one man she forsook all others. Such an idea was mere 'nonsense.'" Whoever "Master" was, he did not prompt Emily's withdrawal from the world. Instead, her anxiety about "Master" was only one of the many forms that her ongoing struggle with renunciation assumed.

In addition to being one of Austin's and Sue's closest friends, Samuel Bowles — one of the candidates for "Master" — received a flurry of letters from Emily in this period. When the Dickinsons came to know him in the late 1850s, Bowles was the editor of one of America's most influential newspapers, the *Springfield Daily Republican*. He regarded Amherst, which was a relatively short distance from Springfield, as a retreat center of sorts. As his biographer explains, "one of his favorite resorts was the house of his friend Austin Dickinson. . . . It was a place where he was perfectly at home; he was on terms of brotherly intimacy with Mr. and Mrs. Dickinson." In later years, Amherst gossip would have it that Susan Dickinson "wanted to have a salon in Amherst with Samuel Bowles & his questionable relationship to Mrs. Austin as a background." Another source spoke of Sue's "flirtations with delightful Sam Bowles, and of how she sent her husband off for a few hours occasionally in order that she might pursue her foolishness with him, untrammelled." But according to Bowles's official biographer, there was a simpler, more innocent explanation. At Austin's and Sue's home, Bowles "was glad to be spared from callers, and would give himself up to lazy enjoyment. . . . Once as he lay on the piazza with the apple-blossoms blowing over him, — 'This,' he said, 'I guess, is as near heaven as we shall ever get in this life!'"

It was a journey of a hundred yards to the east from Austin's to Emily's home, and Bowles made the trip often, especially in the early years of his acquaintance with the Dickinsons. Emily's letters give the impression that his calls made for antic times at the increasingly quiet Homestead. In a letter from 1860, for example, Dickinson apologized for her impulsive behavior during a Bowles visit: "I am much ashamed. I misbehaved tonight. I would like to sit in the dust." Her excuse for her manic manner was that "I am gay to see you — because you come so scarcely, else I had been graver."

When Dickinson's correspondence with Bowles began, his *Springfield Republican* had already published two of her poems. The first, titled "A Valentine," had appeared in the February 20, 1852, edition of the paper. It came into the hands of the *Republican*'s editors by unknown means, but they liked what they saw and wished to publish more: "The hand that wrote the following amusing medley to a gentleman friend of ours, as a 'valentine,' is capable of writing very fine things, and there is certainly no presumption in entertaining a private wish that a correspondence, more direct than this, may be established between it and the Republican." While the poem was published anonymously, many readers appear to have known who had written it. A first cousin of Emily's mother transcribed "A Valentine" into her commonplace book, with the notation "Valentine by Miss E Dickinson of Amherst." The editors of Dickinson's poems conclude that "the knowledge of her authorship [of 'A Valentine'] clearly was abroad." Several years later, the *Republican* printed a second Dickinson poem that had been "surreptitiously communicated" to the editors.

Dickinson's letters to Samuel Bowles in the early 1860s were filled with references to Bowles's ailments and her own unspecified afflictions. She often raised the subject of her physical or emotional distress by means of cryptic poems accompanying her brief letters. "I cant explain it, Mr Bowles," Dickinson wrote to him in 1860 about her anguish:

Two swimmers wrestled on the spar
Until the morning sun,
When one turned, smiling, to the land —
Oh God! the other One!
The stray ships — passing, spied a face
Upon the waters borne,
With eyes, in death, still begging, raised,
And hands — beseeching — thrown!

Other letters mentioned the painful attack of sciatica that Bowles experienced in 1861. It came upon him after he and his wife had returned in a sleigh to Springfield from Amherst during a snowstorm. Seeking treatment for his nerve pain and rest for his general state of exhaustion, Bowles spent more than a month at a "water-cure" in nearby Northampton. He may have suggested that Dickinson consider a similar course of treatment at the "Orient," the new spa two miles east of Amherst. She wrote back to him, "Thank you."

> "Faith" is a fine invention
> When Gentlemen can *see* —
> But *Microscopes* are prudent
> In an Emergency.

"You spoke of the 'East.' I have thought about it this winter," Emily admitted. The harrowing of pain, whether of the body or spirit, reminded her of death. "That *Bareheaded life* — under the grass — worries one like a Wasp," she told Bowles.

While he was convalescing from sciatica, Dickinson sent Bowles a letter containing a poem about the healing art of poetry. She assured him, "We pray for your new health — the prayer that goes not down — when they shut the church — We offer you our cups — stintless — as to the Bee — the Lily, her new Liquors — "

> Would you like Summer? Taste of our's —
> Spices? Buy, here!
> Ill! We have Berries, for the parching!
> Weary! Furloughs of Down!
> Perplexed! Estates of Violet — Trouble ne'er looked on!
> Captive! We bring Reprieve of Roses!
> Fainting! Flasks of Air!
> Even for Death — a Fairy Medicine —
> But, which is it — Sir?

Dickinson's reference to "new Liquors" suggests that in this letter she enclosed a copy of yet another poem, "I taste a liquor never brewed — ," which soon appeared in two different editions of the *Springfield Republican* in May of 1861.

As she was to many people, Emily Dickinson was a source of bafflement to Samuel Bowles. One of the most prominent newspaper editors in America, he had considerable power to shape taste and promote writing careers. Dickinson sent him dozens of poems but did not wish to have them published. She spoke of longing to see him and then sometimes refused to appear when he called. She wrote to him of passion and love but chose to live as a recluse. Bowles did not know what to make of Emily, but he was intrigued by her. In April 1863, he wrote Austin that he had "been in a savage, turbulent state for some time — indulging in a sort of [ ] disgust at everything & everybody — I guess a good deal as Emily feels, — . . . Tell Emily I am here, in the old place. 'Can you not watch one hour?[']"

To a point, Bowles could accept Dickinson's mystifying complexity. But he was a naturally effusive and restless man who needed travel and public contact to thrive. At times, he could only draw back in amusement and amazement as he considered the behavior of his Amherst friend. "To the girls & all hearty thought — Vinnie ditto, — & to the Queen Recluse my especial sympathy," Bowles told Austin, referring to Emily in an 1863 letter " — that she has 'overcome the world.' — Is it really true that they ring 'Old Hundred' & 'Alleluia' perpetually, in heaven, ask her; and are dandelions, asphodels, & Maiden's [*vows?*] the standard flowers of the ethereal?"

One factor complicating Dickinson's relationship with Bowles was that the *Springfield Republican* had published several of her poems without permission. On March 1, 1862, the *Republican* had printed yet another poem. "Safe in their Alabaster Chambers" may have come to Bowles in a letter from Emily, or it may have been forwarded to him by Susan Dickinson. Sue had had an extensive exchange with Emily about the poem the previous summer, and several months after she had offered her final editorial suggestions, the poem suddenly appeared in the *Republican*.

Dickinson may have been expressing her disapproval when she wrote a cryptic note to Bowles in the spring of 1862. "Dear friend," the next letter began, "If I amaze[d] your kindness — My Love is my only apology." The affront for which she apologized may have been her refusal to see him when he called, or she may have been trying to explain why Bowles's "kindness" in publishing her poems had not met with gratitude from her. The edges of this letter are worn away, so only portions of certain words remain. In a crucial passage, Dickinson appeared to say that she, "Daisy," did not need to be published in a "Sunday supplement" in order to know her worth as a poet: "Then I mistake — [my] scale — To Da[isy] 'tis *daily* — to be gran[d] and not a "Sunday Su[pp]." Then, using an image that she used several times to explain her reluctance to publish, Dickinson asked Bowles to "[f]orgive the Gills that ask for Air — if it is harm — to breathe!"

Several months later, Dickinson told Higginson, "I smile when you suggest that I delay 'to publish' — that being foreign to my thought, as Firmament to Fin — ." And during the summer of 1862, while Bowles was vacationing in Europe for his health, Dickinson wrote to him that "a Soldier called — a Morning ago, and asked for a Nosegay, to take to Battle. I suppose he thought we kept an Aquarium." The "Soldier" was likely an editor who had asked Dickinson for poems to print in special publications meant to support the Union war effort. ("Nosegays" and "Bouquets" were names that Dickinson used in several poems for her own poetry.) For Emily Dickinson, publication would remove her from her secure element; she was content to swim in the depths of privacy and feared being stranded in the open air of publicity.

Realizing that her obscurity about these matters must have confused Bowles, Dickinson sent him yet another explanatory letter in the form of a poem:

> Title divine — is mine!
> The Wife — without the Sign!
> Acute Degree — conferred on me —
> Empress of Calvary!
> Royal — all but the Crown!
> Betrothed — without the swoon
> God sends us Women —
> When you — hold — Garnet to Garnet —
> Gold — to Gold —
> Born — Bridalled — Shrouded —
> In a Day —
> "My Husband" — women say —
> Stroking the Melody —
> Is *this* — the way?

Here's — what I had to "tell you" — You will tell no other?
Honor — is it's own pawn —

This poem mixes images of suffering, marriage, and denial to explain the inexplicable. Why would a brilliant and attractive woman shun marriage and society for the sake of poetry, and then refuse to publish that poetry and put her talent on display? At one level, the poem promotes the virtue of celibacy, of being "The Wife — without the Sign." "Renunciation is," after all, a "piercing virtue." By having chosen solitude and celibacy, Dickinson had followed a higher calling and would receive a "title divine" as her reward. At the same time, with this poem she might have been trying to "tell" Bowles of her yearning to be a poet "without the Sign" of publication. Just as a woman did not need to be married to know intimate communion, so a poet did not require publication to sense her worth. She "had to tell" Bowles this and trusted he would "tell no other" — that is, that he would not publish her poems, "honor" being "it's own pawn," after all.

Another letter followed closely after this one, as Dickinson made a final attempt to explain why she did not want Bowles or anyone else to publish her work. "Dear friend," she addressed him, "If you doubted my Snow — for a moment — you never will — again — I know — ." By "my Snow" she may have meant the purity of her decision to keep her poetry and life private. As she explained in a famous poem, written at this time, about publication and purity:

Publication — is the Auction
Of the Mind of Man —
Poverty — be justifying
For so foul a thing

Possibly — but We — would rather
From Our Garret go
White — Unto the White Creator —
Than invest — Our Snow —

Thought belong to Him who gave it —
Then — to Him who bear

Its Corporeal illustration — Sell
The Royal Air —

In the Parcel — Be the Merchant
Of the Heavenly Grace —
But reduce no Human Spirit
To Disgrace of Price — [#709]

Emily explained to Bowles in her letter that "because I could not say — I fixed it in the Verse — for you to read — when your thought wavers, for such a foot as mine — ." The poem she included had martyrdom as its theme:

Through the strait pass of suffering —
The Martyrs — even — trod
Their feet — upon Temptation —
Their faces — upon God —

The imagery of this poem may have been suggested to Dickinson, Karen Dandurand notes, "by an article in the *Republican* on 29 March, titled 'Our Martyrs and Their Resurrection,' on writers who gained recognition only after their deaths." In refusing to publish during her lifetime, Dickinson may well have been equating her anonymity with martyrdom. To seek fame in this life would be to give in to temptation, while to march "Through the strait pass of suffering" would be to secure recognition after death. "To be remembered is next to being loved," she believed.

Fame was much on Dickinson's mind in early adulthood. The deeper her solitude became, the more she dwelt upon the topic. It provided the vital links connecting her renunciation of the world, her poetic endeavors, and her longing for an immortality more substantial than the distant heaven of genteel Christianity. In the winter of 1859, she raised the subject in the first of many letters to her cousin Louise Norcross, who was then seventeen years old. "I have known little of you, since the October morning when our families went out driving, and you and I in the dining-room decided to be distinguished," Dickinson told her cousin. "It's a great thing to be great, Loo." In an exchange of letters with Sue about her poetry two years later, Emily expressed a similar hope for eventual fame: "Could I make you and Austin — proud — sometime — a great way off — 'twould give me taller feet — ."

"It's a great thing to be great," but it is best to be so "a great way off" — such is the balance that Dickinson struck between solitude and notoriety. From her father and Whig culture, she had learned that those who would lead an aristocracy of merit needed patience and self-discipline. Those who exhibited such virtues would be rewarded in due time. By the time she began to write poetry, that Whig world had vanished. If the emerging Republican order of commerce, conflict, and self-promotion no longer valued patient restraint, Dickinson neverthe-less remained willing to bank on the judgment of posterity, which is, after all, the poet's eternity. "We might call her the show-off of eter-nity," notes Leo Braudy, "for the innumerable ways she devised to humble herself in the world even as she asserted herself to posterity and to heaven." The brokers of temporal renown spent the specious currency of the moment, but Dickinson was confident that she owned the ore of immortality:

> Some — Work for Immortality —
> The Chiefer part, for Time —
> He — Compensates — immediately —
> The former — Checks — on Fame —
>
> Slow Gold — but Everlasting —
> The Bullion of Today —
> Contrasted with the Currency
> Of Immortality —
>
> A Beggar — Here and There —
> Is gifted to discern
> Beyond the Broker's insight —
> One's — Money — One's — the Mine — [#406]

To Dickinson, writing for the sake of being published in the *Springfield Republican* would be the same as working for "Time" and "Money." According to the economic perspective that took hold of American culture in her lifetime, "time" was something that one put in at an office to earn "money." In the first half of the nineteenth century, historian Richard Bushman explains, "the home was gradually emptied of its commercial and political functions and devoted mostly to family and culture." Instead of acquiescing to this development, Dickinson sought in her own unique manner to make the home a center of production once again, even though she had no wish to enter the public sphere with what she made there. She was willing to bide her time, "Working for Immortality — ." Like the "Spider" of which she wrote — which "sewed at Night/Without a Light/Upon an Arc of White" — she had her own "Strategy" for "Immortality" [#1138].

After having failed several times to convince Samuel Bowles that she did not want to have her poems printed in his paper, Dickinson finally succeeded, and Bowles stopped pressing for poems to print. Only twice more in her lifetime would the *Republican* publish works by Dickinson, once in 1864 with a reprint of a poem published in a Civil War fund-raising paper, and again in 1866, when Sue apparently passed along to Bowles one of Emily's verses. But for now, from Bowles at least, there would be no more pressure to publish, and Emily was glad. "Dear Mr Bowles," she wrote him, "I cant thank you any more — You are thoughtful so many times."

"THE MAJESTY OF THE ART YOU SEEK TO PRACTISE"

"On April 16, 1862," wrote Thomas Wentworth Higginson almost thirty years later, "I took from the post office in Worcester, Mass., where I was then living, the following letter." Bearing an Amherst postmark, the letter consisted of a series of one-sentence paragraphs and was unsigned, the author having identified herself only by signing her name on a card (in its own envelope) accompanying the letter; also included with the letter and card were four poems transcribed on separate sheets of paper.

Higginson was used to receiving unsolicited manuscripts and letters from aspiring authors. He was a distinguished man of letters prized for the beauty of his style and the sagacity of his judgments. He wrote regularly for the *Atlantic Monthly* and enjoyed the company of the major Massachusetts authors of his day. "Higginson and Hawthorne are," wrote the Boston correspondent of the *Springfield Republi-*

can in 1863, "in point of style, the best of the *Atlantic* writers." Unknown poets, essayists, and fiction writers heard in Higginson's prose a welcoming voice and readily sought out his advice.

Even at that, this letter from a woman in Amherst caught his attention. It had a breathless quality to it, and the poems that accompanied it showed signs of brilliance despite their unconventional images and awkward punctuation. Higginson responded promptly to the letter, and thus began a correspondence and friendship that would endure until Dickinson's death in 1886. Over the next several decades, Dickinson was to send him more than seventy additional letters and scores of poems. Higginson responded to her work with curiosity and courtesy; she intrigued him to such an extent that he encouraged her (unsuccessfully) to come to Boston to read her poems in public, twice came to Amherst to pay her visits, and eventually took part in her funeral. After her death, he served with Mabel Loomis Todd as the editor of the initial editions of her poetry.

The immediate occasion for Dickinson's letter had been the appearance in the April 1862 *Atlantic Monthly* of a Higginson essay, "Letter to a Young Contributor." The piece received lavish praise in the *Republican* and elsewhere, and in this young poet the "Letter" struck a responsive chord. To Dickinson, who longed "to be great . . . a great way off," Higginson offered the reassuring possibility of eventual recognition. In all free governments, Higginson noted in the essay, "it is the habit to overrate the *dramatis personae* of the hour." Yet for each new generation, the names of the gifted politicians and orators of the previous era are nothing but hollow, empty sounds. "Of all gifts, eloquence is the most short-lived. The most accomplished orator fades forgotten, and his laurels pass to some hoarse, inaudible Burke." Rhetoric and public life bring immediate gain but inevitable oblivion. But matters are far different with great literature. "'After all,' said the brilliant Choate, with melancholy foreboding, 'a book is the only immortality.'"

Higginson admitted in his essay that disease, "manifold disaster," and a paucity of talent make the odds against creating books that last so great that "it makes one shudder to observe how little of the embodied intellect of any age is left behind." Yet the fact remains, Higginson argued, that brilliant fiction and poetry do emerge and endure. For those endowed with rare genius, the temporal sacrifices required of them pale in comparison to the immortal glory that is to be theirs.

111

Like other aesthetes in the late nineteenth century, Higginson offered literature as an alternate source for the former force of religious belief. His transfer of the language of spiritual passion from God to literature appealed to Dickinson, who was discovering in poetry the solace that conventional faith no longer provided her. Higginson's "Letter" caught her attention at a point when she was eager to fill the void left by her departure from the church and by what she took to be the increasing irrelevance of much Christian doctrine. "Literature is attar of roses, one distilled drop from a million blossoms," Higginson wrote, and within a year Dickinson would compose a poem that borrowed his image and echoed his lofty praise of literary art: "Essential Oils — are wrung — /The Attar from the Rose," she asserted in a lyric that equated the poet's anguish with the suffering of Christ [#675].

Higginson believed that with the help of literature and the perspective of immortality, "we may learn humility, without learning despair, from earth's evanescent glories." To a young poet toiling in self-imposed seclusion, these words from a man of culture brought encouragement. "War or peace, fame or forgetfulness, can bring no real injury to one who has formed the fixed purpose to live nobly day by day." To put the disappointments of the present in perspective, Higginson asked us as his readers to imagine ourselves as artists chatting in the next life. We look back upon our earthly experience and say to each other, "Do you remember yonder planet, where once we went to school?" From the vantage point of eternity, it will matter little whether "our elective study here lay chiefly in the fields of action or of thought."

Even as he praised the immortal powers of literature, Higginson cautioned those who labored to create it. He specifically advised young authors against rushing into print. "Such being the majesty of the art you seek to practise, you can at least take time and deliberation before dishonoring it," he warned. "Writing rapidly" never brings desirable results. "Haste can make you slipshod, but it can never make you graceful." Considering how slowly thoughts develop and take on coherent form, Higginson wrote, "I certainly should never dare to venture into print, but for the confirmed suspicion that the greatest writers have even done so." The truly great writer is patient and writes for the "vast, unimpassioned, unconscious tribunal, this average judgment of intelligent minds." This "tribunal's" judgment forms slowly but endures

112

forever; it "cancels all transitory reputations, and at last becomes the organ of eternal justice and infallibly awards posthumous fame."

When she came upon Higginson's essay in the spring of 1862, Dickinson had already spent several years musing upon the hope of "posthumous fame." What she lacked was a "tribunal" to assist her in the lonely task of assessing her own work. "Are you too deeply occupied to say if my Verse is alive?" she began her letter to Higginson. "The Mind is so near itself — it cannot see, distinctly — and I have none to ask — ." Dickinson wanted to know if her poetry "breathed," or whether she had made a "mistake" in writing verse of this kind. She included with the letter copies of four of her poems and concluded by repeating an admonition she had also given to Samuel Bowles only months earlier. To both she pleaded that they neither publish nor distribute the poems she had sent them in confidence. She told Higginson: "That you will not betray me — it is needless to ask — since Honor is it's own pawn — ."

Many years later, Higginson wrote that Emily Dickinson's first letter to him "was in a handwriting so peculiar that it seemed as if the writer might have taken her first lessons by studying the famous fossil bird-tracks in the museum of that college town." The day after he received it, he complained to James Fields, editor of the *Atlantic Monthly*, "I foresee that 'Young Contributors' will send me worse things than ever now. Two such specimens of verse as came yesterday & day before — fortunately *not* to be forwarded for publication!" Later that same week his tone was somewhat different, when he wrote to his mother: "Since that Letter to a Young Contributor I have more wonderful effusions than ever sent to me to read with request for advice, which is hard to give. Louise [his sister] was quite overwhelmed with two which came in two successive days."

A total of six letters from Dickinson to Higginson followed in quick order before the end of 1862. In them, she offered considerable information about her family but always came back to the matter of Higginson's judgment of her poetry. In his initial response, Higginson must have been frank in criticizing her verse, which was unlike any other he had ever seen. Dickinson opened her second letter with a word of gratitude: "Thank you for the surgery — it was not so painful as I supposed." His critical scalpel cut deeply, as he labeled her poetic "gait 'spasmodic'" and judged her poems as "uncontrolled" and "wayward." Yet as wounded as she was, Dickinson asked for more. "Will you tell me my fault, frankly as to yourself, for I had rather wince, than die," she explained in a letter two months later. "Men do not call the surgeon, to commend — the Bone, but to set it, Sir, and fracture within, is more critical."

In Higginson, Dickinson hoped to find a critical audience without the risk of exposing herself to public scrutiny through publication. Her experience with Bowles and the *Republican* had proven to her that she could publish if she so desired, but she did not wish to do so. "Two Editors of Journals came to my Father's House, this winter — " she wrote Higginson early in their correspondence. They "asked me for my Mind — and when I asked them 'Why,' they said I was penurious — and they, would use it for the World — ." She turned down their request but knew that she needed a critical response of some kind to what was now pouring from her pen. "I could not weigh myself — Myself — " she told Higginson. "My size felt small — to me — I read your Chapters in the Atlantic — and experienced honor for you — I was sure you would not reject a confiding question — ." That was why she had written to request his help.

In answering this letter — which had been accompanied by seven additional Dickinson poems — Higginson praised his Amherst correspondent's poems but warned her not to rush them into print. In her response, she began by telling how deeply his praise had touched her: "I have had few pleasures so deep as your opinion, and if I tried to thank you, my tears would block my tongue — ." She told him that her "dying Tutor" (Benjamin Newton) had wanted to live "till I had been a poet, but Death was much of Mob as I could master — then — ." Dickinson claimed that she had begun to write poetry on a regular basis only "far afterward," when she discovered its therapeutic powers: when "a sudden light on Orchards, or a new fashion in the wind troubled my attention — I felt a palsy, here — the Verses just relieve — ."

"I smile when you suggest that I delay 'to publish' — " she told Higginson amusedly, "that being foreign to my thought, as Firmament to Fin — ." Emily had no desire for the fame that would mark her as one who had been "selected" by her society. "If fame belonged to me," she observed, "I could not escape her — if she did not, the longest day would pass me on the chase — ." Punning on the term for the metrical measure of poetry, she explained, "My Barefoot-Rank is better — ."

When Dickinson was born in 1830, publishing in America was largely a cottage industry. Books were produced and sold locally, with retail booksellers serving as the primary publishers, and there was no such thing as book promotion or publicity. But by 1862, when she first contacted Higginson, the publishing world had become an enterprise of national scope. Independent publishers now dominated the production and distribution of books. These publishers promoted their products with vigor, working hand in hand with newspapers to generate interest in the works and lives of authors. Newspapers published whatever they could discover about favorite authors, as they tried to satisfy an insatiable appetite for news about the private lives of novelists and poets. Dickinson knew the curiosity of readers firsthand because of her own hunger for information about the beloved George Eliot, Elizabeth Barrett Browning, and other writers she revered.

By the middle of the nineteenth century, the emergence of a national market had led to what literary historian William Charvat has termed the creation of three kinds of poets: the mass poet, the public poet, and the private poet. The mass poet "writes primarily to exploit a market," while the public and private poet write in order to fulfill a need within themselves; their "verse . . . originates from the unique privacies of the poet as person." Of these two types of poets the private poet of the mid-nineteenth century is free "to intensify [her uniqueness] through the writing of verse — even at the cost of writing for unintelligibility." But the public poet of the same period "progressively subordinates or submerges his uniqueness" to become a *"spokesman . . . in his time."* The public poet speaks the "vocabulary and syntax familiar to his audience in his time," while the private poet "creates a vocabulary which the world must *learn* as it learns a new language."

It was easy for Emily Dickinson to choose which type of poet she would be. She neither wished to "speak in a vocabulary and syntax familiar" to her audience nor desired to be subjected to the inquiries of a curious public. Those who tried to persuade her to publish learned quickly of her stubbornness on this score. Mary Elwell Storrs was the wife of one of the few men who ever convinced the reluctant Dickinson to allow at least a few of her poems to be put into print. She knew of the difficulties her husband, Richard Salter Storrs, Jr., had overcome to get Dickinson to part with three poems for a fund-raising newspaper during the Civil War. When the first edition of Dickinson's poems was

115

published in 1890, Mary Storrs paid tribute to her friend by writing of Dickinson's fear of public exposure:

> O soul, made white before the great white throne,
> Past Pain! Dost thou released shrink quivering still,
> Laid open, bare, by earth's publicity!
> Yet comfort thee! thy great heart's sympathy,
> Like shadowing pine, like morning's tearful dew,
> Cheers the drear sands, soothes scorching pain to rest!

From the start, Higginson met two of Dickinson's greatest needs. He served as a confidential yet discerning audience of one for this most private of poets, offering his professional advice about the work she sent him; his judgments strengthened her confidence in her poetry's value and bolstered her hopes for posthumous fame. At the same time, Higginson's advice against publishing meshed nicely with her desire to be told by someone else not to do that which would leave her "laid open, bare, by earth's publicity." The third letter that she wrote to him, in June of 1862, ended with praise and a plea. "Would you have time to be the 'friend' you should think I need?" she asked. "The 'hand you stretch me in the Dark,' I put mine in, and turn away — I have no Saxon, now — ." Her "Saxon" was her language, which failed her as she struggled to thank him adequately for his advice and support. She closed with a simple request: "But, will you be my Preceptor, Mr Higginson?"

For the rest of her life, Dickinson would call upon Higginson's authority to resist pressures to publish. From the start, she turned his concern about not printing work prematurely into a categorical prohibition against publication at any time. "You are true, about the 'perfection,'" she wrote him in the summer of 1862, referring to the many cautions his *Atlantic Monthly* piece had contained against the "haste" that "can make you slipshod." It is true, she told him, that "Today, makes Yesterday mean." By the curious logic of this sentence, Dickinson could justify never-ending delays in publishing. If it was inevitable that each new "tomorrow" would make the work of "yesterday" look mean, then it would be right never to relent when tempted or asked to publish.

"Often, when troubled by entreaty" to publish her poetry, Dickinson was to write Higginson in 1877, "that paragraph of your's has saved me — 'Such being the Majesty of the Art you presume to practice, you can at least take time before dishonoring it,' and Enobarbus said 'Leave that which leaves itself.' " In coupling a critically appreciative appraisal of her poetry with a warning that she should not publish too soon, Higginson had given a greater gift than he knew to a woman in need.

"THE LIGHT OF UNANOINTED BLAZE"

Emily Dickinson's letters from these years seem to raise as many questions as they answer. Who was the "Master" to whom she wrote letters filled with pain and passion? What exactly was she trying to say to Samuel Bowles in the cryptic letters she wrote to him in the early 1860s? What was the deadly pain she felt when she reached out to Higginson in "the dark"? What was the nature of the "terror" that she told Higginson in 1862 she had suffered "since September"? What made that pain something that she "could tell to none"?

There are clues to such riddles in some of the poems that Dickinson wrote at this time. One of them, "Title divine — is mine," she sent to Bowles during the flurry of letters in 1862. The speaker of the poem is "The Wife — without the Sign" whose "title divine" might be interpreted in several ways. It may speak of Dickinson's desire to picture herself as a chaste bride in an imaginary union, a woman who is ravished without being violated, "Betrothed — without the swoon"; it could refer more generally to her deferral of intimacy of any ordinary kind; or it may address her desire to be a poet whose "Stroking the Melody" brought private satisfaction without public recognition.

Or perhaps the poem touches upon each of these separate realities, all of which depict a woman made secure through renunciation and retreat. To be "Royal" with "all but the Crown" would mean to possess the desire in the mind without the burden in the body. As a romantic poet whose imagination had been fed by Christian images of splendor, Dickinson found it sweeter to imagine satisfaction than to taste it. "The stimulus of Loss makes most Possession mean," she was convinced. "I had been hungry, all the Years," a poem from 1862 begins. Yet when she "drew the Table near," the speaker discovered that "The Plenty hurt me — 'twas so new — /Myself felt ill — "

117

> Nor was I hungry — so I found
> That Hunger — was a way
> Of Persons outside Windows —
> The Entering — takes away — [#579]

One out of every ten poems written by Dickinson contains imagery of food or drink, and most of those conclude that it is more satisfying to envision than to consume. As she observed in a late poem, "The Banquet of Abstemiousness/Defaces that of Wine — " [#1430].

For Dickinson, denial brought suffering but also a sometimes exquisite pleasure. Martha once told her aunt of having been sent as a child to sit in a certain room as punishment; in time, she came to enjoy the room so much that she refused to leave when her term of punishment was done. " 'Matty, child,' " her aunt told her, " 'no one could ever punish a Dickinson by shutting her up alone.' " According to her niece, Emily's "love of being alone up in her room was associated with her feeling for a key, which signified freedom from interruption." At times, Emily would look down from the landing outside her room, with her "thumb and forefinger closed on an imaginary key, and say, with a quick turn of her wrist, 'It's just a turn — and freedom, Matty!' "

Dickinson's contemporary Henry David Thoreau said of his decision to live alone that his "purpose in going to Walden Pond was not to live cheaply nor to live dearly there, but to transact some private business with the fewest obstacles." For Dickinson, renunciation and retreat offered a similar opportunity to conduct her particular "private business" as free of distractions as possible. By refusing to marry or publish, she could manage her realities while indulging her possibilities. As a "Wife — without the Sign," Dickinson could embrace the passion of marriage without wedding herself to its pain. And by remaining in the "barefoot" ranks as a poet, she could develop her work hidden from the sight of the public's prying eyes.

Solitude, however, exacted a heavy price. Dickinson might possess the "Title divine," as the poem suggests, but that title was, after all, "Empress of Calvary." As much as her turn inward represented an act of self-preservation, it was also self-consuming to become "Soul at the White Heat." Poem after poem that she wrote in the early 1860s depicts what Richard Sewall has called "humanity at the limits of its sovereignty." Because her pain was both private and intense, Dickinson groped for points of comparison to give her relief; at times she could only fathom her suffering by comparing it to that of Christ. The "Essential Oils" of her poetry had to be "wrung" from her pain, because

> The Attar from the Rose
> Be not expressed by Suns — alone —
> It is the gift of Screws — [#675]

In a similar fashion, if the "ore" of her experience was to be shaped into what Herman Melville called the "fine hammered steel of woe," it had to be tempered in the forge of her suffering. Then, when

>   the vivid Ore
> Has vanquished Flame's conditions,
> It quivers from the Forge
> Without a color, but the light
> Of unanointed Blaze. [#365]

Emily Dickinson's most productive years were also her darkest, just as they were to be the darkest years in the history of the Union. While the cannons roared and the slaughter continued unabated in the fields hundreds of miles to the south of Amherst, Dickinson sat in her room and composed by "the light of unanointed blaze." In privacy and privation, she labored at her lonely forge, hammering away "at the White Heat," all the while "refining these impatient Ores."

7 A More General Sorrow

The Battle fought between the Soul
And No Man — is the One
Of all the Battles prevalent —
By far the Greater One — [#594]

Sorrow seems more general than it did, and not the estate of a
few persons, since the war began, and if the anguish of others
helped one with one's own, now would be many medicines.

IN THESE WRENCHING YEARS, Emily Dickinson's "grand theater
of the mind" played out its acts against the colossal backdrop of the
Civil War. In the period when Dickinson was experiencing an unspecified "terror" of disappointment and "a woe that made me
tremble," and while she was forging hundreds of poems in the "white
heat" of anguish, the war was searing the nation's consciousness and
devouring its sons. On occasion, the shock of battle registered itself
upon Dickinson in her Amherst seclusion, but the war was not her most
pressing concern at the time. When she did refer to the conflict, it was
often for the purpose of using it as a metaphor for a more primary grief.

120

The cataclysmic war between the states, that is, gave her fresh images to describe "The Battle fought between the Soul/And No Man — ."

At the start of 1861, the prospect of war excited Amherst, as it did every city and village across the North and South. On the day after the firing on Fort Sumter, President Abraham Lincoln issued an emergency call for 75,000 troops to join the battle against rebel "combinations too powerful to be suppressed by the ordinary course of judicial proceedings." The country responded to the President's call with fervor. "The heather is on fire. I never knew what a popular excitement can be," wrote George Ticknor, a Harvard professor. "The whole population, men, women, and children, seem to be in the streets with Union favors and flags."

In Amherst, the students and faculty of the college, as well as the citizens of the village, greeted with delight the prospect of a quick and holy war. Less than a week after Sumter, William Tyler, a professor of ancient languages, preached what his son described as "a rousing sermon in the college chapel at Amherst, 'On themes suited to the circumstances, and in a strain intended to inspire courage, heroism, and self-sacrificing devotion.'" Inspired by the service, chemistry professor William Clark told the students that he would go form a company of one hundred recruits, if that many students would enlist along with him. "In less than half an hour," Mason Tyler reported, "one hundred of the college students had given their names."

Charles Hitchcock, son of the former president of Amherst, wrote about the war frenzy to his brother Edward, who was in London: "I never knew Amherst to be so much excited as it is now by the war news. I went up street last night, and found it difficult to work my way along from Cutler's store to Phoenix Row on account of the crowd collected together by the excitement." Hitchcock questioned the ardor for battle and singled out for scorn Professor Clark, who had been "so foolish as to set all College by the ears — so that the College is pretty nearly broken up. It is positively wrong I think to stir up students so much."

Always eager to be at the center of civic affairs, Edward Dickinson quickly caught the martial spirit. On the Monday morning after Sumter fell, he and others hoisted "an elegant national banner" in honor of the Union effort and held an impromptu service filled with worship and war cries. The *Springfield Republican* reported that the ceremony included "addresses by President Stearns, Edward Dickinson, . . . and others," after which there was plenty of "music, of the kind our revolutionary ancestors loved." A week later, Edward Dickinson moved at a town meeting that the "selectmen be authorized to borrow $5000 to provide uniforms and care for the families of needy volunteers." After several years of political uncertainty following the Whig collapse in the 1854 election, Emily's father was happy to be back in his rightful place, leading the public in a noble cause.

His daughter Emily, however, was slow to respond to this flurry of activity and never warmed to the subject of the war, except when it claimed someone she knew or loved. Having neither husband nor son at risk in the conflict, and with her father too old for battle and her brother too frightened to enlist, Emily had nothing immediately at stake in the conflict. Only when someone she knew came into danger did she appear distraught about the carnage that littered the landscape of the nation. For instance, when the health of Samuel Bowles was jeopardized by his tireless efforts to support the Union cause, Dickinson was mobilized to action, sending him poems and letters of sympathy to comfort his weary spirit. In like manner, she grew alarmed at the thought of losing her newly acquired "Preceptor" when Higginson went into battle in South Carolina. And when war struck down one of Amherst's own sons on a distant battlefield, Dickinson felt the loss keenly.

In a December 1861 letter, Dickinson reported to her cousin Louise Norcross that the recently widowed Mrs. Edward Adams "had news of the death of her boy to-day, from a wound at Annapolis. Telegram signed by Frazer Stearns. You remember him. Another one died in October — from fever caught in the camp. . . . Dead! Both her boys!" The Frazer Stearns to whom she referred was the son of Mary and William Augustus Stearns, the President of Amherst College from 1854 to 1876. In concluding her letter to her cousin, Dickinson wrote, "Christ be merciful! Frazer Stearns is just leaving Annapolis. His father has gone to see him to-day. I hope that ruddy face won't be brought home frozen."

At first, the citizens of Amherst, like almost everyone else in the North, thought the war would end quickly and never considered the possibility of stalemate and massive casualties. Each minor skirmish seemed like a prelude to the impending grand finale of the war. On February 20, 1862, for instance, the *Springfield Republican* reported the events of "an exciting day for Amherst" when the "news of the capture of Fort Donelson reached town about 1 o'clock p.m." To commemorate the victory, "the bells were rung, and more tin horns brought into requisition by the students, than the priests blew around the walls of Jericho. The stars and stripes were unfurled from the tower of the chapel, and cheer on cheer rose from College hill." The revelry continued a few days later, albeit in a more formal setting, when the students of the college and the residents of the town crowded into the college chapel for a series of "very interesting exercises." Several Amherst faculty members spoke, as did "President Stearns, who is just getting out after a long illness contracted on a visit to [his son Frazer at] the army camps at Annapolis."

While Dickinson was unmoved by such celebrations, she shared the sorrow of the town two weeks later, when news of Frazer Stearns's death reached Amherst. "Dear Children," Emily wrote her cousins, "'tis least that I can do, to tell you of brave Frazer — 'killed at Newbern,' darlings. His big heart shot away by a 'minie ball.' I had read of those — I didn't think that Frazer would carry one to Eden with him." He "fell by the side of Professor Clark, his superior officer — ," the Amherst professor who had recruited him. Frazer "lived ten minutes in a soldier's arms, asked twice for water — murmured just, 'My God!' and passed!" After a year, the war had come home to Dickinson at last.

When Frazer's body was returned to Amherst for burial, Dickinson reported that "nobody here could look on Frazer — not even his father. The doctors would not allow it." At his funeral, "crowds came to tell him good-night, choirs sang to him, pastors told how brave he was — early-soldier heart. And the family bowed their heads, as the reeds the wind shakes." Faced with the fury of war, Emily could only conclude her letter to her cousins with the plea, "Let us love better, children, it's most that's left to do."

Frazer's death shook all who knew him. From New York, Samuel Bowles wrote to Austin and Sue that "the news from Newbern took away all the remaining life. I shut & threw away the paper after seeing at first glance the great sad fact to all of us who knew him. I did not care for victories — for anything then." Within the week, Emily wrote to Bowles that "Austin is chilled — by Frazer's murder — He says — his Brain keeps saying over 'Frazer is killed' — 'Frazer is killed,' just as Father told it — to Him. Two or three words of lead — that dropped so deep, they keep weighing — ." Her plea to Bowles was more for her own sake than for Austin's: "Tell Austin — how to get over them!" She had offered Bowles generous words of comfort in recent months; what could he now say to her to get over these "three words of lead"?

As the war ground on, Dickinson increasingly personalized it, thinking of the needs it created as well as the dangers it presented. When Bowles traveled to Europe for rest in the spring and summer of 1862, she sorely missed his inspiring energy and reassuring presence. When he returned in the fall, Dickinson told him that she thought that "friends are nations in themselves — to supersede the Earth — ." In his absence, news of the war had been harder to take: "Few absences could seem so wide as your's has done, to us — . . . . We used to tell each other, when you were from America — how failure in a Battle — were easier — and you here — ."

Two years into the war, in February 1863, Dickinson found new cause for concern when Higginson was dispatched to South Carolina at the head of a regiment of black soldiers. Having not yet met her "Preceptor" in person, she wrote to him, "I should have liked to see you, before you became improbable. War feels to me an oblique place — ." The war felt oblique, that is, until it threatened to rob her of what she loved or needed. "I trust you may pass the limit of War, and though not reared to prayer — when service is had in Church, for Our Arms, I include myself." One can only wonder what Higginson thought of the closing request that came to him from the shelter of Amherst, as he ventured out to battle: "Could you, with honor, avoid Death, I entreat you — Sir — It would bereave   Your Gnome — ."

Earlier in the same letter, Dickinson had told Higginson that "Perhaps Death — gave me awe for friends — striking sharp and early, for I held them since in a brittle love — of more alarm, than peace." Death had already taught her much about the contingency of life and the arbitrariness of God. For Dickinson's contemporary, Henry Adams, the message of both science and human suffering was that God was but another name for the impersonal forces that governed the world. As he watched his sister die an agonizing death in 1870, Adams concluded, "God might be, as the Church said, a Substance, but he could not be a person." For Dickinson God was never to become just a force but remained very much a person, one against whose wiles, jealousy, and cruelty she had to protect herself and those she loved. One of her very last poems called frost "The blonde Assassin" who beheaded flowers to the delight of "an Approving God" [#1624]. Lodged in security far from the field of battle, she feared the random power the war embodied. Powerless to protect those she loved from the cruel and cunning force of war, she could only entreat the likes of Higginson to seek to "avoid Death" with appropriate honor.

Eventually, however, Dickinson came to think of the stalemate and slaughter in more general, and less personal, terms. In an unprecedented decision, she consented early in 1864 to allow three of her poems to be published in a paper whose purpose was to raise money for the Union war effort. She had been approached with similar requests earlier but had refused. Now the endless suffering prompted this small sacrifice from her. "Sorrow seems more general than it did, and not the estate of a few persons, since the war began," she wrote to her cousins in 1864, "and if the anguish of others helped one with one's own, now would be many medicines." If publishing a few of her poems could comfort wounded souls and aid wounded soldiers, then so be it, this private poet concluded at a time of dire public need.

"EYES BE BLIND, HEART BE STILL"

As the war raged on the battlefields several hundred miles to the south, life in the Dickinson home went on as usual. With Edward Dickinson well beyond the age of military service and Austin having paid $500 to provide a substitute for his draft call, the family was not directly at risk in the conflict. Freed from the burdens of military commitment, both Austin and Edward practiced law and tended to the affairs of college and town during the war years. At the Evergreens in 1861, Sue gave birth to a son, Edward ("Ned"), the first grandchild in the family, and across the yard at the Homestead, Mrs. Dickinson, Vinnie, and Emily cared for the daily management of the household.

At the start of the war, Emily was thirty years old and had begun to settle into household patterns that would vary little for the rest of her life. On many days the Dickinson family breakfasted together and held devotional exercises led by Edward. "They are religious — except me — " Emily wrote Higginson about her family in 1862, "and address an Eclipse, every morning — whom they call their 'Father.'" After the

125

morning gathering, the members of the family went their separate ways. The volume of correspondence and poetry that Emily produced in the early 1860s would indicate that she must have spent a great number of hours writing in the solitude of her second-floor room. By her own account, her family showed little interest in the life of the mind as she was living it: "My Mother does not care for thought — and Father, too busy with his Briefs — to notice what we do — ." Though they lived under the same roof, the Dickinsons were in many ways strangers to each other. Years later, after his first visit to the Homestead, Higginson described the Dickinson home as "a house where each member runs his or her own selves."

The Dickinson household in these years was of a type perceptively described by Samuel Ward when he read an early edition of Emily's poems. Ward had been a New England transcendentalist but abandoned that faith to become a New York investment banker. When he read Dickinson's poems in 1891, he wrote immediately to Higginson: "She [Emily] is the quintessence of that element we all have who are of Puritan descent. . . . We came to this country to think our own thoughts with nobody to hinder." In analyzing the New England temperament, Ward deftly outlined the poet's particular character and the shape of the Dickinsons' family life. "We conversed with our own souls till we lost the art of communicating with other people. The typical family grew up strangers to each other, as in this case. It was *awfully* high, but awfully lonesome. Such prodigies of shyness do not exist elsewhere." Occasionally, Ward explained, the taciturn New England temperament became inexplicably loquacious. "If the gift of articulateness was not denied, you had Channing, Emerson, Hawthorne a stupendous example, & so many others. Mostly it was denied, & became a family fate. This is where Emily Dickinson comes in. She was the articulate inarticulate."

When not trying to articulate the inarticulate in her poetry during these years, Emily might be found gardening or baking. She had a conservatory in the Homestead, and her letters often enclosed a single pressed petal or might even be accompanied by an entire arrangement of flowers she had grown. Emily spent a good deal of time working the gardens on the family property and no doubt made use in her baking of some of the things she grew there. In 1856, she had placed second in the baking contest for "Rye and Indian Bread" at the Amherst

Cattle Show, winning a 75¢ prize and a place on the panel of judges for the following year's competition. When she met Higginson in 1870, one of the first things she told him was that "she makes all the bread for her father only likes hers & says '& people must have puddings' this *very* dreamily, as if they were comets — so she makes them." Several friends and family members thought so much of Emily's gingerbread that they asked for, and received, copies of her recipe:

1 Quart Flour,
½ Cup Butter,
½ Cup Cream,
1 Table Spoon Ginger,
1 Tea Spoon Soda,
1 Salt

Make up with Molasses —

Dickinson stole what time she could from her household responsibilities to read the fiction, poetry, and popular journalism of her day. Even in her seclusion, the world poured in at her door, the widespread circulation of books and periodicals having made her withdrawal from society much different than it would have been even fifty years earlier. In the early 1860s, the Dickinson family subscribed to fifteen magazines and newspapers, far more than most families in Amherst received. In addition to *The Springfield Republican*, they read three other newspapers; their magazines ranged from the *New England Farmer* to the church publication, *Home Missionary*, the railroading magazine, *American Engineer Monthly*, and the popular literary magazine, *Harper's Magazine*. "If Emily Dickinson gradually withdrew from the world," argues Daniel Lombardo, "the world, at least in the form of an unusual number of magazines and newspapers, arrived for the Dickinsons at Box 207, Amherst."

Emily's constant companion in this period was her "dear, faithful friend Carlo," a Newfoundland her father had given her in the early 1850s. Edward Dickinson thought that a dog might help his daughter overcome her fear of public outings, and for almost a decade Carlo accompanied Emily on her forays around Amherst. She referred to him no less than fifteen times in her correspondence, and even people who had never met her were made aware of Carlo's importance in her life. This was the case when her "Preceptor" Higginson received a brief note from her after a long silence: "Carlo died — ED. Dickinson Would you instruct me now?"

When Carlo died in late January of 1866, Dickinson was still recuperating from a mysterious disorder of her eyes. This affliction may not have been serious in itself, but she and her doctor treated it as such. In the final years of the Civil War, Dickinson was terrified by the thought of losing her sight. For her, such a loss would also have entailed the loss of poetry, both the reading and the writing of it, and that was a prospect that she could not bear.

The evidence provided by the only known photograph of Dickinson suggests that she suffered from *exotropia,* a condition in which an eye turns out. In Dickinson's case, it was her right eye that turned out at least 15 degrees. Of the two forms of *exotropia,* constant and intermittent, it is impossible to tell which is the one from which Dickinson suffered. *Exotropia* is not a dangerous condition in itself, its main symptoms being occasional eye strain, blurring of vision, and heightened sensitivity to light.

Though her mother and Lavinia apparently also had mild cases of *exotropia,* only Emily is known to have received treatment for the condition. Twice, in 1864 and 1865, she traveled to Boston to be cared for by the renowned ophthalmologist Dr. Henry Willard Williams. Perhaps overreacting to his patient's disorder, Williams ordered Emily to stay in Boston far longer than she had planned. Further, he ordered her neither to read nor write while she was under his care. "He is not willing I should write," Emily wrote home to Vinnie in a brief note in May of 1864. She had to stay in Boston for seven months, and for a woman who was not accustomed to be away from home more than a few hours at a time, the separation was unendurable. In November, she apologized to Vinnie: "Emily may not be able as she was, but all she can, she will." Even the plants she left behind in the conservatory "are Foreigners, now, and all, a Foreigner."

Dickinson would look back upon this time as a period of tedium and terror. She later confided to Joseph Lyman about "a woe, the only one that ever made me tremble. It was a shutting out of all the dearest ones of time, the strongest friends of the soul — BOOKS." Dr. Williams had snatched them from her grasp with his prohibition and banished her to a chilly, thoughtless exile. "The medical man said avaunt ye tormentors, he also said 'down, thoughts, & plunge into her soul. He might as well have said, 'Eyes be blind', 'heart be still.' So I had eight months of Siberia."

From her "Siberian" boardinghouse in Cambridge, Emily wrote brief notes filled with images of imprisonment and expressions of remorse. In a letter to Vinnie in July, she called herself "Elijah . . . in the Wilderness." Even though "the Doctor [is] enthusiastic about my getting well — I feel no gayness yet. I suppose I had been discouraged so long." She felt like "the Prisoner of Chillon" who "did not know Liberty when it came, and asked to go back to Jail," she told her sister. In November, only weeks before the end of her seven-month stay, she wrote home to Vinnie that "I have been sick so long I do not know the Sun." To her entire family, she gave thanks "for caring about me when I do no good. I will work with all my might, always, as soon as I get well — ."

Dickinson did "get well," as the crisis ran its course after the second round of "treatments" in the following year. But memories of the trauma remained fixed in her mind for many years. Her doctor's reaction and restrictions had triggered deep anxieties, because, for her, to lose sight would be to lose all. When Dr. Williams finally allowed her to read again, she wrote, "going home[,] I flew to the shelves and devoured the luscious passages [of Shakespeare]. I thought I should tear the leaves out as I turned them."

When Emily returned from "Siberia" after seven months away, it was Vinnie who met her at the station in nearby Palmer, just as it had been Vinnie who had done Emily's share of the family chores in her absence. "I shall go Home in two weeks. You will get me at Palmer, yourself. Let no one beside come," Emily demanded. Vinnie obliged.

As she and Emily aged together, Vinnie assumed an ever larger role in the family, caring for her invalid mother and sheltering her reclusive sister from the world. Like countless educated women in the late nineteenth century, Vinnie faced the problem of vocation, as finance capitalism and the Industrial Revolution did away with the domestic economy that had dominated colonial and early national life. With the middle-class home transformed into a center of consumption by the mid-nineteenth century, the home became the "women's sphere," but what was a woman to do in it? If, as Vinnie said late in life, "Austin had Amherst" and "father believed," what were the women to do?

In assuming her role as a poet with "title divine," Emily found her vocation and made her home, at least for herself, a center of production in a unique, new form of domestic economy. Mrs. Dickinson took upon herself the work of love, ailment, and complaint. That left Vinnie with the job of looking after all of them. ("I had the family to keep track of.") With a warrior's passion and, on occasion, a warrior's recklessness, she plunged into the task of protecting her family, and particularly Emily, against all enemies real and imagined. She was devoted to this sister whose needs she could gauge with precision but whose genius she never fully understood. Millicent Todd Bingham, who came to know Vinnie in the last years of her life, notes that at all times "Vinnie was there . . . to ward off intruders and in general to take the brunt. Thus shielded, Emily could withdraw without explanation."

Emily's younger sister was witty and belligerent. Over the years, she became well known to Amherst residents for her caustic tongue and her readiness to defend the interests of the Dickinsons at any cost. A professor who had known her well wrote of Vinnie at her death that "she abhorred the commonplace in speech almost more than the vulgar." Her views of life, he said, "were at once shrewd and amusing to a remarkable degree." Vinnie could do battle over any number of subjects, but according to Bingham "her fiercest denunciations were reserved for those who ventured to oppose or even call in question, the opinions of her father and brother on matters of public concern."

Emily treasured Vinnie's sheltering care. She was often amused, and occasionally annoyed, by her pugnacious sister, but she also could not imagine life without Vinnie at her side. In 1859, Emily wrote to the Hollands, "Vinnie is sick to-night, which gives the world a russet tinge, usually so red. It is only a headache, but when the head aches next to you, it becomes important. When she is well, time leaps. When she is ill, he lags, or stops entirely. Sisters are brittle things. God was penurious with me, which makes me shrewd with Him." In almost all important respects, after Austin married Sue in 1856 these two sisters were each other's family. No one knew Emily more intimately than did Vinnie, and no one did more to protect her from all unwanted intrusions upon her time and person. In 1873, when the Dickinson parents were still very much alive, Emily wrote again to the Hollands. "She has no Father and Mother but me and I have no Parents but her," she told them. Considering the essential role Emily's younger sister had come to play in her life, there was scant exaggeration in the claim.

IN THE WAKE OF WAR

Just as the start of the Civil War had marked for Dickinson a period of extraordinary productivity and mysterious perplexity, so did its close signal a definitive turn in her life. Her final trip to Boston for eye treatments in 1865 proved to be the last journey she ever took away from Amherst. Several years before that, she had already stopped attending church. Not long after she returned from Boston, she stopped making any trips at all off the grounds of "my Father's House." Her relationship to Austin, Sue, and their children remained strong, but even her walks across the lawn to "the other house" ended.

Emily's immediate family may not have worried about the isolation she chose at this point in her life, but a number of those who knew her did feel concern. Higginson, in particular, wondered about his friend's seclusion. He could not fathom her reluctance to venture out into a world that he had spent his life — as an abolitionist, pastor, soldier, and man of letters — trying to salvage and reform. When they first met in 1870, Dickinson attempted to explain her solitude by telling him, "I find ecstasy in living — the mere sense of living is joy enough." It was when Higginson pressed the point that she told him bluntly of her desire to stay rooted in one place: "I asked if she never felt want of employment, never going off the place & never seeing any visitor. 'I never thought of conceiving that I could ever have the slightest approach to such a want in all future time.'"

To be certain, during the last twenty years of her life Dickinson dreamed of things she had never known — travel to foreign lands, the mysteries of marriage, and the exhilaration of renown — but she never expressed regrets about what she lacked or had failed to do. At times, she felt pinched by the provincial, prosaic life of her family and by the toil of household duties, but at no time did she desire to be free of family or home. More than a century later, we may read Dickinson's experience as a story of relentless frustration and oppression, but she did not see it that way. The woman who claimed never to have thought of having " 'the slightest approach to such a want' " would have been

131

puzzled by the claim of a contemporary critic that "the forces that [Dickinson] felt conspired against her 'real life,' her private life of writing" were "her household responsibilities, the demands of her parents, the condescension of her brother Austin, and the prescriptions of her Calvinist religion."

Knowing full well the constraints of life at the Homestead, Dickinson chose them as her own. Ordinary life attracted her, in part, because it promised so little that it could not easily disappoint her. Marriage, renown, and conversion, on the other hand, promised many things but delivered few. As a young woman, Dickinson had defended her decision not to attend a revival meeting at Mount Holyoke by explaining, "I felt that I was so easily excited that I might again be deceived and I dared not trust myself." There was little in the Homestead that could deceive or surprise her.

Even Dickinson's earliest poems speak of the shocks of deception and disappointment, and the subject grew in importance throughout her adulthood. A verse from 1859, for instance, reads "the days when Birds come back — " as signs of God's trickery, as he employs nature to fool us with the beauty of "the days when skies resume/The old — old sophistries of June — " [#130]. Within a few years, the imagery of disappointment became more searing and terrifying in her poems. Lyrics dating from the time of the Civil War tell of the "Soul *at the White Heat*," of a "Morning after Woe," and of "the Soul/That gets a Staggering Blow — " [#365, #364, #618]. The spectral human beings who float through these poems may be haunted by "a Funeral, in my Brain," cornered by a terror "so appalling — it exhilarates," or startled by a "Horror not to be surveyed — /But skirted in the Dark — " [#280, #281, #777].

Several poems from these years tell stories about the cycle of expectation, devastation, and stunned survival:

> The Soul has Bandaged moments —
> When too appalled to stir —
> She feels some ghastly Fright come up
> And stop to look at her —
>
> Salute her — with long fingers —
> Caress her freezing hair —

Sip, Goblin, from the very lips
The Lover — hovered — o'er —
Unworthy, that a thought so mean
Accost a Theme — so — fair —

The soul has moments of Escape —
When bursting all the doors —
She dances like a Bomb, abroad,
And swings upon the Hours,

As do the Bee — delirious borne —
Long Dungeoned from his Rose —
Touch Liberty — then know no more,
But Noon, and Paradise —

The Soul's retaken moments —
When, Felon led along,
With shackles on the plumed feet,
And staples, in the Song,

The Horror welcomes her, again,
These, are not brayed of Tongue — [#512]

In part, Dickinson stayed at home for the last two decades of her life to avoid the "Horror" of the "Soul's retaken moments," with "shackles" on its feet and with "staples, in the Song." Safely ensconced within her "Father's House," she knew what to expect of others and what could be demanded of her by them. Under that roof, she could shield herself from the claims of others by deferring to the commands of her "preceptors," the authority of her father, and the needs of her family. When Higginson invited Dickinson to Boston in 1866, for instance, she refused him and blamed her father: "I am uncertain of Boston. I had promised to visit my Physician for a few days in May, but Father objects because he is in the habit of me. Is it more far to Amherst?" Similarly, within a few years she would be invoking Higginson's name to ward off those who wanted her to publish her work.

Well versed in the role assigned to her in the Dickinson family, Emily found herself freed by her duties to script and act in the drama staged in "the grand theater of her mind." While committed to the particular needs of her family, she was at the same time free to develop a private world of imaginative alternatives. The very constraints of her daily reality, in other words, made possible the wide latitude of her poetic endeavors.

But what if the reason for Dickinson's seclusion, at least in part, proved to be somehow less sensible and more unsettling? Might it not be that in addition to the generous — and plausible — readings that her family gave of her retreat, there were other disturbing forces at work in her decision, which perhaps contributed to her reclusive inclinations without necessarily determining them? Where the early twentieth century saw a fascination with a doomed love affair as the reason behind Dickinson's retreat, some recent scholarship has shifted to theories of psychological disorder to explain her seclusion.

It does appear that Emily Dickinson suffered from some form of agoraphobia, the fear of open spaces and public places. That fear involves something more than a reluctance to be seen by others; it includes an element of dread, a terror at the prospect of plunging into vast expanses. Any number of Dickinson's poems employ images of trackless immensities and uncharted paths. While searching for God, one poem can discover nothing but "Vast Prairies of Air" [#564]; another poem asserts that the way to God has been lost, because "God's Right Hand — " has been amputated, "And God cannot be found" [#1551]; and in one of her most perfect poems, the dead must await their resurrection for seemingly endless ages, as the constellations make their way across the empty heavens with sickening slowness:

Safe in their Alabaster Chambers —
Untouched by Morning
And untouched by Noon —
Lie the meek members of the Resurrection —
Rafter of Satin — and Roof of Stone —

Grand go the Years — in the Crescent — above them —
Worlds scoop their Arcs —
And Firmaments — row —
Diadems — drop — and Doges — surrender —
Soundless as dots — on a Disc of Snow — [#216]

This poem Emily wrote and revised, after having received Sue's criticism, in 1861. Its picture of the universe is nicely explained by a description C. S. Lewis once offered of the difference between a medieval model of the universe and a modern one. "The medieval universe," he wrote, "while unimaginably large, was also unambiguously finite, . . . containing within itself an ordered variety." Things were to prove very different with the modern picture of the universe: "To look out on the night sky with modern eyes is like looking out over a sea that fades away into mist, or looking about one in a trackless forest — trees forever and no horizon. . . . The 'space' of modern astronomy may arouse terror, or bewilderment or vague reverie; the spheres of the old present us with an object in which the mind can rest, overwhelming in its greatness but satisfying in its harmony." For Lewis, "this explains why all sense of the pathless, the baffling, and the utterly alien — all agoraphobia — is so markedly absent from medieval poetry when it leads us . . . into the sky."

Lewis's observation is extraordinarily useful for an understanding of Dickinson, because it offers a way of setting her personal fear in a greater intellectual and cultural context. The universe had grown unimaginably more vast — especially in terms of time — in her lifetime, and the pattern of design had been shattered and scrambled. For Dickinson, the sense of disorientation in this new universe was palpable. Her apprehensions about the groundless disarray all around her may well have influenced her choice of the Homestead's charted limits over the wilderness outside its gates. There were benefits, after all, to boundaries:

> A Prison gets to be a friend —
> Between its Ponderous face
> And Ours — a Kinsmanship express —
> And in its narrow Eyes —
>
> We come to look with gratitude
> For the appointed Beam
> It deal us — stated as our food —
> And hungered for — the same —
>
> We learn to know the Planks —
> That answer to Our feet —

135

So miserable a sound — at first —
Nor ever now — so sweet —

As plashing in the Pools —
When Memory was a Boy —
But a Demurer Circuit —
A Geometric Joy —

The Posture of the Key
That interrupt the Day
To Our Endeavor — Not so real
The Cheek of Liberty —

As this Phantasm Steel —
Whose features — Day and Night —
Are present to us — as Our Own —
And as escapeless — quite —

The narrow Round — the Stint —
The slow exchange of Hope —
For something passiver — Content
Too steep for looking up —

The Liberty we knew
Avoided — like a Dream —
Too wide for any Night but Heaven —
If That — indeed — redeem — [#652]

This poem shows that Dickinson would have understood the point at the heart of "The Supper at Elsinore," a short story by the Danish writer Isak Dinesen. Set in the early nineteenth century, Dinesen's story is about two sisters and a brother who lead lives of unbridled aestheticism, the brother as a marauding pirate and the sisters as fantasy-spinning spinsters. When the dead brother visits his sisters as a ghost, he tells them: "'We have been amateurs in saying no, little sisters. But God can say no. Good God, how he can say no.'" Having gone through five wives and a series of sensational adventures, he now treasures the "'thought of those great, pure, and beautiful things which say no to us. . . . Those who say yes, we get them under us, and we ruin them and leave them, and find when we have left them that they have made us sick. The earth says yes to our schemes and our work, but the sea says no; and we, we love the sea ever. And to hear God say no, in the stillness, in his own voice, that to us is very good."

The character in the Dinesen story is describing what Hans-Georg Gadamer has called that "insight into the limitations of humanity" which teaches us that human "experience is experience of finitude." In the years of her explosive development and personal trial, Dickinson was learning much about the intimate connections between art and death. As the poet W. H. Auden observes, "aesthetic religion" of the kind championed by Dickinson produces "Tragic Drama" when it comprehends the full extent of good and evil and apprehends the "certainty that death comes to all men, . . . even for the exceptional individual." Dickinson had learned to "close the Valves of her attention — Like Stone — " and bar the door to all intruders, but of all those that knocked, death was the one she could not keep out. He was the "supple Suitor/That wins at Last," and "All but Death, can be Adjusted" [#1445, #749]. "Because I could not stop for Death," she ironically noted in a famous poem, "He kindly stopped for me — " [#712].

Yet even as death knocked at the door of the Homestead, Dickinson still loved to "dwell in Possibility — A fairer House than Prose — ." Here death and disappointment were banished, and poetry and possibility ruled:

> I reckon — when I count at all —
> First — Poets — Then the Sun —
> Then Summer — Then the Heaven of God —
> And then — the List is done —
>
> But looking back — the First so seems
> To Comprehend the Whole —
> The Others look a needless Show —
> So I write — Poets — All
>
> Their Summer — lasts a Solid Year —
> They can afford a Sun

The East — would deem extravagant —
And if the Further Heaven —

Be Beautiful as they prepare
For Those who worship Them —
It is too difficult a Grace —
To justify the Dream — [#569]

The poet Richard Wilbur has a wonderful phrase for Dickinson's approach to the stinginess of God that is hinted at in this and other of her poems. That parsimony drove her to become "the laureate and attorney of the empty-handed." Yet, as Wilbur notes, Dickinson turned poverty into abundance through her view of metaphor and renunciation. Having learned her lessons well from the New Testament, the poet assumed that to "forego what we desire is somehow to gain." Through language, she could own a summer that would "last a Solid Year" and never fade to fall. As she put the matter in a letter written late in life: "Emblem is immeasurable — that is why it is better than Fulfillment, which can be drained — ." There is mercy, after all, in lack: "Remoteness is the founder of sweetness; could we see all we hope, or hear the whole we fear told tranquil, like another tale, there would be madness near."

Emily Dickinson's seclusion freed her to explore and endure the full range of her ambivalence about a number of weighty matters. For every poem of hers that questions the nature or existence of God, another affirms the goodness of the Divine character and power. For every lyric that celebrates the eternity of art, another sees poetry as merely one more mortal creation. Even within single poems, Dickinson engaged in what Sharon Cameron has called the act of "choosing not choosing." Dickinson developed a habit of depositing throughout her manuscripts alternate words or phrases without an indication of a final choice. While many poets refused to choose between alternatives, Cameron argues that the "not choosing in Dickinson's poems is different from not choosing" in other poetry of the Romantic tradition. Poets such as Whitman and Yeats avoided choice by using the conjunction "or" to mean "*both* this and that." In Dickinson's poetry matters are "different because it is assumed [in Dickinson's] poetry that choice is required, even as the requirement is repeatedly, if subversively transgressed."

138

Ambivalence was more than a poetic strategy for Dickinson, for it went to the heart of her uncertainty about life. Like a number of her contemporaries in the late nineteenth century, she found herself caught between the dead assurances of the past and the dynamic uncertainties of the present. Not long before she died, she wrote in a letter that "on subjects of which we know nothing, or should I say *Beings* — . . . we both believe, and disbelieve a hundred times an Hour, which keeps Believing nimble." In choosing not to choose and in shuttling "a hundred times an Hour" between *belief* and *disbelief*, between *infinite possibilities* and *tragic realities,* Dickinson embodied in her life the "polyphonic" quality that Mikhail Bakhtin says animates certain great modern literary texts. In a "polyphonic" novel as Bakhtin defines it, characters espousing diametrically opposed views engage each other and the reader in dialogue. While a certain character may represent the author's point of view, no single character dominates discussion or determines the final meaning of the work. "Several consciousnesses meet as equals and engage in a dialogue that is in principle unfinalizable," write Gary Saul Morson and Caryl Emerson of Bakhtin's view.

What Bakhtin saw in the novels of Fyodor Dostoevsky and others, we can witness in the life and work of Emily Dickinson. Passionately committed to the particular village of Amherst, she nevertheless also roamed the regions of boundless possibilities. She kept her "Believing nimble" both by plumbing the depths of self-conscious doubt and by scaling the heights of spiritual assurance. She barred the door to the world, but death got in. She chose to be a "Bride" but "without the swoon" and a poet who sought everlasting fame but had no present audience to serve as her "tribunal." Having "chosen not to choose" by the time she reached the age of thirty, Dickinson created the conditions that made possible one of the richest literary lives in the history of American culture. Yet at the same time, she consigned herself to a life of civil, internal strife, as she engaged in "the Battle fought between the Soul/And No Man."

8 Vesuvius at Home

Volcanoes be in Sicily
And South America
I judge from my Geography —
Volcanoes nearer here
A Lava step at any time
Am I inclined to climb —
A Crater I may contemplate
Vesuvius at Home. [#1705]

"I HAD NO MONARCH in my life, and cannot rule myself," Emily Dickinson wrote in 1862 to her newfound mentor, Thomas Wentworth Higginson, "and when I try to organize — my little Force explodes — and leaves me bare and charred — ." So it was for Dickinson at the peak of her poetic production. Closeted in her Amherst home, she put out poems at such an alarming rate that she did not know what to do with them.

In her letter to Higginson, Dickinson had thanked him for his corrections of her verse and tried to explain why she wrote in a "Wayward" manner. To Higginson's taste, her surprising metaphors and eccentric rhymes — to say nothing of her odd dashes and curious punctuation — were intriguing but did not seem "orderly" enough to make her poetry pleasing and of lasting value. He recognized that she had brilliance of a kind, but unless she brought her power under control, she could not hope to win the fame that was every true poet's goal.

In replying to Higginson's criticism, Dickinson was tactful — "I thank you for the Truth" — but did not let his strictures change the way she wrote. She took his criticisms in stride and happily accepted his advice against hurrying into print, but she never permitted him to rule her taste or organize her "little Force." Instead, she let it continue to explode, until, within decades of her death, that force had done away with most of the opposition to her ingenuity, and her poetry began to create the very audience and standards by which it would be judged.

A few years before she wrote to Higginson, Dickinson had begun to try to organize her poetic "Force" by assembling her separate poems into loosely bound and thematically unified booklets, which Mabel Loomis Todd called *fascicles*. Over a six-year period from 1858 to 1864, which was the most prolific stretch of her poetic career, Dickinson organized all of her poems into such booklets. To assemble them, she took the cream-colored, lightly ruled sheets on which she had written and stacked several of them together. She then punched two holes in the center margin of the single-folded sheets of paper and threaded them with string to make her books.

In producing the fascicles, Dickinson may have been trying to establish the only form of publication acceptable to her in her lifetime. The booklets provided a form of self-publication and left her work in ordered form for discovery after her death. Over time, the fascicles served as a sourcebook for Dickinson's revisions of her work and provided her a body of texts to copy and send with her letters as she saw fit.

With the making of the fascicles, Dickinson also demonstrated that her work, in Higginson's words, did "belong emphatically to what Emerson long since called 'the Poetry of the Portfolio.'" By introducing her poetry in this manner in his preface to the first edition of the poems in 1890, Higginson was connecting Dickinson's work to a tradition first identified by Emerson a half century earlier. In an 1840 essay, "New Poetry," Emerson had spoken of a "revolution in literature . . . now giving importance to the portfolio over the book." That revolution had been fueled by the dynamic growth of the publishing industry in the early decades of the nineteenth century: "The universal communication of the arts of reading and writing has brought the works of the great poets into every house, and made all ears familiar with the poetic forms." With the breakdown of hierarchies in church, state, and culture, the citizens of the New World were being encouraged in unprecedented ways "to throw into verse the experiences of private life."

As a consequence of this "revolution in literature," Emerson observed, "we are losing our interest in public men . . . and acquiring instead a taste for the depths of thought and emotion as they may be sounded in the soul of the citizen or the countryman." Without mentioning the political specifics, Emerson was chronicling in his essay the demise of the Whig culture of Edward Dickinson and the rise of the private, expressive culture in which his daughter was to play a central role. "Does it not replace man for the state, and character for official power?" Emerson asked about "the Poetry of the Portfolio." In a democracy, each person is to "be treated with solemnity," and when individuals "come to chant their private griefs and doubts and joys," they have, thanks to the Portfolio poets, "a new scale by which to compute magnitude and relation." In cultivating his or her eccentric individual genius, the Portfolio poet contributed to the great healing of humanity: "Art is the noblest consolation of calamity. The poet is compensated for his defects in the street and in society, if in his chamber he has turned his mischance into noble numbers."

In composing her "Poetry of the Portfolio," from the beginning Dickinson took as her guides to technique the patterns of hymnody and the poetic folk tradition. She showed no interest in the iambic pentameter line, which Chaucer, Shakespeare, Milton, and others had made the standard of English poetic form, but turned instead to the metrical patterns of popular lyrics in the English and American traditions. The six- to eight-count lines of the popular tradition were more natural for songs and hymns than the ten-count measure of iambic pentameter. These shorter lines had long been a mainstay of popular culture, and with the revival of folk forms in the romantic movement at the end of the eighteenth century they assumed a new importance in the literary traditions of the educated elites.

Dickinson was an adept pianist and enjoyed the performance of popular songs, so she knew this body of literature well. Her early letters make frequent reference to the making of music, and many of Dickinson's early friends associated her with song in their memories. A Mount Holyoke classmate told years after the fact of a day when young Emily talked her into spending a day singing in the woods with her. "We . . . sang tune after tune, — long metres, short metres, hallelujah metres, *et id omne genus*, — chants, rounds, fugues, anthems, etc., etc. . . . We sang and sang till the valley rang 'with our hymns of lofty cheer.'" Others remembered the Dickinson home as being filled with music in Emily's earlier years; and to the end of her life, the poet would ask visitors to play and sing for her, often while she sat in solitude elsewhere, shielded from view but listening through an opened door.

In the Dickinson home, copies of Isaac Watts's *Christian Psalmody* and his collection of *The Psalms, Hymns, and Spiritual Songs* were fixtures, as they were in many New England households. These and other hymnals of the day named the meter for each song and contained extensive discussions of different meters and their effects. As one of Emily's early biographers explained, "she did not have to step outside her father's library to receive a beginner's lesson in metrics." One of the first references to her poetry in her letters is coupled with the mention of hymnody. In March 1853, she promised her brother that she would send him Asahel Nettleton's supplement to Watts, "*Village Hymns [for Social Worship]*, by earliest opportunity." She teased him about the poem of his own that he had sent to her and told him of her own ventures in verse. "Now Brother Pegasus, I'll tell you what it is — I've been in the habit *myself* of writing some few things, and it rather appears to me that you're getting away my patent, so you'd better be somewhat careful, or I'll call the police!"

Though Dickinson's poetry would always evidence its origins in the hymn and popular song, she quickly went beyond the strict limitations of those forms. She relied heavily on Common Meter, consisting of alternating lines of eight and six syllables. Only sparingly did Emily make use of the extended lines of Long Meter, which has eight syllables to each line, and almost never did she employ the nine-, ten-, or eleven-syllable lines also to be found in the hymnals and in some ballads. As she began to write poetry regularly, Dickinson quickly gained confidence and began to experiment widely with the standard patterns to produce her own distinctive metrical effects.

In similar fashion, as a young poet Dickinson accepted the conventions of rhyming that had governed English poetry since Chaucer but shaped them to her own ends. She experimented with the standard exact rhymes of English poetry by employing such devices as identical rhymes *(move-remove)*; vowel rhymes *(see-buy)*; imperfect rhymes, which consist of identical vowels followed by different consonants, as in *time-thine;* and suspended rhymes, different vowels followed by exact consonants, as in *thing-along.*

Dickinson had no interest in free verse. Like Robert Frost after her, she needed to strain against the restraints of form to develop her own strengths and assert her own poetic prerogatives. Dickinson accepted the limits of metaphor, knowing that it always involved a dynamic transaction between the old and the new, the given and the imagined. In poetry as in life, she considered the most lasting accomplishments to be products of a creative struggle against mortal limits.

SMART MISERY AND THE AMPUTATED HAND

In borrowing freely from the biblical imagery of the Christian faith in general and the hymn tradition of the Protestant churches in particular, Emily Dickinson in these prolific years used such resources to scrutinize her own divided understanding of God. In numerous poems written during the Civil War, she composed her own body of hymns, which alternated in tone between devastating irony and sincere devotion. With intense creativity, she probed the character of God and the vastness of his creation in poems from this period. Read selectively, Dickinson's work of the Civil War years can be called upon to support virtually any conceivable claim about her beliefs. Taken in their entirety, her poems show Dickinson to have been a highly nuanced thinker who took theology seriously and who had an especially keen sense of the peculiar ambiguities of belief in the modern era.

To Emily Dickinson, perhaps the most notable fact about God was that he was, as she had become, so hard to find:

> I know that He exists.
> Somewhere — in Silence —
> He has hid his rare life
> From our gross eyes. [#338]

Belief in the hiddenness of God was, of course, a central part of Dickinson's Protestant heritage. "The splendor of divine glory is so great that the very angels also are restrained from direct gaze," wrote John Calvin in his *Institutes of the Christian Religion*, "and the tiny sparks of it that glow in the angels are withdrawn from our eyes." For Martin Luther, the hiddenness of God had been made necessary by human rebellion: "Because men misused the knowledge of God through works, God wished again to be recognized in suffering, . . . so that those who did not honor God as manifested in his works should honor him as he is hidden in his suffering." But while these theological forebears interpreted God's aloofness as evidence of his mercy, Dickinson saw it as a sign of embarrassment or shame:

> Embarrassment of one another
> And God
> Is Revelation's limit,
> Aloud
> Is nothing that is chief,
> But still,
> Divinity dwells under seal. [#662]

In some poems, Dickinson depicted the absence of God as a boon because of the compensating realities that stood in his place:

> Omnipotence — had not a Tongue —
> His lisp — is Lightning — and the Sun —
> His Conversation — with the Sea —
> "How shall you know?"
> Consult your Eye! [#420]

"'Heaven' has different Signs — to me — " began a poem from 1862. "Sometimes, I think that Noon/Is but a symbol of the Place — ." Dawn sometimes seems to symbolize God and his heaven, as does "The Orchard, when the Sun is on — ":

> The Rapture of a finished Day —
> Returning to the West —
> All these — remind us of the place
> That Men call "Paradise" — [#575]

145

In detecting God in the grandeur of the creation, this poem proved to be the exception rather than the rule for Dickinson's work in this anguished period. More frequently, in the poems from these years, the hiddenness of God becomes a form of absence, and the absence a source of pain. This is most often the case, for example, in the more than twenty poems Dickinson wrote about prayer in the early 1860s. In the history of the church, of course, prayer has long served as an image of the most intimate relationship possible with God. For most devotional poets, prayer reveals the presence of God; in Dickinson's poems, it often discloses his absence.

Several Dickinson poems depict prayer as an act of desperate wish fulfillment. Like her Continental contemporaries, Friedrich Nietzsche and Ludwig Feuerbach, Dickinson at times considered God — or at least the belief in God's loving care — as something we project upon the blank canopy of the heavens, just as prayer is something we fling into the hollow of the divine ear:

> Prayer is the little implement
> Through which Men reach
> Where Presence — is denied them.
> They fling their Speech
>
> By means of it — in God's Ear —
> If then He hear —
> This sums the Apparatus
> Comprised in Prayer — [#437]

We pray without knowing what the worth of our prayers will be or whether they will be heard at all.

After all, who made up the audience for prayer? "My period had come for Prayer — /No other Art — would do — " a poem from this time begins. But as she prayed, "My Tactics missed a rudiment — /Creator — Was it you?" Missing God, the penitent one who prays becomes a fruitless seeker after God:

> God grows above — so those who pray
> Horizons — must ascend —
> And so I stepped upon the North
> To see this Curious Friend —

His House was not — no sign had He —
By Chimney — nor by Door
Could I infer his Residence —
Vast Prairies of Air

Unbroken by a Settler —
Were all that I could see —
Infinitude — Had'st Thou no Face
That I might look on Thee?

The Silence condescended —
Creation stopped — for Me —
But awed beyond my errand —
I worshipped — did not "pray" — [#564]

In almost all cases, what emerges from Dickinson's poems about prayer is stoic resignation rather than confident affirmation. The silence of awe replaces the sound of prayer, and disappointment with prayer leads to doubt about the promises of God. In "I meant to have but modest needs," Dickinson says that she has simply taken God at his word: "Whatsoever Ye shall ask — /Itself be given You —." Taking God up on his offer, the poet asks for "A Heaven not so large as Yours,/But large enough — for me —." And how does God respond to this simple request? "A Smile suffused Jehovah's face," for he, the angels, and the saints are startled to have learned that "one so honest — be extant — /It take the Tale for true —." Embarrassed and disenchanted, having been mocked by God and his cohort, "I left the Place, with all my might — /I threw my Prayer away — ." Naive no longer, the speaker of the poem becomes suspicious of all claims about things divine:

But I, grown shrewder — scan the Skies
With a suspicious Air —
As Children — swindled for the first
All Swindlers — be — infer — [#476]

Prayers that provoke no response lead to embarrassment, doubt, and a questioning of the worth of life itself:

147

Of Course — I prayed —
And did God Care?
He cared as much as on the Air
A Bird — had stamped her foot —
And cried "Give Me" —
My Reason — Life —
I had not had — but for Yourself —
'Twere better Charity
To leave me in the Atom's Tomb —
Merry, and Nought, and gay, and numb —
Than this smart Misery. [#376]

Prayer is depicted here as a gesture as futile as that of a bird "stamping her foot on the air." The "Misery" of knowledge "smarts," because it stings with the disillusionment known by the swindled self. Perhaps it would have been "better Charity" for God to have left the self in the "Atom's Tomb" of unconscious material life than to have saddled it with the "smart Misery" of consciousness.

With her numerous poems about God and faith, Emily Dickinson demonstrated an impressive grasp of intellectual history. She realized that she was living through a revolutionary period, when unbelief had for the first time in history become a lively possibility. James Turner estimates that in the last decades of the eighteenth century — the era in which Emily's grandparents had been born — "the known unbelievers of Europe and America . . . numbered fewer than a dozen or two." Nevertheless, "by the late nineteenth century unbelief had become a fully available option. . . . Modern unbelief burst into full blossom in American culture rather suddenly, in a few decades after 1850."

Dickinson lived through that revolution and contributed to it. With its brilliance and originality, the body of poetry that she produced over a quarter of a century places her in the ranks of her contemporaries Herman Melville, Fyodor Dostoevsky, and Friedrich Nietzsche. Like them, she took the full measure of the loss of God and bravely tried to calculate the cost. In the end, as one who both doubted and believed, she resembled Dostoevsky more than Melville or Nietzsche. Like the Russian novelist, she won her way through doubt to a tenuous but genuine faith. Yet in her moments of deepest uncertainty, Dickinson registered her doubts with a vehemence as blunt as any oath of Melville's Ahab and a defiance as sharp as any hurled at the heavens by Nietzsche's Zarathustra:

Those — dying then,
Knew where they went —
They went to God's Right Hand —
That Hand is amputated now
And God cannot be found —

The abdication of Belief
Makes the Behavior small —
Better an ignis fatuus
Than no illume at all — [#1551]

Past ages, this poem claims, had been eras of belief in which the dying distinctly "Knew where they went — ." They went where the Apostles' Creed affirmed that they went: "to God's Right Hand." But the dead no longer know the way there, for "That Hand is amputated now / And God cannot be found — ." "God's Right Hand" is, of course, a symbol of providential care; it implies that human life and the universe bear the mark of this hand and can be read as signs of his activity. But that hand has been severed and cast away, leaving God without control over life and us without a clue as to where God has gone.

The middle two lines of this poem may be the most succinct description we have of the consequences of modern unbelief: "The abdication of Belief / Makes the Behavior small." Those lines articulate the general argument developed by the sociologist Philip Rieff in his brilliant critiques of the dominance of the therapeutic in modern culture; they bring focus to the argument that the moral philosopher Alasdair MacIntyre has made, in *After Virtue* and later writings, about the loss of coherence in modern accounts of the moral life; and they pithily summarize the anxiety expressed by the political philosopher Leszek Kolakowski in *Modernity on Endless Trial.* "When I try to point out the most dangerous characteristic of modernity," Kolakowski explains, "I tend to sum up my fear in one phrase: the disappearance of taboos. . . . Various traditional human bonds which make communal life possible and without which our existence would be regulated only

149

by greed and fear, are not likely to survive without a taboo system."
"The abdication of Belief," it appears, does indeed "make the Behavior
small."

"MYSELF — THE TERM BETWEEN — "

The poems from this time in Dickinson's life show that hers was not
an unadulterated Enlightenment or romantic faith in human autonomy;
instead, she had a distinctly modern view of the self's vulnerability.
She could not discern in the diminishment of God a source of hope for
the unambiguous exaltation of humanity. If faith in God represented
to Dickinson a ship tossed òn the seas of doubt, then human consciousness was a castaway adrift upon the endless oceans. An 1863 poem
pictures the modern self bobbing between menacing waves:

> Behind Me — dips Eternity —
> Before Me — Immortality —
> Myself — the Term between —
> Death but the Drift of Eastern Gray,
> Dissolving into Dawn away,
> Before the West begin —

For the speaker of the poem, all surmises about what lies beyond the
crest of the waves — "'Tis Kingdoms — afterward — they say" — are
nothing but speculation and fantasy. All that we know for certain is
what we see in the "Term between" the waves:

> 'Tis Miracle before Me — then —
> 'Tis Miracle behind — between —
> A Crescent in the Sea —
> With Midnight to the North of Her —
> And Midnight to the South of Her —
> And Maelstrom — in the Sky — [#721]

What created in Dickinson such a diminished sense of the self?
One source was no doubt the understanding she shared with other
observers of the enormous technological revolution sweeping across

Western Europe and North America in the nineteenth century. Henry Adams, another New England descendant of the Puritans, offered a classic description of those changes in his autobiography. In one chapter of that work, he told of visiting an exposition in Paris in 1900, at the century's end. Adams became enthralled by an exhibit of a dynamo, a device that uses induction to convert mechanical energy into electrical energy. In "The Dynamo and the Virgin," Adams contrasted the worship of the machine in the modern world with the adoration of the Virgin Mary in the Middle Ages. Though he did not believe in the Virgin Mary as a divine being, Adams knew she symbolized a personal, loving, and conscious God; she and God the Father were solicitous of human needs and responsive to human pleas. The dynamo, on the other hand, represented the power dominating the modern world with its ruthless efficiency and utter indifference.

Like Adams, Dickinson took the sobering changes in nineteenth-century material culture to be signs of profound shifts taking place in the thought of the time. As an example, we might consider the fate of an idea that had enchanted Emily Dickinson as a student but that had become badly discredited by the time she began to write poetry. At the Amherst Academy and Mount Holyoke Seminary, Dickinson had been trained thoroughly in the argument from design, which held, in its various forms, that we can read nature like a book and discover the loving intentions of its author in the text. Science reinforced the truths of revealed religion, and the study of nature brought comfort to the troubled soul. "Until the time of the Civil War," writes historian Bruce Kuklick, "the cultured people of New England believed that science and religion were harmonious, that civilized men could avoid both irrationalism and skeptical empiricism."

Emily Dickinson, however, quickly detected the discordant notes being sounded by Darwin and others in the years leading up to the Civil War. As an adult, the poet found it impossible to believe in what had comforted her as a child. In many poems written during the Civil War, she tested the argument from design and found it wanting. In one poem, for instance, she considered the stock image of the butterfly emerging from the cocoon. In her childhood, Dickinson had read this phenomenon as a proof of God's design and a sign of the resurrection. But by the time she came to write a poem about it in 1862, the adult poet drew a far more sobering lesson from the natural process:

151

> From Cocoon forth a Butterfly
> As Lady from her Door
> Emerged — a Summer Afternoon —
> Repairing Everywhere —
>
> Without Design — That I could trace
> Except to stray abroad
> On Miscellaneous Enterprise

The poem tells of the butterfly's flight as it flutters in a field "Where Men made Hay" and of how it struggles "hard/With an opposing Cloud — ." The poem's speaker meets nothing in nature but "Parties — Phantom as Herself — " which, like her,

> To Nowhere — seemed to go
> In purposeless Circumference —
> As 'twere a Tropic Show —

Upon this carnival of random beauty in senseless motion, God looks down without interest: "This Audience of Idleness/Disdained them, from the Sky — " [#354]. Deprived of the attention of its divine audience, the "phantom" self can only play its part in a "Tropic Show," this endless play of signs without design. No longer a *type* of a higher spiritual reality, nature becomes in this poem merely a *trope* of human longing.

In a poem written a year later, in 1863, Dickinson made the case against design even more dramatically:

> Four Trees — upon a solitary Acre —
> Without Design
> Or Order, or Apparent Action —
> Maintain —

The sun and wind meet these trees each day, "The Acre gives them — Place — ," and they receive the "Attention of Passer by — /Of Shadow, or of Squirrel, haply — /Or Boy — ." But what does it all mean? What is the purpose of these different realities in nature? What end do they serve? We cannot answer such questions, Dickinson concludes:

What Deed is Theirs unto the General Nature —
What Plan
They severally — retard — or further —
Unknown — [#742]

Dickinson's poems from this period frequently argue that even when we detect design in creation, there is little to comfort us in the fact. The presence of design may only heighten our sense of the designer's absence:

Just as He spoke it from his Hands
This Edifice remain —
A Turret more, a Turret less
Dishonor his Design —

According as his skill prefer
It perish, or endure —
Content, soe'er, it ornament
His absent character. [#848]

In the absence of God, nature goes on with her business, saying nothing intelligible to us, even as we labor to interpret her:

We pass, and she abides.
We conjugate Her Skill.
While She creates and federates
Without a syllable. [#811]

The muteness of nature in this poem stands in sharp contrast to the talkative role it had long assumed in romantic thought. "Nature is the opposite of the soul, answering to it part for part," Ralph Waldo Emerson wrote in 1837. "Its beauty is the beauty of his own mind. Its laws are the laws of his own mind. . . . In fine, the ancient, 'Know thyself,' and the modern precept: 'study nature,' become at last one maxim." For the American Transcendentalists, nature was never silent for a moment but was always broadcasting her message to the world.

Dickinson struggled to believe that mind and nature were knit together as Emerson had said they were, but she could not do so. More often than not, for the mature Dickinson the most notable fact about the human spirit was its solitary voice in an otherwise silent world:

This Consciousness that is aware
Of Neighbors and the Sun
Will be the one aware of Death
And that itself alone

Is traversing the interval
Experience between
And most profound experiment
Appointed unto Men —

How adequate unto itself
Its properties shall be
Itself unto itself and none
Shall make discovery.

Adventure most unto itself
The soul condemned to be —
Attended by a single Hound
Its own identity. [#822]

"The soul must go by Death alone, so, it must by life, if it is a soul," she wrote in a letter in 1866. Attended by the "single Hound" of "its own identity," the Dickinsonian self is cut off both from the infinite consciousness of God and from the serene unconsciousness of nature. An 1862 poem depicts a person observing a bird hopping "down the Walk." Blissfully unaware of its human observer, the bird ate a worm and hopped "sidewise" to a wall. Suddenly, however, it "glanced with rapid eyes" and espied the alien human presence. To allay the bird's fears, the speaker reports,

Like one in danger, Cautious,
I offered him a Crumb
And he unrolled his feathers
And rowed him softer home —

Than Oars divide the Ocean,
Too silver for a seam —
Or Butterflies, off Banks of Noon
Leap, plashless as they swim. [#328]

With their evocative images of seamless beauty, the last lines portray the human presence as an intruder in nature's perfect peace. Humans may imagine such a realm, but they cannot enter it.

Unconscious nature is beautiful but dumb, Dickinson concluded, for "Nature, seems it to myself, plays without a friend." In a number of poems, she read nature not as a book speaking the language of God but as a series of signs with nothing decipherable to say. "I dreaded that first Robin, so," begins a poem from 1862. The speaker of the poem "dared not meet the Daffodils," "wished the Grass would hurry," and "could not bear the Bees should come." What, after all, do these natural realities have to say to her? "In those dim countries where they go,/What word had they, for me?" That is the crucial question. The poem ends with the poet portraying herself as the "Queen of Calvary," before whom all the citizens of nature march in silent, senseless review:

Each one salutes me, as he goes,
And I, my childish Plumes,
Lift, in bereaved acknowledgment
Of their unthinking Drums — [#348]

As much as Dickinson valued the romantics for their praise of nature, she came, somewhat reluctantly, to suspect that their veneration was rooted in ignorance. Where they heard nature preaching a gospel of human innocence and everlasting life, she detected the strains of mortal sorrow. At the end of *Walden,* for example, Thoreau explained that the "morning of [a] spring day" provided him with "proof of immortality. All things must live in such a light. O Death, where was thy sting? O Grave, where was thy victory, then?" In a poem written in the year of Thoreau's death (1862), Dickinson also wrote of morning but drew a different moral:

The Morning after Woe —
'Tis frequently the Way —

155

Surpasses all that rose before —
For utter Jubilee —

As Nature did not care —
And piled her Blossoms on —
And further to parade a Joy
Her Victim stared upon —

The Birds declaim their Tunes —
Pronouncing every word
Like Hammers — Did they know they fell
Like Litanies of Lead —

On here and there — a creature —
They'd modify the Glee
To fit some Crucifixal Clef —
Some Key of Calvary — [#364]

Only human speech and human song can comfort the one who suffers, for they alone are pitched in the "Key of Calvary." And while suffering humanity sings, nature and God remain quietly distant, safely ensconced "Somewhere in Silence."

In its frank anatomy of the self, Dickinson's poetry reveals both its indebtedness to the Puritan past and its importance for the post-Christian future that it anticipated. "In the history of the New England spirit Emily Dickinson occupies a pivotal place," Albert Gelpi argues. "Her peculiar burden was to be a Romantic poet with a Calvinist's sense of things; to know transitory ecstasy in a world tragically fallen and doomed." Her poetry represents a point at which American romanticism was forced to confront realities harsher than it had ever envisioned. Having emerged at that point in history when the hopes of romanticism were giving way to the bleak realities of naturalism, Dickinson struggled to reconcile her visionary desires with her sober reading of the human plight.

One way she sought to effect that reconciliation was to affirm a modified form of the romantic view of individual development. That is, though she dropped the romantics' belief in the self's inherent divinity, she kept their exalted view of that self's development:

We play at Paste —
Till qualified, for Pearl —
Then, drop the Paste —
And deem ourself a fool —

The Shapes — though — were similar —
And our new Hands
Learned *Gem*-Tactics —
Practicing *Sands* — [#320]

In classic romantic fashion, this poem suggests that the mythical past — the Christian past — was a necessary prelude to the autonomous, secular present. That past supplied the store of images and values that the enlightened modern self could now appropriate entirely as its own. Of the gods of Eastern and Western religion Dickinson's contemporary Walt Whitman wrote, "They bore mites as for unfledg'd birds who have now to rise and fly and sing for themselves." In certain moods, Dickinson would have agreed and welcomed the gods' dismissal.

Indeed, a number of Dickinson poems from the period of the Civil War focus upon the evolution of the self from its dependent origins to an independent destiny. A poem from the same year as "We play at Paste" (1862) speaks of the "education" of the self — "Through the Dark Sod — as Education — /The Lily passes sure — ." Having emerged from that "Dark Sod," the lily grows in the meadow without "fear": "Swinging her Beryl Bell — /The Mold-life — all forgotten — now — /In Ecstasy — and Dell — " [#392].

Poems of this kind put the best possible face on the loss of religious faith. They speak of belief as an inevitable phase — in the life of an individual as well as in the history of the race — when we "play at Paste" and grow in the "Dark Sod," passing through the "Mold-life" that precedes maturity. In its most expansive moments, Dickinson's poetry celebrates the soul's evolution as an exercise in blessed development. Having been nurtured in obscurity by family, community, and church, the self emerges secure and utterly sufficient:

The Props assist the House
Until the House is built
And then the Props withdraw

157

> And adequate, erect,
> The House support itself
> And cease to recollect
> The Auger and the Carpenter —
> Just such a retrospect
> Hath the perfected Life —
> A past of Plank and Nail
> And slowness — then the Scaffolds drop
> Affirming it a Soul. [#1142]

Like the lily in the meadow, this house, which stands "adequate, erect," has "ceased to recollect" the props that assisted it as it was built. Only rarely in her poetry — perhaps in some of her nature poems and in the lyric elegies she wrote late in life — did Dickinson achieve tranquillity of the kind depicted in her poems about "the perfected Life's" development.

In the end, Dickinson proved as divided in her view of the self as she was in her understanding of God. For every poem of hers that celebrates the unimpeded maturation of the soul, another explores the disturbing dimensions of that liberty. An 1862 poem says "There are two Ripenings — ." One of them is "of sight" and is like fruit that ripens perfectly, "Until the Velvet product/Drop spicy to the ground — ." But the other ripening is "A homelier maturing — ." Representing anything but smooth progression or sweet perfection, this ripening is "A process in the Bur — /That teeth of Frosts alone disclose/In far October Air" [#332]. Or, as a late poem puts it, "Traditions ripen and decay" [#1467]. What ripens decays; what is born dies. And it is consciousness that keeps the soul ever aware of that fact: "Of Consciousness, her awful Mate/The Soul cannot be rid — /As easy the secreting her/Behind the Eyes of God" [#894].

Dickinson, in short, knew both the sublime and the terrifying possibilities of the self's development in the modern world:

> A Solemn thing within the Soul
> To feel itself get ripe —
> And golden hang — while farther up —
> The Maker's Ladders stop —

And in the Orchard far below —
You hear a Being — drop —

A Wonderful — to feel the Sun
Still toiling at the Cheek
You thought was finished —
Cool of eye, and critical of Work —
He shifts the stem — a little —
To give your Core — a look —

But solemnest — to know
Your chance in Harvest moves
A little nearer — Every Sun
The Single — to some lives [#483]

Here we find humanity suspended in a perilous state between heaven above and the abyss below. Above the "ripening soul," the "Maker's ladders stop," tantalizingly out of reach, and at the same time, from below "You hear a Being — drop — ." The soul stands exposed to the "cool" and "critical" eye of God the "Sun." However far it has advanced or however mature it has become, that soul remains unsure of its fate. As God "shifts the stem" of your life "a little — /To give your Core — a look — ," it is solemn to ponder that while "Your chance in Harvest moves/A little nearer" every day, so too does the possibility of having your golden soul decay.

The scaffolding of Puritanism can be seen surrounding the view of the modern self that Dickinson was building in and through her poetry. For instance, her apple hanging by its stem recalls Jonathan Edwards's famous depiction of the sinner dangling over the pit of hell:

Your wickedness makes you as it were heavy as lead, . . . and if God should let you go, you would immediately sink and swiftly descend and plunge into the bottomless gulf, and your healthy constitution, and your own care and prudence, and best contrivance, and all your righteousness, would have no more influence to uphold you and keep you out of hell, than a spider's web would have to stop a fallen rock.

159

Though Dickinson would have winced at this picture of God's wrath, she knew the terrors of the self suspended over the abyss. She had inherited from the Puritans a sense of the frightening vulnerability of the self, and she found in the disorienting realities of her own experience — and of modern scientific discoveries — ample warrant for the Puritans' apprehension of danger. She was both appalled and enticed by that danger. In her poetry, critic Daneen Wardrop writes, "Dickinson wants to follow language to the point where it ends, and take one step more."

In Dickinson's poetry, that "one step more" could plunge the self into an eventual encounter with the judgment of God. At times it seemed to her that God had ordained for modern people to live in lonely liberty to the end, at which point he would demand that they account for what they had done in his absence:

> Severer Triumph — by Himself
> Experienced — who pass
> Acquitted — from that Naked Bar —
> Jehovah's Countenance — [#455]

Having chosen the security of seclusion as her vantage point for the judgment of the human spectacle, Dickinson knew the dreadful power of the critical gaze. No test could be greater, and no triumph more profound, than to "pass" before "that Naked Bar — / Jehovah's Countenance — ."

"I SING TO USE THE WAITING"

As she composed poems at a breathtaking pace in her early thirties, Dickinson was also fashioning a theory about her own poetic practice and the nature of poetry in general. She did so in the forum where she thought through most difficult questions — her own verse. In her poetry about poetry, she showed herself to be of as divided a mind about her art as she was about her God and her self. At times, her work extolled the virtues of poetry as a life-giving art. In classic romantic fashion, many of her poems lauded poetry as a way of cheating death. Just as often, however, her poetry self-consciously referred to its own fragility and mortality.

"I sing to use the Waiting," she wrote in 1864, in a poem having to do with the point of poetry. The speaker of the poem is preparing to begin a long journey. After having tied her bonnet and having shut

> the Door unto my House
> No more to do have I,
>
> Till His best step approaching
> We journey to the Day
> And tell each other how We sung
> To Keep the Dark away. [#850]

The speaker in this poem sounds like C. S. Lewis in *Shadowlands*, the dramatized account of the Christian apologist's later life. "We read to know that we are not alone," the Lewis character says at several points, voicing one of the most deep-seated romantic sentiments: the belief that art's primary purpose is to overcome human isolation. In his *An Experiment in Criticism*, Lewis speaks of literature as a "series of windows, even of doors," by means of which we pierce "the shell of some other monad" and discover "what it is like inside." In a similar manner, the speaker in Dickinson's poem refers to poetry as an entirely solitary activity, which is undertaken to "use the Waiting" and "To Keep the Dark away" until "the Day" of judgment. On our way to that "Day," we who "journey to the Day" comfort one another by telling of how we sang "To Keep the Dark away."

Comfort and healing were central to Dickinson's understanding of her art. Her occasional sentimentality on this point has displeased some of her otherwise appreciative critics. Richard Sewall, for example, cites the following 1864 poem as a key example of Dickinson's view of her art:

> If I can stop one Heart from breaking
> I shall not live in vain
> If I can ease one Life the Aching
> Or cool one Pain
>
> Or help one fainting Robin
> Unto his Nest again
> I shall not live in Vain. [#919]

161

With its "doctrine of poetry as message," this poem is, in Sewall's words, "abhorrent to modern ears." Yet he is forced to admit that the poem represents an "unabashed phase of her . . . aesthetic."

For modernist critics of poetry, Dickinson's emphasis upon the rhetorical functions of art is bound to be discomforting. She would have had no interest in theories that questioned the ability of poetry to do things for and to people. The letters she sent out from the Homestead were often accompanied by poems copied from the fascicles. In sending her poems, Dickinson sought to give a gift of healing or solace to someone in need. Knowing too well the stoic solitude of the human heart, she tried to span the gap between herself and others through her art. On numerous occasions, poems had kept her "Heart from break-ing" and "cool[ed] [her] Pain." In turn, she wished to do for others what poems by others had done for her:

> My nosegays are for Captives —
> Dim — long expectant eyes,
> Fingers denied the plucking,
> Patient till Paradise.
>
> To such, if they should whisper
> Of morning and the moor,
> They bear no other errand,
> And I, no other prayer. [#95]

Dickinson's devotion to inwardness strengthened her sense of poetry's force. Greater than any external power for her was the inner source that hounded and haunted the self, "the Tooth/That nibbles at the soul," as one poem puts it [#501]. "One need not be a Chamber — to be Haunted — " she wrote in 1863, for "The Brain has Corridors — surpassing/Material Place — ." More than any "Assassin hid in our Apartment," it is "Ourself behind ourself, concealed — " that "Should startle most — " [#670]. Or as she put it in a letter: "The Giant in the Human Heart was never met outside." Our greatest need in times of duress is for courage to meet "Ourself behind ourself," and nothing served for Dickinson as a better shield than the poetic symbol. Shortly after Edward Dickinson died in 1874, Elizabeth Holland sent his griev-ing daughter a sprig of clover from her father's grave. Emily had never visited that grave, though it was less than a mile from her home, and her gratitude for the token was deep. "Thank you for the Affection," Emily wrote, referring to the clover. "It helps me up the Stairs at Night, where as I passed my Father's Door — I used to think was safety. The Hand that plucked the Clover — I seek."

To Dickinson, poetry was her clover. If a small flower had such power, she thought, how much more might a poem possess. Words can destroy. "A Word dropped careless on a Page" could wreak its havoc long after its maker had died:

> Infection in the sentence breeds
> We may inhale Despair
> At distances of Centuries
> From the Malaria — [#1261]

Words can offer hope to the hopeless in desperate circumstances, as they do in the 1864 poem telling of "'Two Travellers perishing in Snow'":

> The Forests as they froze
> Together heard them strengthening
> Each other with the words
>
> That Heaven if Heaven — must contain
> What Either left behind. [#933]

Those words that "Heaven" must contain were

> given to me by the Gods —
> When I was a little Girl —
> They give us Presents most — you know —
> When we are new and — small.

The presents were words: "I heard such words as 'Rich' — /When hurrying to school — ." To have such words was to possess the very things to which they pointed:

> Rich! 'Twas Myself — was rich
> To take the name of Gold —

163

> And Gold to own — in solid Bars —
> The Difference — made me bold — [#454]

While Dickinson wrote her poetry with present comfort in mind, she also focused on the lasting fame it might give to her name. In a number of instances, she represented poetry as the source of a surrogate heaven in a heartless world. "Essential Oils — are wrung — " affirms that great poetry "expressed" through suffering will continue to give life after the poet's death:

> The General Rose — decay —
> But this — in Lady's Drawer
> Make Summer — When the Lady lie
> In Ceaseless Rosemary — [#675]

For Dickinson, suffering pressed the poetry out of the ordinary stuff of human experience; for her, critic Jane Donahue Eberwein notes, "distillation — despite its inevitable association with distortion and suffering — was the essence of poetry."

> This was a Poet — It is That
> Distills amazing sense
> From ordinary Meanings —
> And Attar so immense
>
> From the familiar species
> That perished by the Door —

The poet is "Himself — to Him — a Fortune — /Exterior — to Time — " because he can wring "amazing sense" from the most mundane material [#448].

Guardedly confident of her own artistic immortality, Dickinson resisted all pressure to seek fame in her lifetime. She took comfort from the contrast between fleeting fame and lasting worth. "The Martyr Poets — did not tell —" begins an 1862 poem. Those poets who never divulged their secrets and "never spoke" publicly become saints to later generations, because instead of trying to shape history they spent their time

Bequeathing — rather — to their Work
That when their conscious fingers cease —
Some seek in Art — the Art of Peace — [#544]

Though at times Dickinson thought that poetry might outwit death, she also knew the limits set to all human effort by mortality. In an 1862 poem, she pondered those limits by playing with one of John Keats's most memorable poetic formulations. "Beauty is truth, truth beauty, — that is all/Ye know on earth, and all ye need to know," Keats's "Ode on a Grecian Urn" concludes. In the Keats ode the permanence of art is contrasted to the mutability of life. In Dickinson's reworking of the Keatsian theme, art itself is forced to recognize its own mortality:

I died for Beauty — but was scarce
Adjusted in the Tomb
When One who died for Truth, was lain
In an adjoining Room —

He questioned softly "Why I failed"?
"For Beauty", I replied —
"And I — for Truth — Themself are One —
We Brethren, are", He said —

And so, as Kinsmen, met a Night —
We talked between the Rooms —
Until the Moss had reached our lips —
And covered up — our names — [#449]

In other poems, Dickinson did develop the opposing theme of the eternity of art. At times during these trying but productive years, she turned to images of Christ-like sacrifice and transcendence to express her sense of the sublime power of poetry to overcome death. A lyric from 1864 alludes to parallels between the writing of poetry and the eucharistic sacrifice of Christ.

The Poets light but Lamps —
Themselves — go out —

The Wicks they stimulate
If vital Light

Inhere as do the Suns —
Each Age a Lens
Disseminating their
Circumference — [#883]

"The significance of the Mass," writes W. H. Auden, is this: "As biological organisms, we must all, irrespective of sex, age, intelligence, character, creed, assimilate other lives in order to live. As conscious beings, the same holds true on the intellectual level. . . . As children of God, made in His image, we are required in turn voluntarily to surrender ourselves to being assimilated by our neighbors according to their needs." As much as she resisted the sacrifice of herself, Dickinson realized that the poet was destined to give her work up to the future, "Each Age a Lens/Disseminating their/Circumference — ."

"TENDER PIONEER"

In comparing the sacrifice of the poets to the crucifixion of Jesus Christ, Dickinson was dwelling upon the one facet of God that consistently afforded her comfort. If God the Father was often her foe, then God the Son was her trustworthy friend. The Trinitarian theological heritage of western Massachusetts provided her with significant resources for the nuanced complexity of God's character. In her search for a satisfying knowledge of the divine, she exploited those resources fully. To what degree she understood precise theological distinctions, we cannot say. Yet it is clear that she intuited the differences between the persons of the Godhead and realized their importance for an understanding of personality and human activity.

In many poems and letters, she identified intensely with the experience of Jesus and was particularly attracted to accounts of his suffering. The depth of Jesus' passion and the breadth of his empathy drew the poet of Amherst to this "man of sorrows." Jesus supplied "Infinitude" with the face that she so longed to look upon, and he gave her fresh ways of thinking about God. The suffering servant was a precious sign of God's presence in an otherwise vacant world, and as the Word become flesh, he broke the silence surrounding God.

The differences between Dickinson's depictions of God the Father and Jesus — and between both of them and the Holy Spirit — display her divided mind about poetry, self, and God. Like God the Father, the poet for Dickinson often seemed omnipotent and deathless, a divinely creative free imagination. It was when she thought of poetry in this way that she was most likely to consider God her rival, a threatening fellow creator. Romanticism had made Satan in Milton's *Paradise Lost* a heroic type of the human spirit; he stood as the dynamic example of all human efforts to share in God's creative power. Like William Blake and Walt Whitman before her, Dickinson knew the impulse for self-creation that pitted the imaginative self against God.

When she thought of poetry not as a power of creation but as a source of solace, however, Dickinson assigned to it many of the attributes of the Holy Spirit. In the Gospel of John, Jesus had spoken of the Holy Spirit as the Advocate who was to come in his place once he had returned to God the Father. The Spirit is the presence of God in the absence of the Son, during that period which stretches between the first and second comings of Christ. In divining the relationship between poetry and God's absence, Dickinson traced analogies between her work and that of the Holy Spirit. As the Spirit gave comfort to the church awaiting Christ's return, so did she offer to others the poems she had sung "to use the Waiting." With its fortifying and therapeutic powers, poetry could supplement the ministry of the Comforter.

Finally, when the self-yielding qualities of poetry and the poet emerged, as they frequently did in her thought, Dickinson had the Son of God in mind. The sorrowful solidarity of Jesus with humanity is a theme, both explicit and implicit, of much of what she wrote. The apostle Paul says that in Jesus, God "emptied himself, taking the form of a slave, being born in human likeness" (Philippians 2:7); so did Dickinson in certain moods view poetry as a divine force giving itself afresh to each age "disseminating [its] Circumference." Poetry had been the "gift of screws" that could "make summer" endlessly.

Dickinson's understanding of her art set her at odds with her romantic contemporaries. The Transcendentalists from Concord were Unitarians, while she remained, however eccentrically, Trinitarian to the core. In the most influential nineteenth-century American essay about poetry, Ralph Waldo Emerson had equated the poet exclusively with the second person of the Trinity, "the Son [or] the Sayer." To Emerson, the poet was the modern embodiment of the ancient *Logos,* the Word become flesh. Emerson, Thoreau, Margaret Fuller, Whitman — they all saw Jesus not as the God-man but as a perfected human form of God-consciousness. He was for them not the revelation of God's transcendence but the realization of God's immanence.

As a result, for Emerson and his associates no distinctions of person ultimately separated God, Jesus, and the poet. They took each to be a divine agent charged with peculiar power. If Jesus is to mediate our experience of God, in Emerson's words, it can be "in that only sense in which possibly any being can mediate between God and man — that is an Instructor of man. He teaches us how to become like God." Emerson refused to distinguish between the persons of the Trinity, because he did not distinguish between God and man: "Alone in history, [Jesus Christ] estimated the greatness of man. . . . He saw that God incarnates himself in man, and evermore goes forth anew to take possession of his world."

In appropriating the Trinitarian distinctions that the romantics had cast aside, Dickinson reserved a unique place for Jesus in her affections. In her poetry, Christ travels with us down the hard path of suffering, and his crucifixion binds him most fully to our experience:

> One Crucifixion is recorded — only —
> How many be
> Is not affirmed of Mathematics —
> Or History —
>
> One Calvary — exhibited to Stranger —
> As many be
> As persons — or Peninsulas —
> Gethsemane —
>
> Is but a Province — in the Being's Centre —
> Judea —
> For Journey — or Crusade's Achieving —
> Too near —

Our Lord — indeed — made Compound Witness —
And yet —
There's newer — nearer Crucifixion
Than That — [#553]

For Dickinson, crucifixion was important as an example of suffering love and not as an act of atonement. Because "Gethsemane — /Is
but a Province — in the Being's Centre — " there are as many crucifix-
ions "As persons." Where her romantic forebears detected Christ in the
innocence of the infant and the imagination of the poet, she apprehended him most fully in the singular intensity of human suffering.

Particularly during the difficult and prolific years of the early
1860s, Dickinson was prone to detect parallels between the crucifixion
and her own renunciation of marriage and a public life. It seemed to
her to be a miracle that Christ could forsake both heaven — to come to
earth — and earth — to die upon the cross:

To put this World down, like a Bundle —
And walk steady, away,
Requires Energy — possibly Agony —
'Tis the Scarlet way

Trodden with straight renunciation
By the Son of God —
Later, his faint Confederates
Justify the Road —
Flavors of that Old Crucifixion
Filaments of Bloom, Pontius Pilate sowed —
Strong Clusters, from Barabbas' Tomb —

Sacrament, Saints partook before us —
Patent, every drop,
With the Brand of the Gentile Drinker
Who indorsed the Cup — [#527]

In times of trauma, it comforted her to know that her trials had the
"Flavors of that Old Crucifixion — ." Because of that crucifixion, the
God who exists "Somewhere — in Silence — " knows something of the
human plight:

169

Jesus! thy Crucifix
Enable thee to guess
The smaller size!

Jesus! thy second face
Mind thee in Paradise
Of ours! [#225]

For Emily Dickinson, Jesus was in many ways that "high priest" of whom the writer of the New Testament letter to the Hebrews speaks. Christ is able "to sympathize with our weaknesses," because "in every respect [he] has been tested as we are, yet without sin" (Hebrews 4:15). We trust him, Dickinson asserted in more than one poem, because he has gone before us as a divine "Preceptor":

Life — is what we make it —
Death — We do not know —
Christ's acquaintance with Him
Justify Him — though —

He — would trust no stranger —
Other — could betray —
Just His own endorsement —
That — sufficeth Me —

All the other Distance
He hath traversed first —
No New Mile remaineth —
Far as Paradise —

His sure foot preceding —
Tender Pioneer —
Base must be the Coward
Dare not venture — now — [#698]

We shape our lives through choices, this poem asserts, but we do not choose our death: "Christ's acquaintance with Him/Justify Him — though — ." In accepting the cross, Jesus gave "His own endorsement" to both life and death. Since he has charted the course, "No New Mile remaineth" from earth to heaven. The "sure foot" of this "Tender Pioneer" precedes each step of our own, and, knowing that, only the basest coward could refuse to venture out into life, into death.

In the last years of her life, Dickinson's suffering seemed to draw her closer to this "Pioneer." If the higher criticism of the Bible and evolutionary theory had created chasms for her faith, Christ himself had nonetheless tested the bridge and found it firm:

> How brittle are the Piers
> On which our Faith doth tread —
> No Bridge below doth totter so —
> Yet none hath such a Crowd.
>
> It is as old as God —
> Indeed — 'twas built by him —
> He sent His Son to test the Plank,
> And he pronounced it firm. [#1433]

This willingness to experiment so daringly on our behalf confirmed for Dickinson the divinely sacrificial nature of Jesus' love:

> The Savior must have been
> A docile Gentleman —
> To come so far so cold a Day
> For little Fellowmen —
>
> The Road to Bethlehem
> Since He and I were Boys
> Was leveled, but for that 'twould be
> A rugged billion Miles — [#1487]

To be sure, there were times when Dickinson sounded the standard romantic note about the infinite potential of Jesus, the God-man whom we strive to emulate. When her friend Charles Wadsworth died in 1882, for example, she celebrated this latency in a poem sent to comfort one of his friends. In it she represented the resurrection as a sign of the inherent potential of Jesus and all humanity:

Obtaining but his own extent
In whatsoever Realm —
'Twas Christ's own personal Expanse
That bore him from the Tomb.

In every facet of life and death — in his humble life, his sacrificial death, and his glorious resurrection — Jesus set the standard for all who came after him:

He gave away his Life —
To Us — Gigantic Sum —
A trifle — in his own esteem —
But magnified — by Fame —

Until it burst the Hearts
That fancied they could hold —
When swift it slipped its limit —
And on the Heavens — unrolled —

'Tis Ours — to wince — and weep —
And wonder — and decay
By Blossoms gradual process —
He chose — Maturity —

And quickening — as we sowed —
Just obviated Bud —
And when We turned to note the Growth —
Broke — perfect — from the Pod — [#567]

The disciples in this poem can only grieve the loss of the "Gigantic Sum" that has "burst the[ir] Hearts" and "slipped its limit — /And on the Heavens — unrolled — ." Like the "bird" that "unrolled his feathers/And rowed him softer home — " [#328], Jesus slipped through the bonds of earth to be "unrolled" on heaven. Left behind, we "wince — and weep — /And wonder — and decay,/By Blossoms gradual process," while "He chose — Maturity — ." Like Jesus, if we have "chosen maturity," we and our works will "[Break] perfect — from the Pod — ."

"He gave away his Life" nicely embodies the complexity of Dickinson's understanding of Jesus, as well as the conflicting views that surfaced in her poems about God, poetry, and the self. In certain moods, the Emersonian view of Jesus as the example of our own infinitude seemed convincing to her. In Dickinson's poems, the romantic view of the godlike self surfaces frequently in metaphors of organic process — if we "decay/By Blossoms gradual process," Jesus nonetheless "chose Maturity." In elaborating their organic theory of art and culture, the American romantics believed that they had come upon the key to poetic development and cultural renewal. Like a stately tree growing from a single seed, all good and holy things develop from a simple inner source. As a poem Dickinson wrote in 1862 explains, "'Tis Duke, or Dwarf, according/As is the Central Mood — ." In all aspects of life "The Inner — paints the Outer — /The Brush without the Hand — " [#451]. As the flower bursts forth inevitably from the seed and as "Christ's own personal Expanse/. . . bore him from the Tomb," so may each human break the bonds of mortality.

But in other moods, Dickinson radically questioned the plausibility of organic views of life and death. It was death that especially puzzled her. What are we to make of its terror? How are we to comprehend its silence? We watch "a Dying Eye/Run round and round a Room" and yet never discover "what it be/'Twere blessed to have seen" [#547]. By forcing us to confront what we have lost, "Death sets a Thing significant/The Eye had hurried by" [#360]. One can tell when "There's been a Death, in the Opposite House/. . . I know it, by the numb look/Such Houses have — alway — " [#389]. That numbness strikes close to the bone in every human being, because in life "All but Death, can be Adjusted." All else can be "repaired," "settled," or "dissolved," but "Death — unto itself — Exception — /Is exempt — from Change — " [#749].

To Dickinson, romantic sentimentalism too easily dismissed the agonies of death and suffering. She had written early in her career, after all, "I like a look of Agony,/Because I know it's true — " [#241]. To counter romantic naiveté, she summoned the resources of her Trinitarian heritage. If God could seem unspeakably cold and death unbearably hard, there was in Jesus a warm and gracious side to divinity. "God is a distant — stately Lover — " asserts a poem she wrote in 1862. Safely situated in his distant heaven, God must "woo" us, "as he states us — by His Son — /Verily, a Vicarious Courtship — ." Like "Miles Stand-

173

ish" of Pilgrim lore, God sends Jesus as his "John Alden" to win the heart of "Priscilla" and all needy humanity:

> But, lest the Soul — like fair "Priscilla"
> Choose the Envoy — and spurn the Groom —
> Vouches, with hyperbolic archness —
> "Miles", and "John Alden" were Synonym — [#357]

At certain points, Dickinson despaired even of Jesus, when she feared that he, too, might become silent and as distant as the heavenly Father. The speaker of one poem is dying and cries out, "And 'Jesus'! Where is *Jesus* gone?/They said that Jesus — always came — /Perhaps he doesn't know the House — " [#158]. In another poem, a person about to pray cries out, "Oh Jesus — in the Air — /I know not which thy chamber is — /I'm knocking — everywhere — " [#502]. And in some cases, the humanity of Jesus seems on the verge of eliminating any sense we might have of his divinity: "When Jesus tells us about his Father, we distrust him. When he shows us his Home, we turn away, but when he confides to us that he is 'acquainted with Grief,' we listen, for that also is an Acquaintance of our own."

In the main, however, Dickinson held on to the rich complexity of Trinitarian categories in her thinking about God and the self. God the Father set the barriers to infinite human aspiration; God the Son assumed human form and shared in the pain we experience as we confront those barriers; and God the Holy Spirit brought healing comfort for the afflicted human spirit. For Emily Dickinson as a poet, the circumference that God had placed around human life spurred the creative efforts that gave birth to art and culture. Jesus broke through that circumference to share in the human lot and the hardness of the world. Inspired by the compassionate courage of such a "Tender Pioneer," the ideal poet might be a creator whose vital works carried speech into the midst of silence and healing comfort into the heart of deepest pain.

"DRAMA'S VITALLEST EXPRESSION"

To claim the abiding influence of Trinitarian theology in Dickinson's life and work is not to argue that she somehow remained consistently orthodox in belief or practice. Her poetry, after all, provided as many challenges to the Christian faith as it did assurances of that faith's efficacy. She was keenly interested in the drama of the Christian story, but her poetry clearly acknowledged the primacy of personal experience over doctrinal beliefs and liturgical practices:

I stepped from Plank to Plank
A slow and cautious way
The Stars about my Head I felt
About my Feet the Sea.

I knew not but the next
Would be my final inch —
This gave me that precarious Gait
Some call Experience. [#875]

This "precarious Gait" of experience was "the Angled Road/Preferred against the Mind/By — Paradox — the Mind itself — /Presuming it to lead" [#910]. That "Angled Road" means very different things to different people, as an 1862 poem explains:

"Morning" — means "Milking" — to the Farmer —
Dawn — to the Teneriffe —
Dice — to the Maid —
Morning means just Risk — to the Lover —
Just revelation — to the Beloved —

Epicures — date a Breakfast — by it —
Brides — an Apocalypse —
Worlds — a Flood —
Faint-going Lives — Their Lapse from Sighing —
Faith — The Experiment of Our Lord — [#300]

How, Dickinson wondered, might we bridge the gap between the myriad meanings of "morning" and our desire to believe that all experience is "The Experiment of Our Lord"? If we take our individual experience with utmost seriousness, how can we detect a pattern in the incidents of even a single morning, let alone of an entire life or the whole of history?

Romanticism had tried to solve this problem, in the words of literary historian M. H. Abrams, by taking the "traditional concepts, schemes, and values" that had been grounded in belief in a transcendent God and reformulating "them within the prevailing two-term system of subject and object, ego and non-ego, the human mind or consciousness and its transactions with nature." The romantics sought to make the drama and development of the self-conscious individual the central spiritual reality of the entire universe. They sought to discern in the order of an individual life the principle of order that ruled in all of creation. That, for example, is the point of Emerson's claim that "nature is the opposite of the soul, answering to it part for part."

For the romantic, what was true for nature was also true for history. There, too, the story of individual development was held to be foundational. If history was to be seen as "The Experiment of Our Lord," then it, too, would have to be seen in light of the drama of individual development. As Emerson boldly put the matter in "Self-Reliance," "history is an impertinence and an injury, if it be any thing more than a cheerful apologue or parable of my being and becoming."

Although she was drawn to this form of romantic optimism, Dickinson ultimately rejected its blithe confidence in the self. She could no more discern history as a "parable of her own being" than she could determine definitively the pattern beneath the grand "Experiment of Our Lord." The self as Emerson had envisioned it was an acquisitive male self, absorbing all that it encountered. In contrast to this consuming spirit, the self Dickinson imagined was more like a stage upon which the actors of the soul played their parts constantly:

> Drama's Vitallest Expression is the Common Day
> That arise and set about Us —
> Other Tragedy
>
> Perish in the Recitation —
> This — the best enact
> When the Audience is scattered
> And the Boxes shut —
>
> "Hamlet" to Himself were Hamlet —
> Had not Shakespeare wrote —

Though the 'Romeo' left no Record
Of his Juliet,

It were infinite enacted
In the Human Heart —
Only Theatre recorded
Owner cannot shut — [#741]

For Dickinson the heart remained divided against itself, and on its stage the most extraordinary drama was enacted. Like the great novelists in American literature — Hawthorne, Melville, James, Wharton, and Faulkner — Dickinson knew that each human heart could play every part of the drama, from the tragic hero to the malevolent villain to the generous, suffering servant. "Other Tragedy/Perish in the Recitation," but this drama plays itself out "When the Audience is scattered/And the Boxes shut — ." Even if the self cannot situate its struggles in some larger context, the drama unfolds each "Common Day" in the "Only Theatre recorded/Owner cannot shut — ."

Thus it was that during the most dramatic years of the American national experience, while the fate of the Union was being decided in the massive struggle of the Civil War, young Emily Dickinson remained at home and wrote the lyric poems that have since secured for her an elevated place in world literature. While the war played itself out hundreds of miles away, this "Vesuvius at Home" recorded assiduously the dialogue of "Drama's Vitallest Expression." With her own singular vision, Dickinson fashioned in these years a remarkably complex understanding of God, poetry, and the self. That vision was informed by her vast knowledge of the Bible and English literature, by the Trinitarian heritage she had assimilated, and by the exceptional power of inwardness that was one of her most unique possessions. Vexed by a distant and forbidding Father-God, heartened by his pioneering Son, and comforted by the Spirit whose presence became palpable for her in the play of words, Dickinson poured her life into poetry in these years.

Not long before Dickinson had begun to write poetry on a regular basis, Henry David Thoreau published *Walden*. Thoreau was, according to one of Dickinson's cousins, "naturally one of [Emily's] favorite authors," and his defense of his retreat to Walden Pond may well have

177

been familiar to her: "My purpose in going to Walden Pond was not to live cheaply nor to live dearly there, but to transact some private business with the fewest obstacles; to be hindered from accomplishing which for want of a little common sense, a little enterprise and business talent, appeared not so sad as foolish." So might Dickinson have justified her own seclusion and vocational choice. The "private business" that she sought to transact "with the fewest obstacles" was the exhaustive exploration of "Drama's Vitallest Expression, . . . the Common Day." Her mind trained itself on all that her inner experience offered for observation. Living through a period of personal trauma, theological upheaval, and unprecedented national peril, Dickinson tried to comprehend the vast changes sweeping across her world, as well as the unique responses her vibrant heart offered to those changes. In doing so, she was fashioning a body of poetry and letters that would prove to be without equal in the history of American literature.

9 The Mind Alone

A Letter always feels to me like immortality because it is the mind alone without corporeal friend. Indebted in our talk to altitude and accent, there seems a spectral power in thought that walks alone —

IN 1862, WHILE Emily Dickinson was composing on average a poem a day within the shelter of her Amherst home, seventeen-year-old John Burgess was making his way desperately through the forests of Tennessee. Burgess's family sympathized with the Union but lived in a secessionist portion of the state, and if he had not fled he would have been drafted into the Confederate army. To reach the safety of the headquarters of the Federal army in western Tennessee, Burgess had to travel more than a hundred miles over difficult terrain through occupied territory. Once in the safety of the Union camp, he swore an oath of allegiance to the United States and enlisted in the Northern army.

It was to be several years before John Burgess would enroll at Amherst College and meet Emily Dickinson. In all likelihood, his encounter with her took place at the annual tea held for Amherst College seniors at the Dickinson home. This reception was sponsored by Edward Dickinson in his capacity as college treasurer and was one of the few events still held at the Homestead rather than at the Evergreens next door. It also provided a rare occasion when Emily Dickinson could still be seen, however fleetingly, in a public setting. Burgess's acquaintance with Emily was slight at best, and she did not impress him as her sister-in-law Susan did. Many years later, Burgess recalled that Susan was "the social leader of the town . . . , a really brilliant and highly cultivated woman of great taste and refinement." Susan Dickinson was "not much of a Puritan in her mentality. She was decidedly aristocratic in her tastes." Emily, on the other hand, "was an invalid" whose "letters and conversation were full of peculiarities which might almost be called oddities." When she appeared at events such as the senior tea, "she seemed more like an apparition than a reality. . . . She would sweep in, clad in immaculate white, pass through the rooms, silently courtesying right and left, and sweep out again. She seemed more like a spirit than a human body." A mystery to all but the few who knew her very well, Emily seemed "vacillating in her mental processes and not always interesting."

For the biographer, Emily Dickinson's life in the years immediately following the Civil War does seem at times more "like an apparition than a reality," for there is little that can be known for certain about her activities between 1865 and 1870. She wrote almost a thousand poems from 1860 to 1865 but composed only a hundred or so in the next five years. The same was true of her letter writing. "The total number of known letters for the four years that conclude the decade of the sixties is the smallest by far that Emily Dickinson is known to have written during her mature years," note the editors of her correspondence. "Psychologically she was dormant." Exhausted by the ordeals of the previous years, Dickinson entered a period of relative silence and inactivity, waiting for a pall to be lifted from her life. Patience and endurance were called for, as she wrote to her Norcross cousins in 1868:

> Would we could mail our faces for your dear encouragement. Remember

> The longest day that God appoints
> Will finish with the sun.
> Anguish can travel to its stake
> And then it must return.

The period of Dickinson's silence coincided with the beginning of an era of remarkable changes in American social and economic life. Like the Whig political party, which had disappeared within a few years in the 1850s, the Whig culture of antebellum New England disintegrated quickly in the wake of the war. "Within a generation after the Civil War the United States was transformed from a predominantly agricultural to a manufacturing nation," explains Sydney Ahlstrom. The center of American life shifted from farm to factory, from village to city, and from college to university. In addition, the antebellum social patterns of hierarchy and deference gave way to the acquisitive individualism promoted by the Republican model of society and the market. In Amherst, the Dickinsons kept toiling away as always, but outside the boundaries of their village — and even within them, to some extent — the world they had ruled was rapidly fading away.

In the decades before the Civil War, Amherst had been a microcosm of the larger nation, yet after the war it soon became an anachronism. When Emily Dickinson was born in 1830, the population of Amherst was 2,631, and Chicago did not exist; only three years later, in 1833, would the seventeen households at Fort Dearborn on Lake Michigan incorporate themselves as a village. By 1900, only a year after Lavinia Dickinson had died, the city of Chicago was home to 1,698,575 inhabitants, while Amherst was still a village with fewer than 5,000 residents.

While the village of Amherst may have changed little in the last two decades of Emily Dickinson's life, Amherst College did adapt to the myriad intellectual developments sweeping across America and Europe. From the beginning, the college had secured its Christian identity in the self-definition of the larger society it served. As long as that society was self-consciously Christian in its professions, then Amherst College would hold to some form of Christian distinctives; but when the culture changed in the final decades of the nineteenth century, the college was also bound to be transformed. In retrospect, the tight bond of college and culture in antebellum Amherst made it inevitable that the college would promote what historian George Marsden has aptly termed "liberal Protestantism without Protestantism." In Marsden's words, to this day, the "heirs to the liberal Protestant universities still equate all good with the social good." The process that led to this state of affairs was well under way in Emily Dickinson's own lifetime.

181

At the end of the war, John Burgess saw these changes coming and did what he could to speed their arrival. In his memoirs, Burgess recounts an evening during the Civil War when he had drawn sentinel duty on the battlefield. That night, the "shrieks and groans of wounded and dying men" mingled with the sounds of thunder to produce a "night of terror . . . awful beyond description. . . ."

> It was, however, in the midst of this frightful experience that the first suggestion of my life's work came to me. . . . I found myself murmuring to myself: 'Is it not possible for man, a being of reason, created in the image of God, to solve the problems of his existence by the power of reason and without recourse to the destructive means of physical violence?' And I then registered the vow in heaven that if a kind Providence would deliver me alive from the perils of the existing war, I would devote my life to teaching men how to live by reason and compromise instead of by bloodshed and destruction.

Committed to rationality, compromise, and an educational career, Burgess received his discharge from the Union Army in the fall of 1864 and promptly enrolled as an undergraduate at Amherst College.

Burgess's autobiography contains sharply drawn portraits of college leaders whom the Dickinsons knew well. Of particular concern to him were William Stearns, who served as president of Amherst College from 1854 to 1876, and Julius Seelye, who succeeded Stearns and led the college until 1890. Stearns, who represented the antebellum piety and Whiggish orthodoxy associated with Edward Dickinson, resisted the dramatic postwar changes. Seelye, on the other hand, proved more comfortable in the value-neutral world that began to govern the academic enterprise in the final decades of the nineteenth century.

In his account of life at Amherst after the war, Burgess adopts a patronizing tone toward Stearns, calling him one of the "sweetest, kindest, most sympathetic natures with whom I have ever come into contact." But this kind man was also a dreadful teacher. Burgess considered Stearns to be a pedant whose course on the evidences of Christianity was centered around "a most stupid book, [Bishop] Butler's *Analogy [of Religion]*." As a teacher, all the president could do was to try to wade "through this tangle of logic, history, and doctrine [which] was dreaded by every . . . clear-headed student." Burgess dismissed out of hand both Stearns and his antiquated arguments from design.

Seelye, on the other hand, "was the most suggestive mind with whom . . . I was ever brought into contact." Burgess considered him a "profound theologian, . . . a great preacher, . . . [and] a clever politician." Most important, he had "a decided bent towards Hegelianism. He believed in a universal reason as the real substance of all things." Some accused Seelye of "setting reason before revelation. He certainly did, . . . but this did not mean that he set reason before God, for with him God was reason," and revelation was merely one of the means "through which God brought reason or himself into the consciousness of men." Seelye was as tolerant and subtle in his reasoning as Stearns was dogmatic and unimaginative.

Having graduated in 1867, Burgess returned to teach at Amherst during the final three years of the Stearns presidency, 1873-76. He came back to his alma mater to establish a department of political science and to initiate a program of graduate education. When a group of students approached him in 1874 to propose that he begin a graduate program, "it seemed to be the fulfillment of my hopes much earlier than I had expected. . . . What I aimed for since that terrible night of 1863 on the sentinel's rounds appeared now to be moving towards realization."

With their request for graduate training, these students spoke for God and made the meaning of their professor's battlefield "conversion" clear at last. To Burgess, the command of Providence was for him to lead benighted Amherst out of the mists of superstition into the bright light of reason and scientific method. Where the young men and women of the antebellum era had heard the call to the mission field or the demand for a devout and holy life, Burgess received instead the command to start a graduate program in the social sciences.

To Burgess's consternation, however, Stearns shut his ears to this call of God. He and the rest of the old guard in 1874 regarded the "college as a place for discipline, not as a place for research." Because "research implied doubt," it was seen as "more or less heretical." As long as the struggle remained "a competition between natural science and theology . . . an accommodation could be maintained." But once "research undertook to account for life and morality, especially under the influence of Darwinism, then its hostility to revelation was recognized and its advance combated." Convinced of the backwardness of Amherst College, Burgess went to Columbia College in 1876 to teach "men how to live by reason and compromise instead of by bloodshed and destruction."

Emily Dickinson knew the Stearns and Seelye families but may have had scant knowledge of the academic and political struggles roiling the postwar college. Yet at the same time she was keenly attuned to the complex issues at stake in the academic debates. She read widely and intuited matters adroitly. The struggles that rattled Burgess and the college at this time also touched Dickinson deeply. In any number of ways, they both troubled and excited her, as the poems and letters from her final years show in countless ways.

The received opinion about Dickinson has long been that her distaste for Puritanism was so great that she would have been more at home in an age later than her own, whether it was the triumphal era of Protestant liberalism at the end of the nineteenth century or the skeptical, fluid world of postmodernity. Interpreting a desire for radical liberty to be the motivating agent behind Dickinson's life choices and artistic achievements, modern readings have often concluded that she would have welcomed whatever liberated her from bondage to a dead orthodoxy.

Dickinson undeniably chafed under the grip of evangelical piety and apologetics, but that discomfort hardly drove her to embrace the rationalistic secularity that was loosening the evangelical hold on the New England mind. As an adult, she came to see the flaws in the argument from design and recognized the limitations of the spiritualized interpretation of nature she had learned from the American romantics and the evangelical scientists before Darwin. The naturalistic assumptions of evolutionary theory seemed plausible enough to her. Yet at best, the account of the world offered by naturalistic science stood as something to be accepted for what it was, an accurate detailing of the operations of nature. Dickinson hardly saw naturalism as a providential agent of progress clearing a path for reason's triumphal procession. Though she did not flinch from the scientific conclusions and historical judgments that undergirded the thought of John Burgess and others, she did not greet such disenchanting views as harbingers of a grand era of rational progress.

Dickinson could not be sanguine about a view that stranded

184

human beings, as naturalism did, in a lonely, lifeless world. As long as nature had been assumed to embody what Charles Taylor calls "an ontic logos" — as long, that is, as nature was seen to be permeated by the Divine presence and driven by the purposive Divine will — then ideas or values could be seen as realities in the world outside the self as well as constructs of the human mind. But as rationalism and materialism discredited belief in a divine word that infused itself through all of nature and informed life from beyond nature, those same ideas and values came to be seen as the exclusive property of the mind. "The valuation is now unambiguously not in the object but in *minds*, ours or God's," Taylor argues. In such a world, the imaginative self is an isolated figure, cut off from divine comfort and communion. Dickinson prized the human imagination but had little desire to inhabit a world where that imagination was the only living presence, the only dynamic force. Unlike John Burgess, she found nothing enchanting about the "disenchantment of the world."

THE BACKGROUND OF ORDINARY LIFE

As the college and country changed rapidly around them in the decade after the Civil War, the Dickinsons went about their lives largely as they had done before the war. The insularity of Amherst allowed them to continue to flourish without requiring them to uproot or dramatically alter their long-established routines. After the war, the law practice of Emily's brother and father still turned a tidy profit; Austin and Sue maintained the reputation of the Evergreens as an Amherst social center, and Sue gave birth to a second child, Martha (Mattie), in 1866; Edward Dickinson remained active in politics up until his death in 1874; and though she struggled with various infirmities, Emily's mother remained reasonably active.

By the end of the Civil War, Emily Dickinson's own patterns had already become set, and it is from the years after the war that the first fabulous characterizations of her solitude emerged. Though he termed Dickinson "vacillating" and "not always interesting," for example, John Burgess also claimed to have found in her a source of otherworldly wisdom. She "seemed almost inspired," he wrote more than half a century later, "and I have heard her express more truth in a sentence

185

of ten words than the most learned professor in the college in an hour's lecture." The stuff of later Dickinson legends is here, with the telltale hints of angelic aloofness and ethereal inspiration. (It was about this time or shortly thereafter that Dickinson began to wear regularly the white dresses so readily associated with her and her "myth.")

Though Burgess was no doubt viewing Dickinson in the glow of the posthumous myths about her, his portrait does capture qualities that others recalled in their memories from these years. Frederic Dan Huntington is a case in point. He was a noted Episcopal bishop and a close friend of Susan and Austin Dickinson. He had met Emily on several occasions in the 1860s, and after her death he wrote to Lavinia about her sister. "It was long ago that she gave me her confidence & made herself my friend, tho' afterwards I scarcely saw her," he explained. "The image that comes before me when I think of her is hardly more terrestrial than celestial, — a Spirit with only as much of the mortal investiture as served to maintain her relations with this present world."

Huntington was one of a relatively small number of people who gained access to Emily Dickinson in the last twenty years of her life. Many stories have come down from this period of friends and relatives rebuffed when they tried to see her. John Graves was one of Emily's favorite cousins and had been a regular visitor at the Dickinson home in the 1850s. Yet, according to his daughter, Graves now found himself turned away at "the Dickinson home, when Cousin Emily sent him one of her little three-cornered notes with a beautiful sprig of white jasmine. The note enclosed the quotation, 'I, Jesus, send mine angel.'" MacGregor Jenkins, the Dickinsons's neighbor and the son of their pastor, tells a similar story about "an elderly lady much loved in Amherst" who called on Emily one day. The Dickinson servant, Maggie Maher, went off "to tell Miss Emily that her friend was there." When Maggie did not return, "the dear lady possessed her soul in patience, walked about among the flowers — and waited." Finally, Maggie arrived to inform the woman that " 'Miss Emily is very sorry but she cannot see you this afternoon. She is very sorry, but it is impossible and she has asked me to give you this.' She thrust forward a tiny silver tray upon which, on a spotless doily, lay a single white clover."

For reasons wholly her own, Dickinson still agreed to meet some people, but only on her own terms. For instance, the Mack family had lived in the Homestead from 1840 to 1855, while the Dickinsons resided several blocks away on North Pleasant Street. When Samuel Mack died in St. Louis in 1866, his wife returned to Amherst. According to her daughter, although "Emily . . . saw no one, and talked to no one," she had formed such a "romantic attachment" to the Mack parents "that she insisted upon meeting my mother, who accordingly went to her home to see her. After being shown into a room that adjoined Emily's she was seated next to a door which stood ajar, on the other side of which was Emily, and thus the conversation was carried on without either seeing the other's face."

Increasingly, Dickinson made this curious form of interview — refusing sight but granting conversation — her preferred means of encounter with others. When Mabel Loomis Todd moved with her husband to Amherst in 1881, she quickly pressed to meet the "lady whom the people call the *Myth*." On September 10, 1882, Mabel recorded in her diary that she "had a walk with dear Mr. D. Senior, & called at the other house to see Miss Vinnie Dickinson. I sang there, & the rare, mysterious Emily listened in the quiet darkness outside. She sent me in a glass of wine & a poem, & in the morning a note & some flowers." She and Emily exchanged letters and gifts over the next four years, but Mabel was never to meet the poet face to face.

Even the physician who cared for Emily Dickinson in her final years was not allowed to see his patient in any customary fashion. When she was suffering from Bright's disease in the early 1880s, Dickinson required Dr. Orvis Bigelow to conduct his examinations in a most unusual manner. "She would walk by the open door of a room in which I was seated," Dr. Bigelow complained. "Now, what besides mumps could be diagnosed that way!" Taking "No!" to be, in her own words, the "wildest word we consign to Language," Dickinson clung to the power of refusal as long as she was conscious. As Jay Leyda explains, "E[mily] D[ickinson] had to be prostrate and unconscious before her doctor could care for her."

"LITERATURE IS FIRM"

As she moved deeper into seclusion after the Civil War, Dickinson maintained contact with the world through her highly selective encounters, her correspondence, her periodicals and books, and her observation of whatever spectacles passed by the Homestead. Her second-floor bedroom, which was also her workroom, commanded an impressive view of Main Street. "It is extraordinary how much of the world can be seen from one window overlooking a village street," noted a late nineteenth-century resident of Amherst. As remote as it was becoming from the main centers of culture and commerce in the Gilded Age, Amherst still offered sufficient spectacles to amuse Dickinson from her Homestead vantage point.

The visit of the circus to Amherst in 1866 was one such spectacle. Flyers announced its coming:

> G. F. Bailey & Co's Great Quadruple Combination!
> will exhibit in Amherst! On Friday, May 4th, 1866.

According to John Burgess, this visit of the circus proved to be a singularly important event in Amherst, where very little happened "to distract our attention from our work. . . . We were all in a fever of excitement to attend the performance." Even the faculty member in charge of Burgess's junior class, "one of the stiffest Puritans in the faculty," gave his class permission to attend, because "as there was a hippopotamus, and he had never seen a hippopotamus, he thought he would go himself." To get from the railroad depot to the grounds where the circus pitched its tent, the animals and acts had to troop past the Homestead. Due east of the Dickinson home, the lively procession wended its way up Triangle Street, as Emily watched. "Friday I tasted life," she wrote to Elizabeth Holland. "It was a vast morsel. A circus passed the house — still I feel the red in my mind though the drums are out."

When the circus was not in town, the periodic revivals at First Church offered the reclusive poet food for thought and targets for satire. The revival of 1873 particularly piqued her interest. No longer tempted or tormented by the call to confession, Dickinson charted the course of spiritual life by looking out her window: "There is that which is called an 'awakening' in the church, and I know of no choicer ecstasy than to see Mrs [Sweetser] roll out in crape every morning, I suppose to intimidate antichrist; at least it would have that effect on me."

The 1873 revival gripped the Dickinson household, with Emily's father especially caught up in the cycle of repentance and renewal. Even though he had made a confession of faith and joined the church years earlier, Edward Dickinson felt called to recommit himself to God. He recorded his decision on a slip of paper that was found in his wallet at his death: "I hereby give myself to God. Edward Dickinson May 1, 1873."

Spurred on by his own recommitment, Edward Dickinson persuaded Jonathan Jenkins, the pastor of the First Church, to examine Emily on spiritual matters. He regretted that his daughter had never joined the church and had even stopped attending services. The pastor's son later reported that "[Emily's] father felt that she needed guidance in spiritual matters. To my father fell the doubtful privilege of providing this guidance." Since neither pastor nor parishioner ever spoke of what transpired at that meeting, MacGregor Jenkins imagines that "there must have lurked in [Emily's] expressive face a faint suggestion of amusement at the utter incongruity of the situation, but she was far too urbane a person to have betrayed it." In a manner characteristic of the early liberal Protestant interpretation of the poet's life and work, Jenkins wrote, "I have no doubt that beneath the hackneyed phrases employed, messages had been exchanged that left each in perfect sympathy with the other." The only result of the meeting was that Rev. Jenkins "reported to the perplexed parent that Miss Emily was 'sound,' and let it go at that."

Jenkins had to go to the Dickinson home for the interview, because Emily never set foot in the new church building, which had been constructed only a few hundred yards away from the Homestead in 1867-68. Austin Dickinson led the drive for the new sanctuary and parsonage and supervised the building of the church as well as the landscaping of the grounds. All Emily knew of the project was what she heard from family members and friends; even her nominal pledge of $25 to the building fund was paid by her father. The new structure was just out of sight of the Homestead, and Emily caught her only glimpse of it one night soon after it was built. "There was a legend," Mabel Loomis Todd reported Vinnie as having said, "that [ED] had crept out one evening with her brother as far as a certain tree in the hedge in order to see the new church."

While the actual circumference of Emily Dickinson's life continued to contract after the Civil War, her imaginative circumference expanded ever larger. What she could see from her window at the Homestead was one thing; what she did with what she saw was quite another matter. Much of what she saw grew in her imaginative reconstructions, and in most cases the transformation took place in her poetry. On some rare occasions, her imagination took shape in narrative rather than lyric form, as was the case when a fire ravaged Amherst's central business district in the early morning hours of July 4, 1879. The buildings it destroyed were only several hundred yards to the west of the Dickinson home. In one of the longest narrative accounts that Emily ever wrote, she told her Norcross cousins of the disaster:

> Dear Cousins,
>
> Did you know there had been a fire here, and that but for a whim of the wind Austin and Vinnie and Emily would have all been homeless? But perhaps you saw *The Republican*.
>
> We were waked by the ticking of the bells, — the bells tick in Amherst for a fire, to tell the firemen.
>
> I sprang to the window, and each side of the curtain saw that awful sun. The moon was shining high at the time, and the birds singing like trumpets.
>
> Vinnie came soft as a moccasin, 'Don't be afraid, Emily, it is only the fourth of July.'
>
> I did not tell that I saw it, for I thought if she felt it best to deceive, it must be that it was.
>
> She took hold of my hand and led me into mother's room. Mother had not waked, and Maggie was sitting by her. Vinnie left us a moment, and I whispered to Maggie, and asked her what it was.
>
> 'Only Stebbins's barn, Emily;' but I knew that the right and left of the village was on the arm of Stebbins's barn. I could hear buildings falling, and oil exploding, and people walking and talking gayly, and cannon soft as velvet from parishes that did not know that we were burning up.
>
> And so much lighter than day was it, that I saw a caterpillar measure a leaf far down in the orchard; and Vinnie kept saying bravely, 'It's only the fourth of July.'

It seemed like a theatre, or a night in London, or perhaps like chaos. The innocent dew falling 'as if it thought no evil,' . . . and sweet frogs prattling in the pools as if there were no earth.

At seven people came to tell us that the fire was stopped, stopped by throwing sound houses in as one fills a well.

Mother never waked, and we were all grateful; we knew she would never buy needle and thread at Mr. Cutler's store, and if it were Pompei nobody could tell her.

The post-office is in the old meeting-house where Loo and I went early to avoid the crowd, and — fell asleep with the bumble-bees and the Lord God of Elijah.

Vinnie's 'only the fourth of July' I shall always remember. I think she will tell us so when we die, to keep us from being afraid.

Footlights cannot improve the grave, only immortality.

Forgive me the personality; but I knew, I thought, our peril was yours.

Love for you each.

Emily

This description of the fire may surprise us, for we associate Emily Dickinson so completely with the short lyric phrase and not with the extended narrative description. Yet while her own talent inclined decidedly to the writing of epigrammatic verse, for intellectual sustenance she drew as deeply from fiction as she did from poetry. Indeed, in her seclusion after the Civil War, fiction served as one of the main links between her and the world outside the gates of the Homestead. Dickinson read widely in the novels and short stories of her time; and in retrospect, her judgment of fiction seems impressive. The writers she admired most — Charles Dickens, Emily and Charlotte Brontë, and George Eliot, as well as Nathaniel Hawthorne and Henry James to a lesser extent — have proved to be among the most enduring English-language novelists from the late nineteenth century.

To be sure, Dickinson's taste in fiction also showed her to be very much a product of her times. In adolescence and early adulthood, she had a fondness for sensational and sentimental tales. She, Austin, and Vinnie had shared with countless numbers a fascination with Henry Wadsworth Longfellow's *Kavanagh* (1849) and Ik Marvel's *Reveries of a Bachelor* (1850). And a decade later, when she was thirty, Dickinson was

191

still reading with delight the sensational fiction of her day. She was especially attracted to the sensational stories of Harriet Prescott Spofford. When Sue let her borrow the copy of the *Atlantic Monthly* in which Spofford's story "The Amber Gods" had appeared, Emily returned the issue with a note: "Sue, it is the only thing I ever read in my life that I didn't think I could have imagined myself!" Already isolated at home, she craved for more to read. "You stand nearer the world than I do, Susan," she wrote to the house next door. "Send me everything she writes." Sue complied, funneling these and other stories to the Homestead, until Emily at times had to turn away in fear from the fiction she loved to read. "I read Miss Prescott's 'Circumstance' [a sensational story of Indian captivity], but it followed me, in the Dark — so I avoided her —."

After the Civil War, Dickinson's tastes in fiction changed, as she turned increasingly to major novelists for the spiritual nurture she no longer received through the church. Among the first novelists for whom she developed a powerful attachment were the Brontë sisters, whose fiction she had first read in adolescence and whose names continued to surface in her letters until her death. There were obvious parallels between the family situations of the brilliant sisters from Haworth and the poet of Amherst. Like Dickinson, the Brontës had developed passionate sibling bonds and fertile imaginative worlds in a home ruled by a distant father; and like the young woman from the Connecticut River valley, these sisters from the Yorkshire moors developed through their experiences a gothic fascination with the macabre.

To Dickinson, the work of the Brontë sisters was marked by clear-sightedness, just as their lives had been distinguished by courage. When Josiah Holland died in 1881, Dickinson wrote to his wife Elizabeth of her "wonder at your self-forgetting." Elizabeth Holland's courage and thoughtfulness during her own grief "reminded [me] again of gigantic Emily Brontë, of whom her Charlotte said 'Full of ruth for others, on herself she had no mercy.' The hearts that never lean, must fall. To moan is justified." And when the poet's beloved nephew Gilbert died suddenly two years later, Dickinson turned again to the Brontës for support. On this occasion, it was Emily Brontë who supplied the help through a poem, "Last Lines," that became one of Dickinson's favorite lyrics at the close of her life. Mourning Gilbert, Dickinson wrote "As Emily Brontë to her Maker, I write to my Lost 'Every Existence would

192

exist in Thee — .'" The reference is to the Brontë passage that Dickinson cited in several letters. In it, "that marvellous Emily Brontë" addresses the "God within my breast":

> Though Earth and man were gone,
> And suns and universes cease to be,
> And Thou wert left alone,
> Every Existence would exist in Thee.
>
> There is not room for Death
> Nor atom that his might could render void
> Since thou art Being and Breath
> And what thou art may never be destroyed.

The fiction of Nathaniel Hawthorne, William Dean Howells, and Henry James also drew Dickinson's attention even if it did not win her unqualified praise. "Hawthorne appalls, entices," she told Higginson in 1879, and "of Howells and James, one hesitates — ." She enjoyed their fiction, especially Hawthorne's stories and novels, which she had first read years before. But in the main, these American writers of social and psychological realism did not fare as well in Dickinson's judgment as they would in history's estimation. Her tastes in novels ran more toward her English Victorian contemporaries than toward her American peers.

Of the English novelists, Charles Dickens was a personal favorite. In her youth and early adulthood, Dickinson read Dickens as everyone did, in monthly installments appearing in serial form. Her early letters are peppered with references to Dickensian scenes and characters; Barkis, Cap'n Cuttle, Mr. Micawber, Little Nell, and others provided her a running commentary on her moods of the moment or the events of the day. Dickinson found in Dickens a kindred spirit; like her, he had discovered in the uncanny resources of language a way to blunt the traumas of experience. "Dear Dickens" she called him in a letter written shortly before her death. Using a phrase she had lifted from his fiction, she praised him for having given " 'the likes of me' " the gifts of verbal inventiveness.

Dickinson's affection for Dickens's fiction was matched only by her reverence for the novels of George Eliot. In April of 1873, she answered a question from her Norcross cousins: "'What do I think of *Middlemarch?'* What do I think of glory — except that in a few instances this 'mortal has already put on immortality.'" There have been few instances of the mortal becoming immortal, but "George Eliot is one. The mysteries of human nature surpass the 'mysteries of redemption,' for the infinite we only suppose, while we see the finite." And when the novelist died, Dickinson grieved the death of "*my* George Eliot." She hoped that "the gift of belief which her greatness denied her" would be given to Eliot "in the childhood of the kingdom of heaven. As childhood is earth's confiding time, perhaps having no childhood, she lost her way to the early trust, and no later came."

Though she guarded her own secrets and privacy jealously, Dickinson enjoyed delving into the lives of the authors she cherished. She had read with delight accounts of the lives of Emily Brontë and Elizabeth Barrett Browning and awaited eagerly the publication of George Eliot's biography. Anticipating its arrival, she wrote to Elizabeth Holland that "Vinnie is eager to see the Face of George Eliot which the Doctor promised, and I wince in prospective, lest it be no more sweet. God chooses repellant settings, dont he, for his best Gems?" When a publisher sent her the Eliot biography, Dickinson thanked him with an elegiac tribute to the English author:

> Her Losses make our Gains ashamed —
> She bore Life's empty Pack
> As gallantly as if the East
> Were swinging at her Back.
> Life's empty Pack is heaviest,
> As every Porter knows —
> In vain to punish Honey —
> It only sweeter grows. [#1562]

In his response to her introductory letter in 1862, Higginson had asked Dickinson what she liked to read. Her answer was brief and direct: "For Poets — I have Keats — and Mr and Mrs Browning." There are important poets missing from this list — Shakespeare was the central poet of her life — but in naming Keats and the Brownings, Dickinson drew close to the core of her concerns as a practicing poet and a devoted reader of verse.

Of these poets, Dickinson was at one level most fond of Elizabeth Barrett Browning. References to her poetry began to appear in Dickinson's letters and poems in late 1861. Browning had died earlier that year, and her passing prompted the beginning of a long process of tribute and assimilation in Dickinson's work. The English poet's 11,000-line blank verse romance, *Aurora Leigh*, became Dickinson's favorite among all of Browning's works. References to it surfaced in a number of her letters, and its metaphors worked their way directly into several of her poems.

In her own copy of *Aurora Leigh*, Dickinson underlined a passage that speaks to the bond of sisterhood between the unknown Amherst poet and the renowned English artist:

> By the way,
> The works of women are symbolical.
> We sew, sew, prick our fingers, dull our sight,
> Producing what? A pair of slippers, sir,
> To put on when you're weary — or a stool
> To stumble over and vex you . . . 'curse that stool!'
> Or else at best, a cushion, where you lean
> And sleep, and dream of something we are not
> But would be for your sake. Alas, alas!
> This hurts most, this — that, after all, we are paid
> The worth of our work, perhaps.

When Browning died in 1861, Dickinson had already begun to produce those "works symbolical" that required her to "sew, sew . . . ,/Producing what?" Like her English forerunner, this New England poet had to struggle her entire life to reconcile her inventive gifts with her allotted roles as a woman. By illuminating the way for women artists to follow, Browning had earned Dickinson's gratitude and high praise:

> Her — "last Poems" —
> Poets — ended —
> Silver — perished — with her Tongue —
> Not on Record — bubbled other,
> Flute — or Woman —
> So divine — [#312]

The Brownings, along with Keats and his fellow romantics — these were poets she read avidly for their substance and from whom she learned much about her craft. But it was Shakespeare, above all others, who served for her as the rock of all poetic practice: "While Shakespeare remains, Literature is firm — ." During the trauma with her eyes in the mid-1860s, Dickinson had been forbidden to read anything for months. For her, that had been a terrifying deprivation. When they met for the first time in 1870, she informed Higginson that "After long disuse of her eyes she read Shakespeare & thought why is any other book needed." She wrote to Joseph Lyman that, when her eye specialist lifted his ban, "how my blood bounded! Shakesper was the first." Having suffered "eight months of Siberia" without poetry, she snatched up a copy of his work and "thought why clasp any hand but this. . . . I thought I should tear the leaves out as I turned them. Then I settled down to a willingness for all the rest to go but William Shakespear. Why need we Joseph read anything else but him[?]" It was as though, of all poets, Shakespeare "so seem[ed]/To Comprehend the Whole — /The Others look a needless Show — " [#569]. She may have been thinking of her own eventual recognition, when she wrote to an acquaintance in 1873, "Had I a trait you would accept I should be most proud, though he has had his Future who has found Shakespeare — ."

The love of Shakespeare stayed with Dickinson until her death. Even when grief seemed to press all other concerns from her life, he remained a vibrant presence in her thought. In 1879, she wrote Higginson, "I . . . have known little of Literature since my Father died — that and the passing of Mr Bowles and Mother's hopeless illness, overwhelmed my moments, though your Pages and Shakespeare's, like Ophir — remain — ." Several years later, Emily tried again to describe the central place of Shakespeare's work in her life, this time by using him as a point of reference in an unusual tribute to her sister-in-law Susan: "With the exception of Shakespeare, you have told me of more knowledge than any one living — To say that sincerely is strange praise."

Like her brilliant contemporary Herman Melville — about whose work she knew very little — Emily Dickinson discovered her true creative voice at the same time that she developed a deep affinity for Shakespeare's tragedies. As Melville did, Dickinson discovered in the

English playwright an unsurpassably rich resource for comprehending the mystery of suffering and the nobility of humanity. For her, as for Melville, the experience of tragedy was a religious one, and in Shakespeare's works she found a powerful supplement to Christian belief.

Lines from Shakespeare's tragedies appear frequently in the letters from her later life, usually in the context of loss or suffering, and the specific citations often seem to lead her into a more general reflection upon life's mysteries. Early in 1878, for example, she cited *King Lear* in a letter to Josiah Holland, who was convalescing from an illness at the time: "We hope that you are happy so far as Peace is possible, to Mortal and immortal Life — for those ways 'Madness lies.' " Having begun her letter with wishes for her friend's recovery, Dickinson moved, by means of the Shakespeare citation, to the real subject gripping her at that time, which was the recent death of Samuel Bowles and her lingering grief over the loss of her father:

But I intrude on Sunset, and Father and Mr Bowles.

> These held their Wick above the West —
> Till when the Red declined —
> Or how the Amber aided it —
> Defied to be defined —
>
> Then waned without disparagement
> In a dissembling Hue
> That would not let the Eye decide
> Did it abide or no

In her adulthood, the only source that Emily Dickinson quoted more often than Shakespeare was the King James Bible. It was, without question, her richest poetic lexicon. She had grown up within the verbal universe of the King James Version; she heard it read from the pulpit several times each Sunday, was drilled in its cadences through her years of schooling, and participated for several decades in the daily family devotional exercises based upon its text. (In the Dickinson collection at Harvard University, there are nineteen Bibles, all of which belonged to members of Emily's immediate family.) And when she was not hearing

197

the prose of the King James Bible read by others, Dickinson was absorbing it quietly through her own extensive reading of it.

In all, Dickinson referred to thirty-eight different books of the Bible one or more times in her poetry and letters. Her most frequent citations came from the book of Genesis; from the Gospels of Matthew, Luke, and John; and from the book of Revelation. In addition, she made frequent reference to 1 Corinthians (especially chapter 15, Paul's treatise on the resurrection), to the Psalms, and to the book of Isaiah. In many cases, she cited scriptural passages from memory; and in some instances, she made changes in wording for her own peculiar purposes. With the Bible, as with all other books, she was willing to raid its verbal stores for resources that could serve her particular spiritual and poetic ends.

In the case of Genesis, Dickinson's interest focused decisively upon Eden and the expulsion of Adam and Eve from it. We have seen how, in adolescence, she playfully chose the name of Eve for herself: "there is no account of her death in the Bible, and why am I not Eve?" In the disenchanted state of adulthood, Dickinson again fantasized on more than one occasion about the deathless bliss of the Garden. Yet when she stirred from her reveries, she always found herself with the rest of humanity, cast out of the Garden and stranded east of Eden:

> The lonesome for they know not What —
> The Eastern Exiles — be —
> Who strayed beyond the Amber line
> Some madder Holiday —
>
> And ever since — the purple Moat
> They strive to climb — in vain —
> As Birds — that tumble from the clouds
> Do fumble at the strain —
>
> The Blessed Ether — taught them —
> Some Transatlantic Morn —
> When Heaven — was too common — to miss-
> Too sure — to dote upon! [#262]

From the Gospels, Dickinson most often drew upon resources for her own encouragement. It was here, of course, that she read the story and heard the words of Jesus, that "Tender Pioneer" and "docile Gentleman" of whom she spoke so warmly in her poems. In Matthew, the assurances of the Sermon on the Mount attracted her, while in the Gospel of John it was the farewell discourses of Jesus that she focused upon in her many citations from the book. When Jesus promised, as he did in John 14, that in his Father's house "there are many mansions," Dickinson wanted to take him at his word:

"Houses" — so the Wise Men tell me —
"Mansions"! Mansions must be warm!
Mansions cannot let the tears in,
Mansions must exclude the storm!

"Many Mansions," by "his Father,"
I don't know him; snugly built!
Could the Children find the way there —
Some, would even trudge tonight! [#127]

Or, as she wrote in one of her earliest poems:

Papa above!
Regard a Mouse
O'erpowered by the Cat!
Reserve within thy kingdom
A 'Mansion' for the Rat! [#61]

Though she often expressed deep affection for the characters and promises of the scriptures, Dickinson also enjoyed parodying biblical texts. She prized the Christian scriptures for their mysteries and assurances but also sensed their unmistakable, alienating strangeness. They spoke, she seemed to think at times, in an antiquated language about an attenuated faith:

The Bible is an antique Volume —
Written by faded Men
At the suggestion of Holy Spectres —
Subjects — Bethlehem —
Eden — the ancient Homestead —

199

> Satan — the Brigadier —
> Judas — the Great Defaulter —
> David — the Troubadour —
> Sin — a distinguished Precipice
> Others must resist —
> Boys that 'believe' are very lonesome —
> Other Boys are 'lost' —
> Had but the Tale a warbling Teller —
> All the Boys would come —
> Orpheus' Sermon captivated —
> It did not condemn — [#1545]

The relationship to the Bible outlined in this poem is a complex one indeed. The opening lines are filled with images of insubstantiality and decrepitude; one can hardly have confidence in the authority of a book that had been "Written by faded Men — / At the suggestion of Holy Spectres — ." The drama of the Bible reads like the playbill of a cheap traveling show, and it has become a "lonesome" matter to believe this story in the modern world, because few are attracted by an ancient account of judgment. What the tale needs is a "warbling Teller" to captivate the vast "lost" audience.

Yet for all its gentle sarcasm concerning the Bible and its stories, this late poem by Dickinson — written around 1882 — expresses an underlying admiration for the very world it parodies. We would do well not to confuse contemporary attitudes toward parody with the kind practiced by Dickinson. Rather than being simple and dismissive, her relationship to the biblical text remained, to the end, complicated and ambiguous. What drew her to Shakespeare and the Bible was the very strangeness that lent itself so well to her parodies and allusions. Those great texts offered her rich alternatives to the poverty of modern understanding. In her poetry and prose, Dickinson both entered into their alien worlds, in order to experience their pleasures and learn their mysteries, and stood back from them, in order to subject them to quizzical critique.

Dickinson's attitude toward the Bible is similar to what Mikhail Bakhtin has described as the medieval style of parody. In the Christian world in the Middle Ages, parody served the purposes of renewal, according to Bakhtin. On feast and festival days, the serious language

200

and ritualistic practices of the Christian faith were held up for laughter and ridicule. In Bakhtin's words, the purpose was "to encourage laughter in the congregation — this was conceived as a cheerful rebirth after days of melancholy and fasting." Holy laughter provided a sanctifying counterpoint to the melody of sacred language and the liturgical year.

Bakhtin's caution against transferring our "contemporary concepts of parodic discourse onto medieval parody" applies to Dickinson as well. "In modern times," he writes, "the functions of parody are narrow and unproductive. Parody has grown sickly, its place in modern literature is insignificant." Living as we do in a "world of free and democratized language," we find it hard to conceive of the "complex and multi-leveled" language of the Middle Ages, which still permeates the world of Shakespearean poetry and King James prose. In Dickinson, parody is not sickly but wistful. Bakhtin writes that in great parody, "it is often very difficult to establish precisely where reverence ends and ridicule begins." Emily Dickinson was astute enough to recognize in Shakespeare and the Bible an incomparable verbal world, but she was also wise enough to know how hard it would be to secure herself in such a world in a "free and democratized" modernity. Here, as elsewhere, she knew what it meant to be "Homeless at home."

"A LETTER IS A JOY OF EARTH"

In the years after the Civil War, then, Emily Dickinson continued to expand her range of reference, as she absorbed Shakespeare, the Bible, and much of the best fiction being written by her contemporaries in America and England. At the same time, as she took in so much from other sources across time and space, she had only the outlet of her letters and poetry for her own thoughts. As it grew ever more difficult for her to negotiate face-to-face encounters, Dickinson turned increasingly to correspondence as her primary form of interaction with other people. There is no other major figure in American history for whom the letter became such an exclusive mode of conducting a public life. More than anywhere else, it was within the pages of her letters that the poet played out her life in her last two decades. It is within the pages of her letters that we meet most closely and fully the adult Emily Dickinson.

To say that is not to deny the artfulness of Dickinson's letters by implying that they are direct transcriptions of her mind. Ever protective of her privacy, she crafted carefully her self-representation in her correspondence, and her letters cannot easily be read as innocently unfiltered accounts of her thoughts. Less than a year after the first edition of her poetry appeared in 1890, Higginson published in the *Atlantic Monthly* an article containing some of her letters to him. In her journal, Mabel Loomis Todd wrote about Higginson's naive reading of the correspondence: "as to the 'innocent and confiding' nature of them [Dickinson's letters to Higginson], Austin smiles. He says Emily definitely posed in those letters, he knows her thoroughly."

Millicent Todd Bingham provides a helpful qualification to Austin's judgment. "Although it may have been true that Austin knew his sister 'thoroughly,'" she suggests, "I . . . question whether he did entirely understand her correspondence with Colonel Higginson. May she not have made light of it in order to conceal from her brother how much it meant to her?" If Emily could be coy in her revelation of herself in her poems and correspondence, could she not be equally artful in keeping her deepest thoughts concealed, on occasion, even from those who knew her best and loved her most? At every level of her life, Dickinson took seriously her own advice to "Tell all the Truth but tell it slant — ." So if her flippant comments make us question the sincerity of her letters, we might also consider how she used such remarks to mask her feelings about what she had revealed.

Those feelings were indeed intense. Over the last two decades of her life, Dickinson prized her correspondence above all else, for it was the only solid bridge connecting her island solitude to the mainland friendships that sustained her. "Take all away from me, but leave me Ecstasy," she wrote a year before her death to a family that had sent her a Christmas card:

And what *is* Ecstasy but Affection and what is Affection but the Germ of the little Note?

A Letter is a joy of Earth —
It is denied the Gods —

Emily,
with Love.

What exactly was the nature of this "joy of Earth" that had been denied to the gods? It was for Dickinson the power to remain in the body while abrogating the limits of the flesh. For the gods in their omniscience, there can be no such thing as a letter, because the essence of a letter is to conceal a world of possibilities and presence under its seal. The gods receive even the most intimate information immediately, but the recipient of a letter stands poised with the presence of another hidden within her hand. "A Letter always feels to me like immortality because it is the mind alone without corporeal friend," Dickinson wrote to Higginson. "Indebted in our talk to attitude and accent, there seems a spectral power in thought that walks alone — ."

That "spectral power" disclosed passion and perceptions otherwise concealed beneath the garb of ordinary life. Stripped of its "corporeal friend," the "mind alone" could transport and reveal itself under the cover of an envelope, without exposing itself to the unwelcome eyes of others. As a young woman, Dickinson had confessed that it made her "shiver to hear a great many people talk, they took [']all the clothes off their souls — .'" Much later in life, she revealed to her friend Helen Hunt Jackson her surprise that Jackson "could consent to publish. 'How can you,' she was to say, 'Print a piece of your soul?'" Yet while appalled by the prospect of indiscriminate publication, Dickinson savored the pleasure of discreet disclosure through letters.

For Dickinson, an unopened letter held promise and peril of the kind that belong to an unfinished life. Like the conclusion of any life, the opening of a letter could reveal the mystery that told whether the risk of the venture had been worthwhile. "The Risks of Immortality are perhaps its' charm — A secure Delight suffers in enchantment," she told Higginson in 1870.

> The Riddle that we guess
> We speedily despise —
> Not anything is stale so long
> As Yesterday's Surprise —

The danger of a letter, of course, was that the surprise within its folds might be news capable of provoking unspeakable sadness rather than unbridled joy. As she grew older, Dickinson came to know that danger well. Less than a year before her own death, Dickinson wrote

203

in desperation to Higginson. She had learned from the *Springfield Republican* that their friend Helen Hunt Jackson lay "at the point of death in San Francisco." Dickinson was "unspeakably shocked" to hear this news. "Please say it is not so," she pleaded with Higginson. "What a Hazard a Letter is! When I think of the Hearts it has scuttled and sunk, I almost fear to lift my Hand to so much as a Superscription."

Letters might break our hearts, heal our wounds, or bring an importunate demand to our door. The latter was the case with an 1872 letter that Emily received from a certain Miss P., most likely Elizabeth Stuart Phelps, the author of the enormously popular *Gates Ajar*. "Of Miss P——— I know but this, dear," Emily explained to her cousin, Louise Norcross. "She wrote me in October, requesting me to aid the world by my chirrup more. Perhaps she stated it as my duty, I don't distinctly remember, and always burn such letters, so I cannot obtain it now. I replied declining. She did not write to me again — she might have been offended, or perhaps is extricating humanity from some hopeless ditch."

Containing mystery and the unknown within itself, a letter for Dickinson had uncanny power and needed to be handled with tantalizing care:

> The Way I read a Letter's — this —
> 'Tis first — I lock the Door —
> And push it with my fingers — next —
> For transport it be sure —
>
> And then I go the furthest off
> To counteract a knock —
> Then draw my little Letter forth
> And slowly pick the lock —
>
> Then — glancing narrow, at the Wall —
> And narrow at the floor
> For firm Conviction of a Mouse
> Not exorcised before —
>
> Peruse how infinite I am
> To no one that You — know —

And sigh for lack of Heaven — but not —
The Heaven God bestow — [#636]

Letters offered Dickinson the pleasures of friendship and communion without many of the attendant pressures or perils of ordinary
relationships. Lodged within the Homestead, she retained tight control
over the access of others to her; and through her letters, she could efface
herself without withdrawing entirely from the public world. By means
of letters, Dickinson could live vicariously in a time before modern
forms of diversion made vicariousness as easy as it has become.
Through letters, she received reports of the exotic Middle East from her
childhood friend Abby Wood Bliss, she asked Samuel Bowles to touch
the London grave of Elizabeth Barrett Browning for her, she heard
reports of travel and literary culture from the Hollands, and through
her correspondence with Higginson she gained protected access to the
literary elites of her day. What she could not or would not know in
person, Dickinson experienced as fully as possible through the letters
that crossed the threshold of the home on East Main Street in Amherst.
They were to her one of the undoubted "joys of Earth."

LIFE BY LETTER: DICKINSON'S ADULT FRIENDSHIPS

Of all the adult friendships she enjoyed through letters, none was more
important to Dickinson than her relationship with Elizabeth and Josiah
Holland. After a few initial visits she paid to the Hollands in nearby
Springfield in the 1850s, the friendship flourished almost exclusively
by mail. From her young adulthood, when she was discovering and
testing her remarkable powers, to the painful days of her final illness,
Emily kept little from her Springfield friends. They heard of her theological doubts, shared in her bereavements, and were regaled with
accounts of the Dickinson family's many eccentricities.

Especially in her later years, Dickinson often wrote to Elizabeth
Holland alone, using her friend as a sounding board for her thoughts
about her family. In 1873, Emily employed hyperbole to press a point
about the gap between the Dickinson daughters and their parents:
"[Vinnie] has no Father and Mother but me and I have no Parents but
her." Then in the same letter, she teasingly chided both her sister and

205

her father. Writing at the height of the 1873 revival, Emily gently made fun of them for having permitted themselves to be "defrauded" by the promise of eternal life. Anticipating heaven, Vinnie and her father failed to recognize that they themselves already "[dwelt] in Paradise," a place that Emily "never believed to be a superhuman site." Even her brother Austin could perplex Emily and prompt her to seek an outlet in Mrs. Holland. On more than one occasion she commented to Elizabeth about Austin's remoteness. "It seemed peculiar — pathetic — and Antediluvian. We missed him while he was with us and missed him when he was gone," she wrote after he had stayed, in the absence of Susan and their children, at the Homestead for a month. And several years later she lamented to her friend that "Austin seldom calls — . . . He visits rarely as Gabriel."

After Mrs. Dickinson suffered a debilitating stroke in 1875, it was Elizabeth Holland to whom Emily turned most often for a sympathetic ear. Elizabeth heard how Emily's mother missed her "power to ramble" and "the stale inflation of the minor News"; she received a report from Emily that "Mother does not yet stand alone and fears she never shall walk"; and she read of the consolation Emily offered her paralyzed mother: "I tell her we all shall fly so soon, not to let it grieve her, and what indeed is Earth but a Nest, from whose rim we are all falling?"

Emily also kept Elizabeth Holland updated about Mrs. Dickinson's ongoing disappointments with her children's heterodox religious views. "Austin and I were talking the other Night about the Extension of Consciousness, after Death," Emily reported. "Mother told Vinnie, afterward, she thought it was 'very improper.'" There is a hint of pathos in this account of two children, both near the age of fifty, troubling their disabled mother with their conversations about scientific naturalism and the higher criticism of the Bible: "She forgets that we are past 'Correction in Righteousness — ' I dont know what she would think if she knew that Austin told me confidentially 'there was no such person as Elijah.'"

Dickinson felt free to share her spiritual confusion with the Hollands. She wrote to them of her refusal to join the church and take communion, as well as about her unhappy memories of church in childhood: "When a Child and fleeing from Sacrament I could hear the Clergyman saying 'All who loved the Lord Jesus Christ — were asked to remain' — My flight kept time to the Words." In another letter, she

206

confided in Elizabeth about her doubts concerning the Bible's authenticity: "The Fiction of 'Santa Claus' always reminds me of the reply to my early question of 'Who made the Bible' — 'Holy Men moved by the Holy Ghost,' and though I have now ceased my investigations, the Solution is insufficient — ." At least Santa Claus *"illustrates* — Revelation." And in reporting to Elizabeth that Vinnie was angry with God for his failure to "help" her with her garden, Emily flippantly assessed the situation: "I suppose he is too busy, getting 'angry with the Wicked — every Day.'"

"Why the Thief ingredient accompanies all Sweetness Darwin does not tell us," Dickinson wrote to Elizabeth Holland in 1871, wondering why loss follows every gain and death hounds life at every step. In another letter two years later, she lamented to her friend the fact that "science will not trust us with another World. Guess I and the Bible will move to some old fashioned spot where we'll feel at Home." Science speaks with certainty about senseless matter in motion, while theology tries to comfort us with guesses about other worlds. To overcome such troubling thoughts, Dickinson often reiterated her stubborn belief in human immortality: "How unspeakably sweet and solemn — that whatever await us of Doom or Home, we are mentally permanent," she assured Elizabeth Holland. "'It is finished' can never be said of us."

By means of her letters, Dickinson also gave comfort to the Hollands as she did to many others. Over the years, she sent notes to encourage them in their sickness or to wish them well on their journeys; but in the fall of 1881 she had a much more difficult task to perform. When she heard by telegram of Josiah Holland's fatal heart attack, she wrote immediately to Elizabeth: "Our hearts have flown to you before — our breaking voices follow. How can we wait to take you all in our sheltering arms?" In this and the other letters that she wrote in rapid order, the poet strained to do what she feared might be impossible. While chafing at the limits of language, she struggled to give healing solace through her words. "Nor would we dare to speak to those whom such a grief removes," her first letter of sympathy concluded, "but we have somewhere heard 'A little child shall lead them.'" A few days later Emily wrote again about grief and the weakness of language: "Panting to help the dear ones and yet not knowing how, lest any voice bereave them but that loved voice that will not come, if I can rest them, here is down — or rescue, here is power." She offered "rest and rescue" while acknowledging that "One who only said 'I am sorry' helped me the most when father ceased — it was too soon for language." She and Vinnie tried unsuccessfully to keep the news of Josiah's death from their paralyzed mother. Someone "disclosed it unknown to us. Weeping bitterly, we tried to console her. She only replied 'I loved him so.' Had he a tenderer eulogy?"

In these letters to Elizabeth Holland, Dickinson offered to another spiritual assurance that she could not so readily generate for herself. She promised her friend, "After a while, dear, you will remember that there is a heaven — but you can't now. Jesus will excuse it. He will remember his shorn lamb." In giving this and other assurances, Emily was no doubt seeking to have her own anxieties calmed. Emily had a "yearning to know if he knew he was fleeing — if he spoke to you. Dare I ask if he suffered?" Elizabeth Holland responded quickly, and her letter soothed Dickinson's spirit. "How sweet that he rose in the morning — accompanied by dawn," Emily noted. In the case of Josiah Holland, death had "mislaid his sting," and "because the flake fell not on him, we will accept the drift, and wade where he is lain."

As she often did, Dickinson concluded her series of sympathy letters with a poem. To her grieving friend, the poet offered both a poignant acknowledgment of loss and a gentle note of hope:

> The Things that never can come back, are several —
> Childhood — some forms of Hope — the Dead —
> Though Joys — like Men — may sometimes make a Journey —
> And still abide —
> We do not mourn for Traveler, or Sailor,
> But think enlarged of all that they will tell us
> Returning here —
> "Here!" There are typic "Heres" —
> Foretold Locations —
> The Spirit does not stand —
> Himself — at whatsoever Fathom
> His Native Land — [#1515]

During and immediately following the Civil War, another of Dickinson's frequent correspondents was Joseph Lyman, Austin's schoolboy friend and Vinnie's onetime suitor. Before he died in 1872, Lyman established a considerable reputation as an author on domestic economy. As his publishing career prospered, he kept in touch with the Dickinsons through letters and occasional visits. Though his correspondence with Emily was destroyed, his transcriptions of portions of her letters were found among his papers long after his death.

Lyman was in central Massachusetts for more than a year near the end of the Civil War. A visit from this period is the likely source of his dramatized description of the adult Emily Dickinson. "EMILY. 'Things are not what they seem. Night in Midsummer,'" Lyman titled his portrait of her. Picture a "library dimly lighted. . . . Enter a spirit clad in white, figure so draped as to be misty[,] face moist, translucent alabaster, forehead firmer as of statuary marble." Though written during Dickinson's life, Lyman's description bears an unmistakable resemblance to the legends that sprang up after her death: "Eyes once bright hazel now melted & fused so as to be two dreamy, wondering wells of expression," wrote Lyman, "eyes that see no forms but gla[n]ce swiftly to the core of all thi[n]gs — hands small, firm, deft but utterly emancipated from all claspings of perishable things, very firm strong little hands absolutely under control of the brain, types of quite rugged health[,] mouth made for nothing & used for nothing but uttering choice speech, rare thoughts, glittering, starry misty figures, winged words."

Lyman was intrigued by what Dickinson had to say about her family in her letters. Her father "seems to me often the oldest and oddest sort of a foreigner," explained Emily, using island imagery that could just as well have described the daughter as the father: "[He] says that his life has been passed in a wilderness or on an island." Even Vinnie, the sister who "sleeps by my side," whose "care is in some sort motherly," and "who is in matter of raiment greatly necessary" to Emily, seems remote: "the tie is quite vital; yet if we had come up for the first time from two wells where we had hitherto been bred her astonishment would not be greater at some things I say."

Emily's comments about her family speak of physical propinquity and emotional distance. Like others in the romantic tradition, Dickinson spent a lifetime trying to understand the mystery of what Charles Taylor has called the modern discovery of "an inexhaustible inner domain." Though her sister slept at her side and her father ate at the same table with her, Dickinson considered them at times to be as unknowable as the fathomless depths of the sea. "What mystery pervades a well," began a poem she wrote late in life. In 1877, Emily sent a variation upon the last two stanzas of this poem across the lawn to her sister-in-law. Of Sue, whom she had known for almost thirty years, the poet wrote:

> But Susan is a stranger yet —
> The One who cite her most
> Have never scaled her Haunted House
> Nor compromised her Ghost —
>
> To pity those who know her not
> Is helped by the regret
> That those who know her know her less
> The nearer her they get —

For Dickinson, inwardness was an isolating reality but also a sign of immortality. "So I conclude," she explained to Lyman, "that space & time are things of the body & have little or nothing to do with our selves." When she was emphatic about the vast "inner domain," Dickinson could sound like a gnostic hymning the praises of disembodied life. Especially in the seclusion of her adulthood, she cultivated that "doubleness" that Thoreau knew could make us "poor neighbors and friends sometimes." At the conclusion of one of his transcriptions, Lyman recorded Dickinson's defiant thoughts about the domain she considered her own: "My Country is Truth. Vinnie lives much of the time in the State of Regret. I like Truth — it is a free Democracy."

Dickinson wrote to Lyman about the power of words as well as about the conflicts of consciousness. She told him that she had fallen "to reading the Old & New Testament. I had known it as an arid book but looking I saw how infinitely wise & how merry it is." Anyone "that knows grammar must admit the surpassing splendor & force of its [the King James Version's] speech," but "fathomless gulfs of meaning" remained for the poet. As she meditated upon the gap between words and their objects, Dickinson anticipated the postmodern preoccupation with the distance separating language and reality. The words of the Bible were evocative but unconvincing, giving "hints about some celestial reunion — yearning for a oneness." Though she knew many people for whom those biblical words were "very near & necessary," she could only "wish they were more so to me." To those with the capacity for belief, the words of the Bible shed "a serenity quite wonderful & blessed. They are great bars of sunlight in many a shady heart." But for her, the letters to Lyman implied, the shadows remained.

It was not that words lacked the power to move her. "We used to think, Joseph, when I was an unsifted girl and you so scholarly[,] that words were cheap & weak. Now I dont know of anything so mighty," she confessed. As an adult, she found herself tempted to worship words rather than the realities they pointed to. "There are those to which I lift my hat when I see them sitting princelike among their peers on the page. Sometimes I write one, and look at his outlines till he glows as no sapphire." She knew that words could stir the sluggish will and quiet the restless heart, but she could not determine to her satisfaction the source of their power. Did it rest in a divine scheme of things, grounded in the will of God and revealed in his Son, Jesus Christ, the incarnate Word? Or was their power nothing more than the grasping action of the groundless human will and boundless human appetite? Throughout adulthood, Dickinson shuttled back and forth between these two dramatically different alternatives.

Dickinson wrote her letters to Lyman in the 1860s, her most prolific period as a poet. When Lyman had first met Dickinson, she was a witty woman of about twenty. She was at that time an "unsifted girl" whose letters and early poems gave evidence of considerable ability and an outgoing temperament. It is her later letters to Lyman that document how her seclusion in the Homestead had signaled her removal to the "inexhaustible inner domain." It was at that point, she told him, in her mid and late twenties, that she discovered the inexhaustible richness of books and words in general, and of Shakespeare and the Bible in particular.

Dickinson's letters to Lyman also show the changes her style underwent when she began to write poetry regularly. In her seclusion, she abandoned the breezy epistolary style of her youth and perfected a gnomic brevity in her letters. After 1860 or so, the wit and verbal play of her earlier letters remained, but the expansive development of her early correspondence increasingly gave way to the cryptic metaphors peppering her later prose. At the same time, her poems became tantalizingly compressed and increasingly elliptical as she moved ever more deeply into her inner domain. The closer Dickinson came to an almost complete social silence, the more evocative and extravagant the language of her letters became.

One of the persons most frequently called upon to decipher Dickinson's prose after the Civil War was Thomas Wentworth Higginson, who remained one of her most faithful correspondents. He proved to be the most helpful of all her acquaintances as she tried to negotiate a career as a private "poet of the portfolio." Higginson offered Dickinson comfort for her anxieties and losses, encouraged her (unsuccessfully) to leave her seclusion and enter the literary world, and accepted her invitation to visit her at her home in Amherst.

Higginson repeatedly failed in his efforts to draw Dickinson into his Boston literary world. After a two-year hiatus in their correspondence, he asked her in 1866 to come to Boston. She refused and cited her father's prohibition as the reason — "I had promised to visit my Physician for a few days in May, but Father objects because he is in the habit of me" — just as several years earlier she had invoked Higginson's authority to resist requests that she publish her poetry. And when Higginson renewed his offer a month or two later, Emily once again pressed her father into service as the "Preceptor" who forbade travel: "I must omit Boston. Father prefers so. He likes me to travel with him but objects that I visit."

Three years later, in the spring of 1869, Higginson made his final plea for Dickinson to leave her isolation to taste the cultured world in which he thrived. He needed to see her, he explained, to know that she was real. He wrote of rereading her poems and letters and feeling "their strange power." Could she not come to Boston? "I have the greatest desire to see you, always feeling that perhaps if I could once take you by the hand I might be something to you." He longed to be the "Preceptor" she had asked him to be, but, he wrote, "you only enshroud yourself in this fiery mist & I cannot reach you, but only rejoice in the rare sparkles of light."

A gregarious man, Higginson was happy to travel with the schools of respectable literary culture. He could not comprehend how his Amherst friend was able to survive on her own, swimming in the seas of lonely speculation. "It is hard [for me] to understand how you can live s[o alo]ne, with thoughts of such a [quali]ty coming up in you

& even the companionship of your dog withdrawn." Yet though he wanted her to visit and worried about her solitude, Higginson was enough of a transcendentalist to realize that when consciousness was concerned, place did not matter. Dickinson could detach herself wherever she was: "It isolates one anywhere to think beyond a certain point or have such luminous flashes as come to you — so perhaps the place does not make much difference."

In refusing yet another request for her to travel to Boston, Dickinson begged her correspondent and "Preceptor" to come to Amherst, so that she might thank him: "Could it please your convenience to come so far as Amherst I should be very glad, but I do not cross my Father's ground to any House or town." She wanted to thank him for the "great kindness" he had shown her in her time of dire need. "Of our greatest acts we are ignorant," she explained. "You were not aware that you saved my Life. To thank you in person has been since then one of my few requests."

Higginson complied with this request. He paid his first visit on Tuesday, August 16, 1870, combining a trip to Amherst with other business in western New England. That evening, after he had visited the Homestead in the afternoon, he wrote a long letter to his wife. In describing for her the events of the day, he painted the fullest portrait ever to be drawn of the adult poet. When he visited, Dickinson was less than four months shy of her fortieth birthday. Once admitted to the "large county lawyer's house, Higginson was left to wait in a "parlor dark & cool & stiffish." He noticed that in addition to some "engravings & an open piano," the Dickinsons had on display two of his own books. He then heard

> A step like a pattering child's in entry & in glided a little plain woman with two smooth bands of reddish hair & a face a little like Belle Dove's; not plainer — with no good feature — in a very plain & exquisitely clean white pique & a blue net worsted shawl. She came to me with two day lilies which she put in a sort of childlike way into my hand & said 'These are my introduction' in a soft frightened breathless childlike voice — & added under her breath Forgive me if I am frightened; I never see strangers & hardly know what I say — but she talked soon & thenceforward continuously — & deferentially — sometimes stopping to ask me

213

to talk instead of her — but readily recommencing. Manner between Angie Tilton & Mr. Alcott — but thoroughly ingenuous &
simple which they are not & saying many things which you would
have thought foolish & I wise — & some things you wd. hv. liked.

"I never was with any one who drained my nerve power so much,"
Higginson concluded. "Without touching her, she drew from me. I am
glad not to live near her."

It was Dickinson's conversation that wore out Higginson. She had
many things to say to him, the most memorable of which he recorded
for his wife. "Women talk: men are silent: that is why I dread women,"
she informed him, before proceeding to talk about every manner of
subject. She began, quite naturally, with the subject of books and poetry,
always a favorite of hers. "My father only reads on Sunday — he reads
lonely & *rigorous* books," Dickinson explained, but she was interested
in another kind of literature and anything but a "lonely and rigorous"
reading experience. "If I read a book [and] it makes my whole body so
cold no fire ever can warm me I know *that* is poetry. If I feel physically
as if the top of my head were taken off, I know *that* is poetry. These
are the only way I know it. Is there any other way."

The interview confirmed the judgment Higginson had made the
year before that "it isolates one anywhere to think beyond a certain
point or have such luminous flashes as come to you." Emily did indeed
think a great deal about thinking. "How do most people live without
thoughts," she wondered aloud to Higginson. "There are many people
in the world (you must have noticed them in the street) How do they
live. How do they get strength to put on their clothes in the morning."
At another point, she asked, perhaps apropos of nothing, "Is it oblivion
or absorption when things pass from our minds?" And when Higginson pressed her about seclusion and contact with the outside world,
her reply was firm: "I never thought of conceiving that I could ever
have the slightest approach to such a want in all future time." What
need did she have of travel or visitors, when truth, ecstasy, and joy
were her daily companions? "Truth is such a *rare* thing it is delightful
to tell it," Higginson reported her as saying. "I find ecstasy in living —
the mere sense of living is joy enough."

As much as Higginson was intrigued by the woman who called
herself his "Scholar," he had little clue as to her genius. "The impression

214

undoubtedly made on me was that of an excess of tension, and of an abnormal life," he wrote years later, describing his first meeting with the poet from Amherst. One can understand how he came to admire her, even though he did not fully comprehend her. "She was much too enigmatical a being for me to solve in an hour's interview."

THE DICKINSON ENIGMA

What made Emily Dickinson an enigma to Higginson has fascinated generations of readers who have been drawn to her poetry. She wrote at a time when the likes of Higginson, a former Unitarian minister, and John Burgess, a rationalist agnostic, were charting the course for a culture once governed by her father and the Whig tradition he had championed. The shift from the Whig to the Republican party — which coincided almost exactly with the start of Dickinson's serious poetic career — entailed a move "away from paternalism toward a more impersonal, secular society," in the words of Daniel Walker Howe. The cultural order represented by Higginson and Burgess was one in which tastes were to become ever more refined and mysteries ever more rationalized.

In religion, Higginson's genteel Unitarianism was a forerunner of the liberalism that would eventually dominate mainline denominations in the twentieth century. More than half a century ago, Reinhold Niebuhr traced modern liberalism to its nineteenth-century sources. "The belief that human virtue is guaranteed by the rational preference for the benevolent as against the egoistic impulses becomes a definite strand in modern thought," he argued. "Saint Simon erected his structure of a 'New Christianity' upon it and Auguste Comte made it the cornerstone of his positivist sociology." And Reinhold's brother, H. Richard Niebuhr, gave classic expression to the liberal creed that had been forwarded by Higginson and others at the end of the nineteenth century: "A God without wrath brought men without sin into a kingdom without judgment through the ministrations of a Christ without a cross."

Where Higginson's views show the general theological drift of late nineteenth-century American culture, John Burgess's career charts the more particular transition taking place in American colleges and

215

universities at the time. Within two decades of the Civil War — the last two decades of Emily Dickinson's life — the pastors who had ruled American colleges with their Scottish Common Sense realist views were replaced by a new breed of professors fueled by European agnosticism. In the last decades of the nineteenth century, both academics and clergymen were embracing in increasing numbers what the British statesman A. J. Balfour described at the time as "that general habit of thought which . . . refuses all belief in anything beyond phenomena and the laws connecting them, and . . . attempts to find in the 'worship of humanity,' or, as some more soberly phrase it, in the 'service of man,' a form of religion unpolluted by any element of the supernatural."

These changes began in Emily Dickinson's lifetime and became all but complete within decades of her death. Much of the received scholarly opinion about Dickinson, in turn, has issued from women and men who take what Balfour said for granted. As one Dickinson biographer, Cynthia Griffin Wolff, approvingly wrote, in 1986, "the hundredth year after Dickinson's death, Amherst College graduated no more than one or two students who went into the ministry. No longer an outpost of latter-day Puritanism, Amherst College trains young men and young women who will take their places in law, business, medicine, and teaching. Though it is still situated upon a hill, it has become a thoroughly secular institution."

For the critic committed to some variation of this view of modernity, it is perhaps irresistible to interpret the life of Emily Dickinson largely as a moral lesson about liberation from bondage. Yet is it accurate to assume that because Dickinson rejected membership in the church and wrestled with doubt, she would have welcomed the triumph of secular liberal individualism? When the secular transformation of religious belief began in earnest in the college and culture of Amherst after the Civil War, Dickinson was no more in harmony with it than she had been with the Whig revivalism of her early adulthood. Her letters to the Hollands, Lyman, and Higginson, as well as her responses to the voluminous reading she did in the decade after the Civil War, attest to her passion for the perennial questions about language, consciousness, and God. Though the emerging positivism of her day was ready to dismiss such questions as irrelevant, she could never do so. "Truth is such a *rare* thing it is delightful to tell it," she had told Higginson at their first meeting. In no small measure, Dickinson's reputation has flourished because she apprehended the truth in ways that the rationalism, scientism, and sentimentalism of her age — and ours — could not and cannot begin to understand.

10 A Blissful Trial

"This tabernacle" is a blissful trial, but the bliss predominates.

HAVING SURVIVED the physical and emotional harrowing of the Civil War period, Emily Dickinson spent the better part of a decade trying to restore order to her emotional life. If the crises of those years represented, in the words of one of her poems, the time of "a great pain," then the next decade was to be her period of "formal feeling." As Thomas Johnson, editor of Dickinson's letters, explains, she was "trying to restore her strength and build up a new reserve" in the years after the Civil War.

As a consequence of her inner turmoil, Dickinson's poetic production and letter writing slackened significantly after 1865. Artistically considered, the years between the end of the Civil War and the death of her father in 1874 represent the most fallow period in her adult life. While she had written about 850 poems during the years spanning the Civil War, she produced a little more than 200 in the decade after the war; and of the well over 1,000 letters of hers that have survived, fewer than 100 can be traced to the 1866-1874 period.

The letters from this period — especially those written to the Hollands, to Joseph Lyman, and to Thomas Wentworth Higginson — indicate that Dickinson spent this decade of seclusion seeking to experience the simple "ecstasy in living" that she considered "joy enough." In her normal round of activities, she savored "the Happiness/That too competes with Heaven" [#1601]. "I saw the sunrise on the Alps since I saw you," she informed Elizabeth Holland in 1866. "Travel why to Nature, when she dwells with us? Those who lift their hats shall see her, as devout do God." Whether it was the grandeur of the Pelham hills espied from her bedroom window or the aromatic savor of an ordinary meal, simple pleasures brought the poet contentment in these quiet years. "I cooked the peaches as you told me," she wrote her cousin Louise Norcross in 1870, "and they swelled to beautiful fleshy halves and tasted quite magic. The beans we fricasseed and they made a savory cream in cooking that 'Aunt Emily' liked to sip." As she put it succinctly in a letter to Elizabeth Holland in October of 1870:

> Life is the finest secret.
> So long as that remains, we must all whisper. . . .
> We are by September and yet my flowers are bold as June.
> Amherst has gone to Eden. . . .
> How fine it is to talk.
> What Miracles the News is!
> Not Bismark but ourselves.
>
> > The Life we have is very great.
> > The Life that we shall see
> > Surpasses it, we know, because
> > It is Infinity.
> > But when all Space has been beheld
> > And all Dominion shown
> > The smallest Human Heart's extent
> > Reduces it to none.
>
> Love for the Doctor, and the Girls.

While she was savoring everyday life, Dickinson wondered about the need of a heaven to come. It was only the shortness of life, she concluded, and not the waywardness of the human will, that made that heaven necessary. "Immortal is an ample word/When what we need is by," explains one of the poems she wrote after the Civil War, "But when it leaves us for a time/'Tis a necessity":

> Of Heaven above the firmest proof
> We fundamental know
> Except for its marauding Hand
> It had been Heaven below. [#1205]

Dickinson could plead, "Oh Sumptuous moment/Slower go/ That I may gloat on thee — " [#1125], but she knew that

> No lodging can be had
> For the delights
> That come to earth to stay,
> But no apartment find
> And ride away. [#1186]

The Christian faith claimed to explain death, but Dickinson was dubious about the explanation:

> Paradise is that old mansion
> Many owned before —
> Occupied by each an instant
> Then reversed the Door —
> Bliss is frugal of her Leases
> Adam taught her Thrift
> Bankrupt once through his excesses. [#1119]

During these years, she resisted the thought that her plight had anything to do with the rebellion of Adam and Eve. She considered the idea of imputed sin to be nonsensical at best and repulsive at worst. Romantic theory and democratic practice had made her leery of claims about inherited guilt; like many who came to question the Christian faith in nineteenth-century America, she could not accept responsibility for something she had never done. She asked in 1873:

> Is Heaven an Exchequer?
> They speak of what we owe —

But that negotiation
I'm not a Party to — [#1270]

God may know why we need to be forgiven, but "The Crime, from us, is hidden — ."

"EXODY"

The equilibrium that Dickinson had reestablished by the mid-1870s was shattered when what she called the "Dyings" began. Between the passing of her father in 1874 and her own death in 1886, she was to lose virtually every person of importance to her, save her brother, sister, and sister-in-law. Each death struck her hard, and their cumulative effect was to drain and dishearten her in a way that no other suffering had done. "The Dyings have been too deep for me, and before I could raise my Heart from one, another has come," she wrote to an acquaintance in 1884. By that time, her own health had begun to be impaired by the repeated losses. "The doctor calls it 'revenge of the nerves,'" Dickinson told her cousins to explain a fainting spell in the summer of 1884, "but who but Death had wronged them?"

The death of her father on June 16, 1874, was the first great loss of many, and in some ways it proved to be the hardest. In life Edward Dickinson had always been a riddle to his daughter, who had never quite known how to respond to his stiff and distant bearing. Like the remote God he himself worshiped, Edward was for his daughter an object of puzzlement and a frequent source of curious dismay. At times his remoteness made him seem humorously out of step with his surroundings: "Father steps like Cromwell when he gets the kindlings." And at other times, his distance presented a frightening prospect to his daughter. "Father was very sick. I presumed he would die, and the sight of his lonesome face all day was harder than personal trouble," Emily wrote her cousins in 1871. "I hope I am mistaken, but I think his physical life don't want to live any longer. You know he never played, and the straightest engine has its leaning hour."

For Edward Dickinson, the engine gave out in Boston, where he was serving in the Massachusetts House of Representatives. He had just returned to the capitol from Amherst, where he had spent the weekend

221

with his family. He had worked in his Amherst office into the night on Saturday and spent much of Sunday with Emily. "The last Afternoon that my Father lived, though with no premonition — I preferred to be with him, and invented an absence for Mother, Vinnie being asleep," she later told Higginson. Her being with her father "peculiarly pleased" him, because "I oftenest stayed with myself, and [he] remarked as the Afternoon withdrew, he 'would like it to not end.' His pleasure almost embarrassed me and my Brother coming — I suggested they walk. Next morning I woke him for the train — and saw him no more."

At about noon on Monday, "a cruelly hot day," Edward Dickinson was nearing the end of a speech on a favorite subject, the railroads of western Massachusetts, when he became faint. With help he struggled the short distance back to his hotel, where he suffered an "apoplectic attack" and died within hours. "We were eating our supper," Emily explained, "and Austin came in. He had a despatch in his hand, and I saw by his face we were all lost, though I didn't know how. He said that father was very sick, and he and Vinnie must go. The train had already gone. While horses were dressing, news came he was dead."

Emily and Austin were stunned in their customary ways, so, as always, the task of organizing matters fell to Vinnie. Years later, a friend remarked of Emily's younger sister that "because she was sure her father would have wished it, [she] denied herself to no one in the hours that succeeded his death, could weep with those who wept, and tried in gentle ways to ease the burden." She handled the details of the funeral, shielded her brother from a troubling newspaper article about their father's death, and served as the main point of contact between the family and the village. "I thought Vinnie's character as it shone out in her face today was beautiful," remarked the Amherst postmaster a week after Edward's death.

In the meantime, Austin and Emily tended to their own griefs. According to an Amherst neighbor, when Edward's body was brought to the Homestead from Boston, "Austin leaned over his father's face, kissed his forehead and said, 'There, father, I never dared do that while you were living.'" Austin's daughter Martha wrote years later of her "terror at my father's grief. The world seemed coming to an end." The postmaster, J. L. Skinner, was as surprised by Austin's desolation as he had been impressed by Vinnie's serenity: "Austin is . . . the most

222

shocked, stunned by the loss of his father." Skinner wrote to his wife that only several days after the funeral, Austin had little memory of the events. "He did not know at all who acted as bearers or who were present from abroad & various other details," Skinner explained.

"And where was Aunt Emily?" asked her niece. She was upstairs in her room, with her door cracked open so that she could hear the service below. She did not accompany her mother, sister, brother, and sister-in-law to the church for the memorial service the week after the funeral, and she refused to see any of the family members or friends who came to mourn Edward Dickinson and to console his family. Outside her immediate family, only Samuel Bowles was allowed to see Emily at this time, as she wandered aimlessly through her trackless grief. "We take him [Father] the best flowers, and if we only knew he knew, perhaps we could stop crying. . . . I cannot write any more, dears," she told her Norcross cousins. "Though it is many nights, my mind never comes home."

Instead of mourning her father publicly, Dickinson meditated privately on the meaning of his life and death. Within months, she began to turn his life into poetry by means of lofty elegiac lyrics that had him as their subject. There was in Emily's descriptions of her father after his death not a trace of the whimsical flippancy she had used so often when discussing him in life. In his daughter's memory, Edward Dickinson rapidly became a grand and tragic figure, a symbol of a vanished heroic era. Shortly after he died, Emily wrote to Higginson that her father's "Heart was pure and terrible and I think no other like it exists."

The transformation continued over the following months. In January of 1875, she described for Elizabeth Holland the scene in the Dickinson household on a winter's afternoon. Less than a year after his death, Edward Dickinson had assumed a god-like status in his daughter's mind:

Mother is asleep in the Library — Vinnie — in the Dining Room — Father — in the Masked Bed — in the Marl House.

> How soft his Prison is —
> How sweet those sullen Bars —
> No Despot — but the King of Down
> Invented that Repose!

When I think of his firm Light — quenched so causelessly, it fritters the worth of much that shines. . . .

'I say unto you,' Father would read at Prayers, with a militant Accent that would startle one.

Forgive me if I linger on the first Mystery of the House.

It's specific Mystery — each Heart had before — but within this World. Father's was the first Act distinctly of the Spirit.

Images of divinity and royalty suffused Emily's tribute poems to her father. One depicted him as a departed king who rules, like God, in majestic silence at a distance:

> From his slim Palace in the Dust
> He relegates the Realm,
> More loyal for the exody
> That has befallen him. [#1300]

"The righteous flourish like the palm tree, and grow like a cedar in Lebanon" (Psalm 92:12), and through the transforming power of Emily's memory the awkward stiffness of Edward Dickinson's life became a regal strength in death:

> To break so vast a Heart
> Required a Blow as vast —
> No Zephyr felled this Cedar straight —
> 'Twas undeserved Blast — [#1312]

For several years, Emily was to puzzle over the meaning of her father's life and death in her writing. In a number of instances, her poems and letters about him gave frank expression to the feelings of disorientation that came from living in a home that no longer had him as its compass. She explained to a family friend in the spring of 1875 that "home itself is far from home since my father died" and worried that her father's new "homelessness" was much like her own.

> Lives he in any other world
> My faith cannot reply

Before it was imperative
'Twas all distinct to me — [#1557]

Her father had been "gathered" out of the common human "story" and gathered into another, far stranger story:

Gathered into the Earth,
And out of story —
Gathered to the strange Fame —
That lonesome Glory
That hath no omen here — but Awe — [#1370]

Her father's death reminded Emily sharply of her own sense of belatedness. He became for her a symbol of vanished grandeur:

The vastest earthly Day
Is shrunken small
By one Defaulting Face
Behind a Pall — [#1328]

Edward Dickinson's death confirmed for his daughter that the earthly happiness that "too competes with heaven" cannot compete with death. When "the vastest earthly Day" could be "shrunken small" by a "Defaulting Face," how could one pretend that the fragility of earth could withstand the caprices of heaven? Only by granting immortality could God give back in heaven what he had stolen from the earth. "I suppose even God himself could not withhold that now —" she said about immortality two years after her father's death. "When I think of my Father's lonely Life and his lonelier Death, there is this redress —."

Take all away —
The only thing worth larceny
Is left — the Immortality —

In 1877, a full three years after Edward Dickinson's death, Emily wrote perhaps her finest poetic tribute to him. She enclosed the poem in a letter to Higginson, explaining to him that "Since my Father's dying, everything sacred enlarged so —." She told him of an experi-

225

ence that had taken place when she was only "a few years old." She had attended a funeral where "the Clergyman asked 'Is the Arm of the Lord shortened that it cannot save?'"

> He italicized the 'cannot.' I mistook the accent for a doubt of Immortality and not daring to ask, it besets me still, though we know that the mind of the Heart must live if it's clerical part do not. Would you explain it to me?
>
> I was told you were once a Clergyman. It comforts an instinct if another have felt it too. I was rereading your 'Decoration.' You may have forgotten it.

> Lay this Laurel on the One
> Too intrinsic for Renown —
> Laurel — vail your deathless tree —
> Him you chasten, that is He!

> Please recall me to Mrs — Higginson —

> Your Scholar.

In imagining the "immortality" granted to one "Too intrinsic for renown," Dickinson may have been thinking of the fate of her poetry as well as the destiny of her father. There were, after all, unmistakable parallels between them; and in memorializing her father, Emily was perhaps anticipating the fame she hoped would be hers after death. "To them both," remarked Martha Bianchi of her grandfather and aunt, "father and daughter, their inner lives were solemn and private things." Memorial notices portrayed Edward Dickinson as a man of principle who had been largely unappreciated in his own day but was destined to be honored by future generations. The *Amherst Record*, for instance, was confident that Edward Dickinson "will be even more respected and honored now that he is dead, and his character is more fully understood." In the *Springfield Republican*, Samuel Bowles described Edward Dickinson as "a Puritan out of time for kinship and appreciation, but exactly in time for example and warning." According to Bowles, his "failing was that he did not understand himself; consequently his misfortune was that others did not understand him."

Nevertheless, "he possessed and exhibited that rarest and yet most needed of all qualities in these days of cowardly conformity and base complaisance, *the courage of his convictions.*"

At the memorial service held a week after the funeral, Jonathan Jenkins developed the same theme, when he compared Edward Dickinson to the prophet Samuel whose apparition had been conjured up after death by the witch of Endor. "It is a condition of human life that men are not known by contemporaries," Jenkins observed. "Here influences that warp and distort judgments are many and strong." But we also know of "the great illumination which death diffuses," and if the people of Amherst "remain blind and refuse to see the excellencies made apparent" in Edward Dickinson's character, then that proves the "presence and power of inveterate prejudice, or wicked hate" in the community. "In the apparition in which [Samuel] was evoked after death, there was something terrific," and yet this man "whom a whole village feared . . . was gentle in nature, and no more gentle in nature, than our friend and father whom we mourn to-day." There was in the elder Dickinson "a finer fibre in the gentleness which was in him, but which he carefully, and may I say, so unwisely, concealed?" Perhaps after Edward Dickinson's death, others would finally see what he had hidden from them in life. As Jenkins asked rhetorically: "Had he the Puritan notion that sentiment betrayed weakness, or was it his training in that elder school whose primal precept was repression?"

The lessons drawn from the father's life and death could not have been lost on his daughter. Just as Edward had been judged greater in death than he had been considered in life, so might Emily and her poetry be worthy of fame one day. Like her father's concealment and "primal repression," her seclusion and reluctance to publish would prove to have been justified by that fame. Death could and would transform, as Ariel had sung in Shakespeare's *Tempest:*

> Full fathom five thy father lies;
>   Of his bones are coral made;
> Those are pearls that were his eyes;
>   Nothing of him that doth fade
> But doth suffer a sea-change
> Into something rich and strange.

So it was that through the "sea-change" of poetic memory, this man whom Higginson had once called "thin dry & speechless" became for his brilliant, grieving daughter "something rich and strange."

"YOU ARE A GREAT POET"

Within a year of her father's death, Dickinson was to find her seclusion and resolve not to publish sorely tested once again. In late 1875, she renewed her friendship with Helen Hunt Jackson, one of the most celebrated American writers of her day. Over the next decade, the two would exchange a number of letters, and in that time Jackson became the most astute and encouraging critic Dickinson had ever had for her poetry. Jackson lavished praise upon the work of her childhood friend, but that praise came with a price, for Jackson was to place intense pressure on her friend to publish.

Born in 1830, the same year as Emily, Helen Fiske was the daughter of a professor of Greek and philosophy at Amherst College. She moved away from Amherst for good when she was orphaned at the age of sixteen. She was married in 1852, but by 1865 had lost her husband and only child. The widowed Helen Hunt moved to Newport, Rhode Island, in 1866 and took up residence in the same boardinghouse as Thomas Wentworth Higginson and his wife. Higginson befriended Hunt and encouraged her to pursue a writing career. Within several years, in the words of one literary historian, "she was on her way to being America's most successful, energetic, and envied woman writer." Higginson told his new protégé about his correspondence with the reclusive poet of Amherst. "I have seen [a lady] who once knew you, but could [not] tell me much," he informed Dickinson that year. But it would be several years before the two childhood friends renewed their relationship.

The occasion for the contact came when the widowed Helen Hunt married William Jackson of Colorado in 1875. To congratulate her now famous friend, Dickinson sent a cryptic note:

> Have I a word but Joy?
>   E. Dickinson.
> Who fleeing from the Spring

> The Spring avenging fling
> To Dooms of Balm —

Helen Jackson returned the letter with a scribbled request for an interpretation and with a demand — "This is *mine*, remember, You must send it back to me, or else you will be a robber." Dickinson neither sent back the poem nor provided a convincing interpretation of it, for Jackson wrote again, "But you did not send it back, though you wrote that you would. . . . Thank you for not being angry with my impudent request for interpretations. I do wish I knew just what 'dooms' you meant, though!"

In this letter, Jackson pressed to renew their acquaintance and declared her unstinting admiration of Dickinson's poetry. She told her friend that she had received, probably from Higginson, "a little manuscript volume with a few of your verses in it — and I read them very often — ." On the basis of her having read that slim volume, Jackson had formed a confident and generous judgment of Dickinson's ability. She closed her initial letter with a bold declaration: "You are a great poet — and it is a wrong to the day you live in, that you will not sing aloud. When you are what men call dead, you will be sorry you were so stingy." In Emily Dickinson's lifetime, no one else ever gave such telling, unadulterated praise to her work.

Jackson's encouragement soon took the form of pressure to publish. She implored her friend to contribute to a "No Names Series" of poetry and fiction to be published by Roberts Brothers of Boston, each book of which was to be written by a "great unknown." Jackson's own novel, *Mercy Philbrick's Choice*, had been the first book to be published in the series, and she hoped that a volume of Dickinson poetry would soon follow. "Surely, in the shelter of such *double* anonymousness as that will be, you need not shrink," she wrote. "I want to see some of your verses in print. Unless you forbid me, I will send some that I have [to Roberts Brothers]."

The pressure unsettled Dickinson. After Jackson paid a call at the Homestead in October 1876 to press her point in person, Dickinson wrote to her "Preceptor" Higginson in haste. "Are you willing to tell me what is right? Mrs. Jackson — of Colorado — was with me a few moments this week, and wished me to write for this — I told her I was unwilling, and she asked me why? — I said I was incapable and she

seemed not to believe me." Jackson would not accept Dickinson's refusal to be included in the series; she told her that she would write in
several days, expecting a positive response. Not wishing to "estrange"
one "so sweetly noble" as Helen Hunt Jackson, Dickinson asked Higginson to send "a note saying you disapproved it, and thought me
unfit."

Higginson completely misread Dickinson's letter. He assumed
that Jackson had asked the Amherst poet to write a collection of stories
for the series, and that suggestion mystified him: "It is always hard to
judge for another of the bent of inclination or range of talent; but I
should not have thought of advising you to write stories, as it would
not seem to me to be in your line." He wrote that perhaps "Mrs. Jackson
thought that the change [from poetry to fiction] & variety might be
good for you." Higginson was not about to write a note excusing
Dickinson from such a ludicrous task; he could only suggest that his
Amherst "Scholar" follow the advice of a "celebrated prison-reformer,
Mrs. Fry," who "made it one of her rules that we must follow, not force,
Providence; & there is never any good in forcing it."

At about the same time, Dickinson received the promised letter
from Helen Jackson, who realized that she may have made her case too
forcefully in person. "[I feel] as if I ha[d been] very imperti[nent that]
day [in] speaking to you [as] I did, — accusing you of living away from
the sunlight — and [telling] you that you [looke]d ill," Jackson explained. (The bracketed portions of the letter have been cut away.) Yet
although she apologized for the abruptness of her manner, Jackson was
still blunt about her concerns for Dickinson's health:

> Re[al]ly you look[ed] so [wh]ite and [mo]th-like[!] Your [hand]
> felt [l]ike such a wisp in mine that you frigh[tened] me. I felt [li]ke
> a [gr]eat ox [tal]king to a wh[ite] moth, and beg[ging] it to come
> and [eat] grass with me [to] see if it could not turn itself into beef!
> How stupid. —

"You say you find great pleasure in reading my verses," Jackson wrote
at the letter's close. "Let somebody somewhere whom you do not know
have the same pleasure in reading yours."

Unable to resist the pressure on her own, Dickinson wrote to
Higginson again in late October of 1876. She told him that "It was not

230

stories she [Helen Jackson] asked of me. But may I tell her just the same that you dont prefer it? Thank you, if I may, for it almost seems sordid to refuse from myself again." As she had done almost fifteen years before, Dickinson once again sought shelter under Higginson's name. She was using him to keep from doing something she did not want to do, just as she had invoked her father's name years before to turn down Higginson's request that she travel to Boston. And when Helen Jackson finally let up, Dickinson wrote to thank Higginson once more: "Often, when troubled by entreaty, that paragraph of your's has saved me — 'Such being the Majesty of the Art you presume to practice, you can at least take time before dishonoring it.'"

Jackson did eventually win one small concession from the woman she had called "a great poet." In the spring of 1878, she asked Dickinson not for an entire volume of poetry to publish but only for one or two lyrics to be printed anonymously in a "No Name" series anthology. "I will copy them — sending them in my own handwriting — and promise never to tell any one, not even the publishers, whose the poems are," Jackson assured her friend. "Could you not bear this much of publicity?"

Once again, Jackson followed up her written request with a visit to the Homestead, this time on October 24, 1878. But even here Dickinson hesitated, for Jackson had to write from Hartford: "Now — will you send me the poem? . . . If you will, it will give me a great pleasure. I ask it as a personal favor to myself — Can you refuse the only thing I perhaps shall ever ask at your hands?" Perhaps fearing that a refusal of such a request might indeed appear "sordid," Dickinson forwarded a copy of "Success is counted sweetest." In a letter of thanks, Thomas Niles, the publisher of the volume, informed Dickinson that her anonymity had been protected, because "for want of a known sponsor Mr Emerson has generally" been assumed to have been the author of "Success."

"WHEN A HEART IS BREAKING"

Having relied upon Higginson for support for almost fifteen years, Dickinson felt called upon at last to be of help to him, when his wife died on September 2, 1877. For the first time with this "Preceptor," she found herself in the position of lending strength and consolation rather than receiving them. Higginson had seen the world and knew all the major authors, but his "Scholar" was acquainted with grief in ways he had not yet experienced. Several days after Mary Channing Higginson died, Dickinson wrote to her mentor:

If I could help you?

Perhaps she does not go so far
As you who stay — suppose —
Perhaps comes closer, for the lapse
Of her corporeal clothes —

Did she know she was leaving you? The Wilderness is new — to you. Master, let me lead you.

Dickinson knew the "wilderness" of death so well, because she had traversed its territory so often. Although she never came to accept death without protest, she was beginning to grow strangely accustomed to the grip of the "marauding hand"; and even as she lamented her own losses, she continued to comfort others. In reassuring them, she found repeatedly that she also strengthened herself. "I know we shall certainly see what we loved the most," she wrote to an aunt who had just lost a son. "There are no Dead, dear Katie, the Grave is but our moan for them."

For one who lived inwardly as intensely as Dickinson did, affirming the promises of the Christian faith objectified the faith in helpful ways. At times Dickinson approached the state theologian Helmut Thielicke has described in a book about the Apostles' Creed. "He who finds Christ becomes so filled with him that he literally forgets his faith," explains Thielicke. "That is why the people of the Bible bore witness to their *Savior* and not to their faith. One of them was not even sure whether he believed at all, but when Jesus stood there before him he said, 'I believe; help my unbelief' " (Mark 9:24). In giving sympathy, Dickinson found strength to surmount her own grief and help her own unbelief.

To that end, in the fall of 1877 she sent lines of poetry and a note to neighbor Richard Mather when his wife died. She had not known

Elizabeth Mather well, but she included in her condolences some lines by James Russell Lowell and a brief "sermon" of her own on everlasting life: "That the Divine has been human is at first an unheeded solace, but it shelters without our consent — To have lived is a Bliss so powerful — we must die — to adjust — but when you have strength to remember that Dying dispels nothing which was firm before, you have avenged sorrow — ." Of all the articles of the Christian creed, the one that Dickinson most fervently longed to believe was that of the resurrection of the body and the life everlasting; and in assuring others of its truth, she steadied her own wavering faith.

That faith was shaken badly several months later, when her beloved friend Samuel Bowles died. The editor of the *Springfield Republican* was one of the few people outside the Dickinson family whom the poet had continued to see with regularity. He had for a long time treated Austin's and Sue's home, the Evergreens, as a rest center, where he could retreat from the manifold pressures of public life. Invariably, when he came to Austin's home, Bowles also paid a visit to the woman he called the "Queen Recluse" in the house next door. Emily often admitted him, but sometimes even he was denied access, as was the case on a visit in the last year of his life. While next door, Bowles dropped in at the Homestead to borrow a book and see Emily. Unnerved and unwilling to come downstairs to greet him, she hid herself in her room. Bowles, however, refusing to accept the rebuff, called upstairs: "Emily, you wretch! No more of this nonsense! I've traveled all the way from Springfield to see you. Come down at once, you damned rascal." A repentant Emily sought to make amends with a poem and an apology several days later:

I went to the Room as soon as you left, to confirm your presence — recalling the Psalmist's sonnet to God, beginning

I have no Life but this —
To lead it here —
Nor any Death — but lest
Dispelled from there —
Nor tie to Earths to come —
Nor Action new

> Except through this extent
> The love of you.

It is strange that the most intangible thing is the most adhesive.

Your "Rascal."

I washed the Adjective.

Less than a year after this visit, Bowles was dead at fifty-one, having worked himself to the point of exhaustion. Of all of Dickinson's friends in adulthood, he had been one of the most intimate. As she struggled to master her own grief and to comfort the Bowles family after his death on January 16, 1878, she underwent the process she had described so memorably in "After great pain, a formal feeling comes — ." Bowles's passing was for Dickinson "the Hour of Lead" remembered "As Freezing persons, recollect the Snow — /First — Chill — then Stupor — then the letting go — " [#341]. When news reached her of her friend's death, she dashed off a note of grief-stricken solace to his widow: "To remember our own Mr Bowles is all we can do. With grief it is done, so warmly and long, it can never be new."

On the day of Bowles's private burial service, the disconsolate Emily sent a brief letter to Higginson, as much to hearten herself as anything else. Austin and Vinnie were among the few family and friends who had traveled to Springfield to be "with Mr Bowles, who is buried this afternoon" in a private service. It would have been, of course, out of the question for Emily to have traveled with them. Instead, she grieved alone at home. What came to her mind on that desolate day was "the last song that I heard — ." It was the Twenty-third Psalm, which had been sung for her the previous February by Nora Green, the Village Church soloist. Green had sung the number in church for Jonathan Jenkins's farewell service, and Vinnie's report so impressed Emily that she asked to hear it. With her brother and sister, Green visited the Homestead, where she sang in the drawing room, while Emily listened from her room upstairs. " 'He leadeth me — he leadeth me — yea, though I walk [in death's dark vale],' " Dickinson quoted to Higginson. "Then the voices stooped — the arch was so low — " that it was hard, so hard, to follow the shepherd into the vale.

234

Once again, in the weeks after Bowles's death, Dickinson strained to allay her own fears by consoling others. "His nature was Future — " she wrote to Susan about this man whose optimism had been infectious. "He had not yet lived — David's route was simple — 'I shall go to him — .'" When the child born to him through the widow of Uriah the Hittite died, David had asked, "Can I bring him back again? I shall go to him, but he will not return to me."

"I hasten to you, Mary," Dickinson wrote to Mrs. Bowles not long after the memorial service, "because no moment must be lost when a heart is breaking. . . . I am glad if the broken words [of her January 16 letter] helped you. I had not hoped so much, I felt so faint in uttering them." The "broken words," of course, had strengthened the one who offered them as much as they comforted their recipient: "Love makes us 'heavenly' without our trying in the least. 'Tis easier than a Saviour — it does not stay on high and call us to its distance; its low 'Come unto me' begins in every place." The only difficulty with this love — its "one mistake" — is that "it tells us it is 'rest' — perhaps its toil is rest, but what we have not known we shall know again, that divine 'again' for which we are all breathless." So, we press on, buoyed by fragile hope and spurred on by our "breathless" longing. "I am glad you 'work,'" Dickinson told Bowles's widow. "Work is a bleak redeemer, but it does redeem; it tires the flesh so that can't tease the spirit."

In spite of the great loss, "dear 'Mr. Sam' is very near, these midwinter days," Dickinson observed. "When purples come on" the Pelham hills east of Amherst, "in the afternoon we say 'Mr. Bowles's colors.' I spoke to him once of his Gem chapter, and the beautiful eyes rose till they were out of reach of mine, in some hallowed fathom." A favorite of both Bowles and Dickinson, chapter 21 of the book of Revelation speaks of the "new heaven and new earth," where "death will be no more; mourning and crying and pain will be no more." Dickinson's letters and poems contain no fewer than ten references to this single chapter of the Bible and its unblushing promises.

Those glorious promises of life still had to contend in Dickinson's mind with the ghastly reality of death. The first of her several letters to Maria Whitney, a close friend of Samuel Bowles, began by acknowledging the impotence of consolation: "I have thought of you often since the darkness, — though we cannot assist another's night." Dickinson wished for Whitney what she wished for herself: "I hope you have the power of hope." But as her next letter indicated, she also wondered about the meaning of hope in the midst of grief, for "to relieve the irreparable degrades it." To accept death one must resign oneself to the inevitable. Here, as elsewhere, Shakespeare offered the clue, in this case in *Othello:* "Brabantio's resignation is the only one — 'I here do give thee that with all my heart, which, but thou hast already, with all my heart I would keep from thee.'"

Dickinson's brief letters to Maria Whitney contained hints of a way out of the grief that had crippled all who mourned the great "Mr. Bowles." "The crucifix requires no glove," Dickinson told her. We can clasp the cross of Jesus, because such suffering is familiar to our touch. Here in the crucifixion of his son, God has put himself at our disposal and made it possible for us to grasp him through our own abundant sorrows. Unlike the "Father above," this man who had been "'acquainted with Grief'" can become our friend, because we know that grief so intimately ourselves. Samuel Bowles's new "acquaintance" with eternity made that alien realm seem more appealing and less remote: "That he has received Immortality who so often conferred it, invests it with a more sudden charm."

There are genuine theological limits to the effort Dickinson made here and elsewhere to apprehend God all but exclusively through the sufferings of Jesus. Without question, her stress on the humanity of Jesus was an attempt to counter the otherworldly austerity of Puritan views of God. The Whig character type that Dickinson knew in her own father — so "lonely" and "rigorous" — had descended from Calvinist beliefs about the majesty of God the Father. The heresy of Docetism — the belief that the humanity and suffering of Jesus were more apparent than real — had always tempted the New England mind. It was to counter the Docetic tendency that Emily Dickinson so passionately embraced the exemplary qualities of Christ's suffering and crucifixion.

In doing so, however, she ran the risk of engaging in what Helmut Thielicke has termed "anthropological over-compensation." Offended by the sterile rationalism of orthodox treatments of the atonement, romantic theologians and artists responded by pressing the point of Jesus' humanity. Yet as they did battle with arid orthodoxy, the romantic theologians initiated, perhaps unwittingly, the "increasing transformation of theology into anthropology" that has become a distinguishing mark of modernity. In their eagerness to establish solidarity with the human, suffering Jesus, they made the second person of the Trinity into a prophet who fortified and illuminated our experience. But at the same time, Jesus decidedly became something less than a God who could forgive sins and raise the dead. He was, in the end, trapped with us within our finitude in a universe of death. The suffering Jesus, it appeared, turned out to be as lonely and desperate as those who came to him for deliverance.

In the early nineteenth century, a stunning expression of Jesus' loneliness was offered in a fable by the German writer Jean Paul Richter, who was a favorite among Emily's circle of friends. The week that she returned from Mount Holyoke, in early August of 1848, Austin shared the Amherst College commencement week program with George Gould, who recited Thomas Carlyle's translations of Richter's "Speech of Christ." Whether or not Emily heard this recitation of Jean Paul's story, the themes of her poetry were to resonate with many of those sounded by the German fabulist.

In Richter's story, Christ descends upon the altar in a church that adjoins a graveyard. As Jesus appears, the dead awaken and cry out to him, " 'Christ! is there no God?' " The response of Jesus is indeed plaintive. "There is none! . . . I went through the Worlds, and flew with the Galaxies through the wastes of Heaven; but there is no God! I descended as far as Being casts its shadow, and looked down into the Abyss and cried, Father, where art thou? But I heard only the everlasting storm which no one guides; . . . And when I looked up to the immeasurable world for the Divine *Eye,* it glared on me with an empty, black, bottomless *Eye-socket."*

When the dead children who have awakened in the churchyard stream into the temple, they throw themselves before Jesus and ask him in desperation, "Jesus! have we no Father?" It grieves him to tell them, "We are all orphans, I and you; we are without Father!" Christ looks down upon the children, and with "his eyes filled with tears" he tells them, "Ah, I was once there; I was still happy then; I had still my Infinite Father, and looked up cheerfully . . . and pressed my mangled breast on his healing form." Like them, Christ once expected to be welcomed by God after death and to have his wounds healed for eternity. Yet having scoured the heavens unsuccessfully in search of God, Christ has nothing to proclaim save the sad refrain, *"we are all orphans, I and you."*

237

Several Dickinson poems echo the themes of Jean Paul's "dream," and the crisis of his Christ enacts the anxious drama the poet underwent whenever she tried to reconcile faith with death. In the twelve years between her father's death and her own, she surrendered "to the deep Stranger" all but a few of those who mattered most to her. For herself and others, she sought peace in the shadow of heaven's "marauding Hand." Yet she found it hard to see the suffering servant as the Son of God. Instead of revealing to us the merciful heart of the heavenly Father, Jesus seemed to her at times to disclose a Divine indifference about human anguish. Jesus was "acquainted with grief," but Dickinson could not help but wonder whether that acquaintance meant anything to God. It was always possible that her prophetic Jesus would prove as fruitless as Jean Paul's Christ had been in his search for God: "Majestic as the Highest of the Finite, he raised his eyes towards the Nothingness, and towards the void Immensity, and said: 'Dead, dumb Nothingness! Cold, everlasting Necessity! Frantic Chance! Know ye what this is that lies beneath you? When will ye crush the Universe in pieces, and me?"

In grappling with death and the character of God as she did, Dickinson laid bare conflicts that were challenging and changing American Protestantism at the end of the nineteenth century. In 1830, when she was born, a variation of Scottish Common Sense Realism held sway over the intellectual, religious, and cultural life of New England. It was, according to historian Henry May, a credo with three articles: the trustworthy reality of moral values, the certainty of progress, and the importance of a narrowly defined literary culture. With its emphasis upon an innate moral sense, Common Sense Realism provided a foundation for evangelical thought and sentimental piety, just as, in modified form, it would later give Emersonian romanticism grounds for its confidence in the powers of the unaided self. Dickinson's early letters and poems show the imprint of this intuitionism, derived from Common Sense Realism, and its elevated view of the unimpeded human agent.

Charles Darwin and the Civil War changed all that. In the words of historian Allen Guelzo, Darwin's *Origin of Species* trampled "under its feet any divinity erected on Scottish intuitionism and [reawakened] the nightmare of hard, materialistic determinism." A God who was the sum of human perfection could not remain intact under the weight of biological determinism, nor could he emerge with his reputation intact from the clockwork carnage of the Civil War. Before the war, Americans looked to providence; after it, they cast their lot with chance. For Emily Dickinson, the "nightmare of determinism" took the form of the horrifying possibility that nature and recent events had disclosed either a malicious God or no God at all behind the scheme of things. For Dickinson in the last decades of her life, nature, history, and death often appeared as texts that could be scanned but not deciphered; each had something crucial to say, but who could hear or interpret them rightly?

" 'This tabernacle' is a blissful trial, but the bliss predominates," Dickinson wrote to Elizabeth Holland in the wake of Bowles's death. A tabernacle is a dwelling place in which a divine spirit or power is housed temporarily, and a trial is a test endured in time for the sake of eternity. After the death of her father, Dickinson wondered whether the tabernacle housed anything of ultimate importance and whether the trial led to any holy site at all. Was Christ the Son whose suffering pointed to the forgiving heart of God his Father and the heavenly mansion filled with many rooms? Or was Jesus just another orphan, like all the rest of us, destined to discover nothing but "Frantic Chance" at the very heart of things? To the end, Emily Dickinson longed to believe that human suffering was a type of the divine mystery and not merely a trope of human desire. She trusted Jesus because he had suffered unspeakable grief, and she strained to believe that in his compassion there was healing balm for the deepest of human wounds.

11 Rendezvous of Light

Pass to thy Rendezvous of Light,
Pangless except for us —
Who slowly ford the Mystery
Which thou hast leaped across! [#1564]

WHEN SAMUEL BOWLES DIED in 1878, Emily Dickinson herself had less than a decade to live. In her final years, death was to take an enormous toll on her emotional and physical resources. Over one span of less than three years, she would lose her mother, her nephew, a beloved friend, and the only man she ever seriously considered marrying. Yet even as she endured these losses and her health deteriorated, Dickinson carried on her self-styled ministry of consolation. She remained, as she styled herself in a letter only a month before she died, both a "Pugilist and Poet," one who wrestled with God and who continued to write in his shadow until the very end.

"SAYING 'MOTHER, GOOD-NIGHT'"

In most important respects, the course for the last decade of Emily's life was set when her mother suffered a debilitating stroke on June 15, 1875, almost exactly a year after Edward Dickinson's death. Mrs. Dickinson was not paralyzed, but her physical and mental functions were so badly impaired that she could no longer care for herself. For seven years, Vinnie and Emily were to share the responsibility for nursing their invalid mother. With some assistance from hired help, they fed, bathed, and read to her, attending to her needs as well as the management of the entire household. While Emily never complained about her mother's illness and the added duties that fell to her as a result of it, the burdens of care exhausted her.

A letter to her Norcross cousins in 1880 offers a glimpse of the grueling round of responsibilities Emily and Vinnie faced each day. "I have only a moment, exiles, but you shall have the largest half," Dickinson told her cousins. "Mother's dear little wants so engross the time, — to read to her, to fan her, to tell her health will come tomorrow, to explain to her *why* the grasshopper is a burden, because he is not so new a grasshopper as he was, — this is so ensuing, I hardly have said 'Good-morning, mother,' when I hear myself saying 'Mother, good-night.'" The following day, Dickinson wrote to Elizabeth Holland and expanded upon what she had told her cousins: "The responsibility of Pathos is almost more than the responsibility of Care. Mother will never walk. She still makes her little Voyages from her Bed to her Chair in a Strong Man's Arms — probably that will be all." The mother's impatience tested the patience of her daughters: "Her poor patience loses it's way and we lead it back — . . . Time is short and full, like an outgrown Frock — ."

The pathos of her mother's life frequently drew gently ironic responses from Emily. "Mother pines for you, and says you were 'so social,'" she informed Elizabeth Holland in 1877. "Mother misses power to ramble to her Neighbors — and the stale inflation of the minor News." Several years later, she reported to Elizabeth that Mrs. Dickinson had overheard a conversation between Emily and Austin. Their mother complained that she found it "very improper" for her children to be questioning life after death and the historical accuracy of the Bible. To their mother's concerns, Emily's flippant response was that her mother "forgets that we are past 'Correction in Righteousness.'"

241

Emily's irony was often mixed with pity, when she reported on her mother's confusion about even the most simple matters. In an 1878 letter to the family's former pastor, Jonathan Jenkins, Emily explained that "Mother asked me last Sabbath 'why Father did'nt come from Church,' and [']if Mr Jenkins preached'? I told her he did and that Father had lingered to speak with him — ." Her mother's defenselessness evoked sympathy from Emily. When her mother became her "child," the "Affection came"; Emily was at last able to become for her mother what her mother, in some way, had never been for her. Left, with Vinnie, to care for this elderly child, Emily developed for her mother a tenderness that she had never known before.

"EMILY 'JUMBO' LORD"

As her mother lay immobilized in an upstairs bedroom and in need of constant care, the drama of Emily Dickinson's own life continued to play itself out in the other rooms of the Homestead. To the end of her life, Dickinson kept up with household responsibilities and continued both to test her poetic abilities and to explore a remarkable range of relationships. With some people she continued correspondences begun decades earlier, while in several other instances she launched entirely new friendships through her letters. On rare occasions, she still saw certain visitors, and in one case, most remarkably, Dickinson came close to accepting an offer of marriage and moving away from Amherst.

The relationship that blossomed into a romance in the last decade of Dickinson's life had begun as a casual acquaintance decades before. Otis Phillips Lord was eighteen years older than Emily Dickinson and had graduated from Amherst College when she was one year old. Lord became active in the Massachusetts Whig party, where he met Edward Dickinson. Eventually, in the words of one who knew the Dickinson family, he became Edward Dickinson's "best friend." When he came to court Emily Dickinson in the late 1870s, Lord stood as a throwback to an earlier era; in the words of Susan Dickinson, his principles were founded upon a "rock bed of old conservative Whig tenacities, not to say obstinacies." Alternately tough and tender, he was a complex man of many facets, as Emily wrote of him a year after his death:

242

"Abstinence from Melody was what made him die. Calvary and May wrestled in his Nature."

Though he lived across the state in Salem, as a member of the Massachusetts Superior Court and an alumnus of Amherst College Lord had cause to visit in the Amherst area on many occasions in the 1850s and 1860s. On these trips to the western portion of the state, he and his wife Elizabeth stopped whenever they could at the Dickinson Homestead to visit with his friends Edward and Emily Norcross Dickinson and with their two adult daughters, Emily and Lavinia, whom Lord teasingly called his "little 'Playthings.'"

The visits continued, even after the death of Edward Dickinson in 1874 and the passing of Elizabeth Lord three years later. According to Martha Dickinson Bianchi, while the judge's nieces and Amherst young people took trips to neighboring towns in his hackney coach, "Aunt Emily and he enjoyed their own adventures in conversation at home." They bantered back and forth about any number of things, according to Dickinson's niece, for "their enjoyment of the comedy of every day was . . . broadly akin." The poet called a certain type of humor "the Judge Lord brand," and at her death she left behind a yellowed newspaper clipping "'Returned by Judge Lord with approval!'":

NOTICE!

My wife Sophia Pickles having left my bed and board without just cause or provocation, I shall not be responsible for bills of her contracting.

SOLOMON PICKLES

NOTICE!

I take this means of saying that Solomon Pickles has had no bed or board for me to leave for the last two months.

SOPHIA PICKLES

The Judge and his Amherst friend "relished" this kind of wit. As Emily said to him, "you have a good deal of glee in your nature's corners."

The banter turned decidedly more serious after Elizabeth Lord died in late 1877, as Emily Dickinson plunged into the one love affair in her life for which there is evidence and not just conjecture. Within

243

months of Mrs. Lord's death, the Judge and Dickinson began to write to one another, perhaps on a weekly basis. All of Emily's letters to Lord were lost after his death, just as Vinnie, at Emily's request, destroyed all of the letters from Lord that Emily had left behind. Yet one set of papers survived the general conflagration of the correspondence; it was a collection of drafts and fragments of letters that were found among Emily's papers and preserved by her brother Austin. It is from these documents that we know of the full extent of the passion between Emily and her friend from Salem.

There is nothing else like these drafts in the whole canon of Emily Dickinson's works, for the letters to Lord make explicit an ardor unexpected from the mythic "Belle of Amherst." Within a year or two of Elizabeth Lord's death, Dickinson was declaring openly her love for her widowed friend. "My lovely Salem smiles at me. I seek his Face so often — but I have done with guises," she wrote to him around 1878. "I confess that I love him — I rejoice that I love him — I thank the maker of Heaven and Earth — that gave him me to love — the exultation floods me. I cannot find my channel — the Creek turns Sea — at thought of thee — ." Employing the metaphors of property and negotiation that were to figure so importantly in her letters to Lord, Dickinson asked him, "Will you punish me? 'Involuntary Bankruptcy,' how could that be Crime? Incarcerate me in yourself — rosy penalty — ."

Lord pressed his claims upon Dickinson forcefully, perhaps even demanding sexual intimacy before their marriage. She loved him but refused to deed the rights to her "property" before the marriage contract had been signed. "Dont you know you are happiest while I withhold and not confer — " she challenged him, "dont you know that 'No' is the wildest word we consign to Language?" She longed "to lie so near your longing — to touch it as I passed, for I am but a restive sleeper and often should journey from your Arms through the happy night, but you will lift me back, wont you, for only there I ask to be — ." Dickinson told Lord that she feared she would not be able to resist his requests: "if I felt the longing nearer — than in our dear past, perhaps I could not resist to bless it, but must, because it would be right."

"The 'Stile' is God's — My Sweet One — " Dickinson told Lord, referring to marriage as the step he must climb. "For your great sake — not mine — I will not let you cross — but it is all your's, and when it is right I will lift the Bars, and lay you in the Moss — ." She did not

244

want him to think her penurious or unkind but implored him to respect her needs: "It is Anguish I long conceal from you to let you leave me, hungry, but you ask the divine Crust and that would doom the Bread."

There proved to be many stiles blocking the path to marriage for Dickinson and Lord. Neither was in good health, as he approached the age of seventy and she fifty. Emily had the added burden of caring for her ever more needy mother and of continuing to manage the operation of the Homestead. The emotional and physical drain upon her resources may have made her pause at the thought of a lasting commitment.

Whatever the impediments were to their marriage, Dickinson's passion remained intense. On May 1, 1882, she wrote to Lord, "I do — do want you tenderly. The Air is soft as Italy, but when it touches me, I spurn it with a Sigh, because it is not you." Of her love for him, she lamented, "Oh, had I found it sooner! Yet Tenderness has not a Date — it comes — and overwhelms."

The day that she composed this letter, Lord was taken seriously ill and lay near death for several days. When he recovered, Dickinson wrote to him of "my own rapture at your return." She told him that when she had learned of his grave condition from Vinnie, she sought solace in the arms of a Dickinson family servant: "Meanwhile, Tom [Kelley] had come, and I ran to his Blue Jacket and let my Heart break there — that was the warmest place. 'He will be better. Dont cry Miss Emily. I could not see you cry.'"

Later that year, when Lord had recovered, he and Emily seriously considered marriage. In the fall, he wrote a humorous letter to his Amherst lover and suggested that she call herself "Emily 'Jumbo!'" Her reply took his suggestion a step further: "Emily 'Jumbo!' Sweetest name, but I know a sweeter — Emily Jumbo Lord. Have I your approval?" Lord must have accepted this humorous proposal, because at the beginning of December 1882, Dickinson wrote to him: "You said with loved timidity in asking me to your dear Home, you would 'try not to make it unpleasant.' So delicate a diffidence, how beautiful to see!" Lord had no need of such timidity, she told him, noting, "You even call me to your Breast with apology!" Her lover does not seek to ask for what has already been offered to him: "The tender Priest of Hope need not allure his Offering — 'tis on his Altar ere he asks."

Members of both families knew of the intimacy between Dickinson and Lord. Mabel Loomis Todd later claimed to have been warned by Susan Dickinson about the dangers of contact with Emily. When Mabel received an invitation to "call at once" at the Homestead, Sue blurted out, "You will not allow your husband to go there, I hope!" When Mabel asked, "Why not?" Sue replied, "because they have not, either of them, any idea of morality." Pressed for details, she explained, "I went in there one day, and in the drawing room I found Emily reclining in the arms of a man. What can you say to that?"

Long after Dickinson and Lord had died, their relatives continued to dwell upon their romance. Martha Dickinson Bianchi possessed a ring that had belonged to her Aunt Emily; she enjoyed showing it to visitors and watching "their mystification when they read the name 'Philip' engraved inside. 'Little Phil' Lord may have solved that mystery," argues Dickinson scholar Jay Leyda. And decades after her uncle Otis Phillips Lord had died, Abbie Farley West still complained bitterly about the woman who had threatened to replace her as the beneficiary of the Judge's will. When a visitor to West's home picked up a copy of Dickinson's poems, she said, "Take it away. Little hussy — didn't I know her? I should say I did. Loose morals. She was crazy about men. Even tried to get Judge Lord. Insane, too."

It is hard to square the image of Emily Dickinson as a "little hussy" who had "loose morals" with the standard picture of the woman dressed in white. But it is also difficult to imagine the Dickinson of legend writing the following lines, which she most certainly did: "I have written you, Dear, so many Notes since receiving one, it seems like writing a Note to the Sky — yearning and replyless — but Prayer has not an answer and yet how many pray! While others go to Church, I go to mine, for are not you my Church, and have we not a Hymn that no one knows but us?" What transformed the Queen Recluse, the champion of renunciation, into someone who could write lines such as these?

Fragments of two letters that Dickinson wrote to Lord, probably in 1883, may explain in part the mystery of her changes. The first fragment plays upon a theme dear to the poet:

> The withdrawal of the Fuel of Rapture does not withdraw the Rapture itself.
> Like Powder in a Drawer, we pass it with a Prayer, it's Thunders only dormant.

Dickinson liked to dwell upon the relationship between intense affection and its missing object. In some cases, she wrote of absence and loss that had been willed through acts of renunciation; in other instances, she focused upon death, God's "Burglar," and its power to steal what we love; and in still other cases, absence was to her a sign of hope, because of art's power and the poet's confidence that when she lies "in Ceaseless Rosemary," the "Essential Oils" of her verse will still "Make Summer." But in this letter to Lord, the "Fuel of Rapture" is neither stolen nor renounced, for it will soon become real again. The "Thunders" of the "Powder in a Drawer" are latent, ready to crack and resound.

By the time she fell in love with Phil Lord, Dickinson had become weary of renunciation and expectation. She wanted satisfaction, and she wanted it *now*, she told her Judge:

> I feel like wasting my Cheek on your Hand tonight — Will you accept (approve) the squander — Lay up Treasures immediately — that's the best Anodyne for moth and Rust and the thief whom the Bible knew enough of Banking to suspect would break in and steal.

There is a similar intermingling of sexual, psychological, and Christian arguments in some of Dickinson's earlier poems, but those poems make the dynamic of sexuality and spirituality a matter of eschatology; the "Queen of Calvary" endures deprivation, because fulfillment has been promised at the end of time. Gratification had been like fame for the younger Dickinson; it was something that would be even more satisfying when it finally came, having been delayed for so long. But now, having passed the age of fifty, Dickinson had lost her faith in waiting, at least as far as Otis Lord was concerned. She wanted to break out the treasures on earth and forget about storing them up for heaven.

Like Austin in his affair with Mabel Loomis Todd, Dickinson was trying to grasp the tangible bliss that had been denied her so long. Not long before Otis Phillips Lord died, she wrote:

> The Summer that we did not prize,
> Her treasures were so easy
> Instructs us by departing now
> And recognition lazy —

247

Bestirs itself — puts on its Coat,
And scans with fatal promptness
For Trains that moment out of sight,
Unconscious of his smartness. [#1773]

Like the life that was slipping away from many whom she loved, love itself now seemed part of that "Summer that we did not prize,/Her treasures were so easy." In her fondness for Lord, Emily stirred herself to search for the love "that moment out of sight." In the love of this complex, powerful man, she grasped what she had only dreamed of up to this point. In her letters to Lord, the passions that had been phantoms for so long at last took on a human form. But even at that, they never married, and less than two years after she had teased about becoming "Emily 'Jumbo' Lord," he was dead.

"THE DRIFT CALLED 'THE INFINITE'"

Dickinson's urge to seize whatever was tangible was intensified by the many losses she was suffering, beginning with the death of Charles Wadsworth in April of 1882. Though she had met the famed preacher only several times, he occupied a central place in her emotional life. His importance to her was made clear in letters she wrote to two of his friends, James and Charles Clark, after his death. Dickinson told James Clark of an "intimacy of many years with the beloved Clergyman." Though Wadsworth was a famous preacher, Dickinson found in him a kindred spirit of seclusion. Because "his Life was so shy and his tastes so unknown," her "grief for him seems almost unshared," she told Clark. Wadsworth had been her "Shepherd from 'Little Girl'hood,'" and she could not "conjecture a world without him, so noble was he always — so fathomless — so gentle." The clergyman had paid the second of his two visits to the Dickinson home only two years before, she explained. (The first had taken place twenty years earlier, in 1860.) "He rang one summer evening to my glad surprise," she wrote. "'Why did you not tell me you were coming, so I could have it to hope for,' I said — 'Because I did not know it myself. I stepped from my Pulpit to the Train,' was his quiet reply."

"I knew him a 'Man of sorrow,'" Dickinson observed in a subsequent letter, "and once when he seemed almost overpowered by a spasm of gloom, I said, 'You are troubled.' Shivering as he spoke, 'My Life is full of dark secrets,' he said." She had probably heard Wadsworth preach in 1855 and had read copies of his sermons over the years. In reading them, Dickinson warmed to Wadsworth's intimate grasp of human suffering. Though stiff in his outward bearing, Wadsworth as a preacher played masterfully upon his audience's emotions and fed the insatiable appetite for sentiment in the age. "In illustrating such phrases as 'Jesus wept,' and 'watching the dying Savior,' the plaintive wail of his tremulous voice is singularly subdued and effective," reported the *Springfield Republican* in 1850. Wadsworth was one of those "warbling Tellers" of which the poet felt the Christian faith was in such desperate need. She told James Clark, who had sent her a volume of Wadsworth's posthumously published sermons, "I am speechlessly grateful for a friend who also was my friend's, and can scarcely conceal my eagerness for that warbling Silence." These sermons were "Gifts from the Sky," written by a man who was too good for this world:

He was a dusk Gem, born of troubled Waters, astray in any Crest below. Heaven might give him Peace, it could not give him Grandeur, for that he carried with himself to whatever scene —

Obtaining but his own extent
In whatsoever Realm —
'Twas Christ's own personal Expanse
That bore him from the Tomb.

Wadsworth's was the first of many deaths that seemed to drain Dickinson herself of life in the final years. On November 14, 1882, her mother died at last. "The dear Mother that could not walk, has *flown*," Emily wrote to Elizabeth Holland. Emily Norcross Dickinson had suffered a "violent cold" a few weeks earlier but "seemed entirely better the last Day of her Life and took Lemonade — Beef Tea and Custard with a pretty ravenousness that delighted us," Emily reported. "After a restless Night, complaining of great weariness, she was lifted earlier than usual from her Bed to her Chair, when a few quick breaths and a 'Dont leave me, Vinnie' and her sweet being closed." To another friend she explained that she and Vinnie were "both benumbed," because they had been assured by Mrs. Dickinson's physician that their mother was recovering "and only the night before she died, she was happy and hungry and ate a little Supper I made her with such enthusiasm, I laughed with delight, and told her she was as hungry as Dick [the Dickinson stableman]."

As she had done with her father, Emily effected a poetic reshaping of her mother's life after her death. "She was scarcely the aunt you knew," she wrote to her Norcross cousins within days of her mother's passing. "The great mission of pain had been ratified — cultivated to tenderness by persistent sorrow, so that a larger mother died than had she died before." Twenty years before, Emily had written of the "Essential Oils" wrung from the rose by "the gift of Screws." Now she found in her mother's suffering an instance of the sublime process through which pain mysteriously produced beauty. With her mission of pain "ratified," Mrs. Dickinson was no longer a "General Rose" but an "Essential Oil," a "larger mother" than if she had died before her suffering came. "She slipped from our fingers like a flake gathered by the wind, and is now part of the drift called 'the infinite.'"

Yet while Mrs. Dickinson had "slipped" into "the infinite," Emily and her cousins were left behind with their questions: "We don't know where she is, though so many tell us." Emily spoke of her faith that "we shall in some manner be cherished by our Maker," that the maker of "this remarkable earth" must have the power to create something even greater than it, but "beyond that all is silence." She closed with the admission to Fanny and Loo Norcross: "I cannot tell how Eternity seems. It sweeps around me like a sea. . . . Thank you for remembering me. Remembrance — mighty word. 'Thou gavest it to me from the foundation of the world.'"

Grief drove Emily to transform her mother through memory and metaphor. To James Clark she wrote, "As we bore her dear form through the Wilderness, Light seemed to have stopped." And then the wilderness became a void: "Her dying feels to me like many kinds of Cold — at times electric, at times benumbing — then a trackless waste, Love has never trod." Days later, she told Otis Phillips Lord, "I cannot conjecture a form of space without her timid face." The death of her mother, like so many other deaths Emily had survived, sapped her of her emotional strength. "Speaking to you as I feel, Dear, without that

Dress of Spirit must be worn for most, Courage is quite changed," she explained to Lord. Grief had unhinged her, Emily told Elizabeth Holland: "I have thought of you with confiding Love, but to speak seemed taken from me — Blow has followed blow, till the wondering terror of the Mind clutches what is left, helpless of an accent — ."

"Mother has now been gone five weeks," Dickinson continued to her friend. That would have seemed a "long Visit, were she coming back," but the fact that she was dead — "the 'Forever' thought" — made the daughter realize that she and her sister Vinnie were "nearer rejoining her than her own return — ." Vinnie and Emily had never been very close to their mother while they were growing up, but her illness and suffering changed Mrs. Dickinson in their sight: "We were never intimate Mother and Children while she was our Mother — but Mines in the same Ground meet by tunneling and when she became our Child, the Affection came — ." As the suffering of Jesus had put a human face upon God for Emily, so did her mother's helplessness break down the barriers separating parent and child. "When we were Children and she journeyed, she always brought us something. Now, would she bring us but herself, what an only Gift — Memory is a strange Bell — Jubilee, and Knell."

In transforming her father and mother through the elegiac mode, Dickinson never suggested that she, as a poet, was gilding them with a luster they did not intrinsically possess. Instead, when she described her father as a man of royal stature and her mother as a woman of Christ-like suffering, Emily thought she was only bringing to the surface the ore trapped within the seams of their lives. As she had done for the father whom so many had esteemed, the daughter now paid tribute to the mother whom so few had known:

All is faint indeed without our vanished mother, who achieved in sweetness what she lost in strength, though grief of wonder at her fate made the winter short, and each night I reach finds my lungs more breathless, seeking what it means.

To the bright east she flies
Brothers of Paradise
Remit her home,
Without a change of wings,

251

Or Love's convenient things,
Enticed to come.

Fashioning what she is,
Fathoming what she was,
We deem we dream —
And that dissolves the days
Through which existence strays
Homeless at home.

The sunshine almost speaks, this morning, redoubling the division, and Paul's remark grows graphic, 'the *weight* of glory.'

As hard as it was to absorb the shock of losing Wadsworth and her mother — and as difficult as the deaths of Otis Phillips Lord in 1884 and Helen Hunt Jackson in 1885 would prove to be — nothing in her final years devastated Emily as dramatically as the loss of her beloved eight-year-old nephew, Thomas Gilbert Dickinson. Young "Gib" was a favorite of hers, and in mysterious ways he served as a bond holding together the members of a fragmenting family. Aunt Emily never fully recovered from his death.

When Gilbert was born in 1875, his father and mother were already estranged in spirit; and by the time of his death, an icy hostility gripped their marriage. Temperamentally distant from the start, Austin and Sue grew ever further apart over the years. She worked tirelessly to make their home the center of Amherst culture and spent the family resources liberally on entertainment and outings. Diffident and reclusive in his own way, Austin looked with a critical eye on his wife's activities, referring, for example, in an 1882 diary entry, to his house as "my wife's tavern." Partisans on both sides of the marriage discord have long disputed which of the parties was most to blame. But while that question may never be resolved, one fact is indisputable: by the time Gilbert died, his father had already begun an affair with Mabel Loomis Todd and had become a virtual alien in his own home. As Austin complained in a letter to his cousin, Clara Turner, less than a year before Emily's death, "a man with an expensive family relying on his daily labor for the delights of Life isnt reliable for a good time."

Austin's and Sue's two oldest children, Ned and Mattie, were inevitably drawn into the dispute between the parents. In 1883, Ned was twenty-two, and it had become apparent that he had few if any of the intellectual abilities possessed by his father, mother, grandfather, and aunt. He was a painfully slow learner and a victim of epilepsy. His father and mother kept from him the true nature of his illness, thus leaving him to suffer from the double bind of being both inept by Dickinson standards and ignorant of the source of his impediments. Hounded by his intellectual inadequacies and physical infirmities, Ned still labored to keep up the appearances. His Dickinson name won him a special dispensation at Amherst College, where he continued as a non-degree student for many years.

Martha was five years younger than Ned and considerably more talented. Mattie was close to her Aunt Emily, enjoying access to the Homestead that was denied to almost everyone else. It is difficult to tell from the jocular tone of Emily's letters to Mattie what the aunt truly thought of the niece's character and abilities. But there is no doubt about her affection for the young woman next door. "Be true to yourself, Mattie," Emily wrote when her niece went away to school in Connecticut in the fall of 1884, "and 'Honor and Immortality' — although the first will do — the last is only inferential, and I shall be prouder of you than I am, which would be unbecoming — ."

As their parents grew apart, Ned and Mattie had to choose sides. Mattie quickly aligned herself with Susan and never wavered in her support until her own death in 1943. Ned was more confused about his parents' conflict. By nature insecure and prone to manipulation by his mother, he was also enamored of the reputation won by the Dickinson men of earlier generations. According to one party close to the Dickinson family, "Ned put most of the blame upon his Mother. He said that he and Mattie had grown up in an atmosphere of Hell." Yet at the same time, there is evidence that Ned saw his father as his antagonist and dreamed of living with his mother and sister in unbroken peace. He clumsily competed with his father for the affections of Mabel Loomis Todd and was no doubt vexed by their affair. In the spring of 1885, more than a year after the death of Gilbert and the start of his father's affair, Ned wrote to Mattie that "if there is any beautiful, peaceful, restful place hereafter and [Mother] dont have a seat among the Saints & martyrs — I dont care to go there — ." He told her he had but one "ambition in life" — "to have a quiet pleasant little house somewhere — with you and Mother in it, where things can be *pleasant* — No fame, no brains, no family, no scholarship." Thus it was that the century that had begun with Samuel Fowler Dickinson dreaming of Amherst College as a "city upon a hill" came to an end with his great-grandson wanting nothing more than "a quiet pleasant little house somewhere."

To some degree, the animosity in Austin's and Sue's marriage spread into the relationship between the Evergreens and the Homestead. The friendship between Emily and Sue had cooled before these marital difficulties began to develop. There remained a great degree of respect and cordiality between the sisters-in-law, but there was also a palpable tension in some of the brief notes that Emily sent next door over the years. As early as 1861, Emily and Sue had exchanged notes that alluded to hurt feelings and a breach of some kind. Emily wrote a three-line note:

Could *I* — then — shut the door —
Lest *my* beseeching face — at last —
Rejected — be — of *Her?*

During the same months in late 1861, Sue sent a message of her own over to Emily, perhaps in response to her sister-in-law's challenge:

Private I have intended to write you Emily to day but the quiet has not been mine — I should send you this, lest I should seem to have turned away from a kiss —

If you have suffered this past Summer I am sorry. *I* Emily bear a sorrow that I never uncover — If a nightingale sings with her breast against a thorn, why not *we?* When I can, I shall write — SUE

The tension in the relationship between Sue and her sisters-in-law was heightened by the affair between Austin and Mabel Todd. As late as Christmas of 1882, Emily was complaining that "Austin seldom calls — I am glad you were glad to see him — He visits rarely as Gabriel — ." But within months, the situation had changed dramatically. In March 1883 she wrote, "my Brother is with us so often each Day, we almost forget that he ever passed to a wedded Home." The reason for the change was simple. When Austin's affair began in late 1882, the Homestead offered a convenient place of assignation, and his sisters provided a sympathetic audience for his tales of marital woe. On July 12, 1885, Austin wrote to Mabel, "I have two or three little visits with my sisters everyday, and we talk you over, always. . . . I see Vin and Em more than I did and you are the constant theme." Emily must have known of the intimacy between Austin and Mabel, and her refusal to condemn it may have antagonized Sue without completely alienating her. As Emily wrote in one of her last notes to her sister-in-law, "the tie between us is very fine, but a Hair never dissolves."

In this swirl of discord and deceit, young Thomas Gilbert Dickinson had provided a unique common bond between the battling parties. Having conceded Ned's infirmities and Mattie's allegiance to her mother, Austin concentrated his hopes upon Gilbert. (To emphasize his displeasure with his two eldest children, Austin put the following clause in his own will: "I make no special mention of Ned and Mattie because they are practically one in interest and feeling with their Mother, and would I presume prefer it in this way to any division.") Sue was also enormously fond of her youngest child, as was his Aunt Emily, and as long as Gilbert lived there was someone to bridge the widening gaps between the Dickinsons. "There was in him also," the *Amherst Record* obituary said of Gilbert, "a self-reliance, rare in a boy so gentle and sensitive, which seemed, somehow, to lift him into the sphere of men. . . . When the village heard of his death we felt as if one had gone who had established a place for himself among us. We loved him as one in whom the qualities that men 'Tie to' were freshened by the dew of childhood."

Gilbert's death came suddenly, on October 5, 1883, after he had battled for his life for several days against typhoid fever. The night he died, his Aunt Emily came to his home, having left the grounds of the Homestead for the first time in many years. A Dickinson neighbor, Harriet Jameson, wrote to her son that "Miss Emily Dickinson . . . went over to Austin's with Maggie [the household servant at the Homestead] the night Gilbert died." According to Mrs. Jameson, this was "the first time she had been in the house for 15 years — and the odor from the disinfectants used, sickened her so that she was obliged to go home about 3 A M — and vomited — went to bed and has been feeble ever since, with a terrible pain in the back of her head — ." In November, Vinnie wrote to friends in Rhode Island that "Emily received a nervous shock the night Gilbert died & was alarmingly ill for weeks — . . . You can imagine my anxiety for all that's left of this home — Emily was devoted to Gilbert & was there the night of his death — ."

Somehow, while prostrated by grief and sickness, Dickinson struggled to compose a letter of sympathy for Sue. It is a remarkable piece of writing. Though stunned by the loss of Gilbert, Emily rallied herself again to provide comfort to a loved one in extreme need:

Dear Sue —

The Vision of Immortal Life has been fulfilled —
How simply at last the Fathom comes! The Passenger and not the Sea, we find surprises us —
Gilbert rejoiced in Secrets —
His Life was panting with them — With what menace of Light he cried "dont tell, Aunt Emily"! Now my ascended Playmate must instruct *me*. Show us, prattling Preceptor, but the way to thee!
He knew no niggard moment — His Life was full of Boon —
The Playthings of the Dervish were not so wild as his —
No crescent was this Creature — He traveled from the Full —
Such soar, but never set —
I see him in the Star, and meet his sweet velocity in everything that flies — His Life was like the Bugle, which winds itself away, his Elegy an echo — his Requiem ecstasy —
Dawn and Meridian in one.
Wherefore would he wait, wronged only of Night, which he left for us —
Without a speculation, our little Ajax spans the whole —

> Pass to thy Rendezvous of Light,
> Pangless except for us —
> Who slowly ford the Mystery
> Which thou hast leaped across!
>   Emily.

Late in 1883, two months after Gilbert's death, Emily confided to Elizabeth Holland, "The Physician says I have 'Nervous prostration.'

Possibly I have — I do not know the Names of Sickness. The Crisis of the sorrow of so many years is all that tires me — ." Several months later, while she was still mourning the death of Gilbert, Otis Phillips Lord died unexpectedly. In thanking her Norcross cousins for their note of sympathy, Emily told them, "I hardly dare to know that I have lost another friend, but anguish finds it out." She offered them a poem about weariness and the wearing away of love and life:

> Each that we lose takes part of us;
> A crescent still abides,
> Which like the moon, some turbid night,
> Is summoned by the tides.

"Thank you once more for being sorry," the letter concluded. "Till the first friend dies, we think ecstasy impersonal, but then discover that he was the cup from which we drank it, itself as yet unknown."

The days grew increasingly difficult for Dickinson, as grief and sickness continued to assail her. She wrote to her cousins in August of 1884 about an initial indication of what proved to be her final, fatal illness:

> Eight Saturday noons ago, I was making a loaf of cake with Maggie, when I saw a great darkness coming and knew no more until late at night. I woke to find Austin and Vinnie and a strange physician bending over me, and supposed I was dying, or had died, all was so kind and hallowed. I had fainted and lain unconscious for the first time in my life. Then I grew very sick and gave the others much alarm, but am now staying. The doctor calls it 'revenge of the nerves'; but who but Death had wronged them?

As she had done on more than one occasion at this time, Dickinson brought the discussion back to the departed Gilbert:

> The little boy we laid away never fluctuates, and his dim society is companion still. But it is growing damp and I must go in. Memory's fog is rising.

> The going from a world we know
> To one a wonder still

Is like the child's adversity
Whose vista is a hill,
Behind the hill is sorcery
And everything unknown,
But will the secret compensate
For climbing it alone?

"Will the secret compensate for climbing it alone?" — that question haunted Emily Dickinson in the last years of her life, and the death of Gilbert and others only intensified her bewilderment. "'Open the Door, open the Door, they are waiting for me,' was Gilbert's sweet command in delirium," she reported to Elizabeth Holland. Young Gilbert's assurance left his skeptical aunt wondering and uncertain: "*Who* were waiting for him, all we possess we would give to know — Anguish at last opened it, and he ran to the little Grave at his Grandparents' feet — All this and more, though *is* there more? More than Love and Death? Then tell me it's name!" Dickinson had no certainty about the life beyond the grave; but she also refused to believe that, having created the entire universe, God would let it all be given over to death. She wrote as much to Sue in 1884, when they were discussing an anticipated biography of Samuel Bowles. Having reminded her sister-in-law of Bowles's lively wit and "the prance that crossed his Eye," Emily offered this promise:

Though the Great Waters sleep,
That they are still the Deep,
We cannot doubt —
No Vacillating God
Ignited this Abode
To put it out —

By this time, less than a year after Gilbert's death, Emily was suffering the early stages of Bright's disease, an earlier name for what is now known as nephrotic syndrome. Because of the primitive state of medical diagnosis in Dickinson's day, it is impossible to say which of several conceivable causes was responsible for the kidney or urinary disorder that led to her death. The collapse she had reported to her cousins in August 1884 may well have been an early sign of general

258

renal failure. As a result of that episode, Dickinson had to take her "summer in a Chair," as she reported to Helen Hunt Jackson. "I have not been strong for the last year," she confessed to Rebecca Mack a few weeks later. It was in this letter that the poet commented that "the Dyings have been too deep for me, and before I could raise my heart from one, another has come — ." In between attacks of illness, she continued to keep up her correspondence and work on her poems, but the work grew increasingly difficult for her.

Throughout the following year, Dickinson struggled through several bouts of sickness. She had, in her words, "twice been very sick . . . with a little recess of convalescence, then to be more sick." By November she had become so ill that she was confined to her bed, and her family feared for her life. Austin was so concerned that he canceled a business trip in late November of 1885. On the 30th of that month, Austin wrote to Mabel Loomis Todd, "I came down to go — but found Emily so poorly I dont dare — ." In her journal entries for the 30th and the first of December, Mabel made note that "Emily is quite sick" and that Austin dared not leave.

Emily rallied from this round of illness, only to be laid up again until April of the following year, 1886. When she recovered slightly in that month, she wrote to Higginson, "I have been very ill, Dear friend, since November, bereft of Book and Thought, by the Doctor's reproof, but begin to roam in my Room now — ." Her handwriting, always bold, became dramatically stretched and slanted in these last months. Relentlessly, the disease continued to tighten its grip upon her. In April she told Charles Clark, "I am better. The velocity of the ill, however, is like that of the snail."

Emily knew that she had little time to live. In early May she sent her final letter. It was to the Norcross cousins, and the only portion of it that they permitted to be published was the cryptic message, "Little Cousins, Called Back. Emily." The allusion is to the best-selling sentimental Hugh Conway novel, *Called Back*, published in 1883. The cryptic reference to Conway's melodramatic story may have been intended to assure Emily's cousins that she was now confident of her eternal destiny.

On Thursday morning, May 13, 1886, "Emily seemed to go off into a stark unconscious state toward ten — and at this writing 6 P.M. has not come out of it," Austin recorded in his diary. Dr. Bigelow spent the better part of the day with Emily, prescribing a mixture of chloroform and olive oil for her convulsions. Vinnie, as always, was with her sister every moment, sitting by her and caring for her.

There was no change in Emily's condition the following day. Austin noted that she had "been in this heavy breathing and perfectly unconscious" for an entire day. Mabel Loomis Todd and her daughter Millicent stopped by twice to see Lavinia but were not allowed into Emily's sick room. In the evening, Emily was "still unconscious, & losing constantly." Austin called at the Todds and, true to form, was again paralyzed by the suffering of another. "He is terribly oppressed," Mabel confided to her diary.

During the night on Friday, "it was settled before morning broke that Emily would not wake again this side," according to Austin. On Saturday, Harriet Jameson went to be with Vinnie. "How can I live without her?" Vinnie cried. "Ever since we were little girls we have been wonderfully dear to each other — and many times when desirable offers of marriage have been made to Emily she has said — I have never seen anyone that I cared for as much as you Vinnie." Jameson stayed with Vinnie through the afternoon, along with Sarah Montague. "The day was awful," Austin wrote in his diary. Emily finally "ceased to breathe that terrible breathing just before the whistles sounded for six." After Emily died, Jameson's daughter Helen observed, Vinnie "seems very calm so far. Austin is much shaken." To the very end, the family members played their parts.

On Tuesday, May 18, the day before the funeral, an unsigned obituary appeared in the *Springfield Republican*. It had been written by Susan Dickinson and remains one of the most perceptive of all early judgments of Emily Dickinson's life and art. Reading it more than a century later, one is struck by the astuteness and balance of Sue's rendering of her sister-in-law. However strained their relationship had become at times, Sue understood Emily and her rare abilities better than any other member of the Dickinson family did.

Sue began by depicting the Homestead as a place redolent of "old-fashioned times, when parents and children grew up and passed maturity together, in lives of singular uneventfulness unmarked by sad or joyous crises." When Emily secluded herself within that home, few came to know her directly, "although the facts of . . . her intellectual brilliancy were familiar Amherst traditions." Many who had never even met Emily, however, nevertheless became the objects "of her unselfish consideration," receiving from her "treasures of fruit and flowers and ambrosial dishes for the sick and well."

As Austin and Vinnie did, Sue portrayed Emily's withdrawal as a natural development rather than an extraordinary event. She described her as a woman whose "sensitive nature shrank from much personal contact with the world, and more and more turned to her own large wealth of individual resources for companionship, sitting thenceforth, as some one said of her, 'in the light of her own fire.'" As Sue understood her, Emily was neither disappointed with the world nor "insufficient for any mental work or social career." Instead, it was a matter of "the mesh of her soul" being "too rare, and the sacred quiet of her own home prov[ing] the fit atmosphere for her worth and work." Sue was convinced that Emily's seclusion had to do with a need to preserve her resources rather than with a fear of friendship or acquaintance.

"Her talk and her writings were like no one else's," Sue noted, offering a judgment to be echoed through the years. Emily refused to publish a line, but word of her activity and ability inevitably leaked out. Thus it was that "frequently notable persons paid her visits, hoping to overcome the protest of her own nature and gain a promise of occasional contributions at least, to various magazines." But they almost always failed, for Emily had no desire, in her lifetime, to broadcast her work abroad and take upon herself the burdens of fame.

"A Damascus blade gleaming and glancing in the sun was her wit." Emily, Sue was the first to recognize, possessed an extraordinary ability to capture and name the fleeting, intangible activities of human consciousness: "Like a magician she caught the shadowy apparitions of her brain and tossed them in startling picturesqueness to her friends, who . . . fretted that she had so easily made palpable the tantalizing fancies forever eluding their bungling, fettered grasp." Here again, Sue was the first to identify a key element of Emily's poetic genius — the ability to create poetic forms and startling metaphors that were both profoundly original and immediately recognizable.

Sue called her sister-in-law "keen and eclectic in her literary tastes" and "quick as the electric spark in her intuitions and analyses." Endowed with enormous gifts, Emily "seized the kernel instantly, almost impatient of the fewest words, by which she must make her

261

revelation." Sue correctly noted that Emily had "no creed, no formulated faith"; and despite the hagiographic tone, there is ample truth in her characterization of the poet as one who "walked this life with the gentleness and reverence of the old saints, with the firm step of martyrs who sing while they suffer."

The funeral took place on Wednesday, May 19, on a "deliciously brilliant sunny afternoon." The private service was held in the Homestead, as Edward Dickinson's had been a decade earlier. With Vinnie's permission, Sue had prepared both Emily for burial and the home for the service. Shortly after noon, Vinnie invited Harriet Jameson, who had sat with her during the dreadful final hours on Saturday, to come over to "see Miss Emily — and very glad was I of the privilege — ." Emily lay in an expensive white casket furnished with white flannel and white textile handles. "She looked more like her brother than her sister," Jameson reported in a letter to her son, "with a wealth of auburn hair and a very spirituelle face — She was robed in white — with a bundle of violets at her throat."

Higginson came down from Boston for the funeral and noted in his diary that there was "an atmosphere of its own, fine & strange about the whole house & grounds — a more saintly & elevated 'House of Usher.' " The lawn of the Homestead was "full of buttercups violet & wild geranium," and in the house "a handful of pansies & another of lilies of valley on piano." But it was the face of Emily Dickinson, which Higginson had not looked upon for more than a decade, that most interested him: "E.D.'s face a wondrous restoration of youth — she is 54 [55] & looked 30, not a gray hair or wrinkle, & perfect peace on the beautiful brow." Sue had seen to every detail: "There was a little bunch of violets at the neck & one pink cypripedium," and before the casket was closed "Vinnie put in two heliotropes by her hand 'to take to Judge Lord.' "

The service took place in the middle of the afternoon. The Dickinson family favorite, Jonathan Jenkins, returned from Pittsfield to officiate, along with Rev. George Dickerman, the current pastor of the First Church. Julius Seelye, the president of Amherst College, served as an honorary pallbearer, along with several other notable friends of the family. Higginson read Emily Brontë's "Last Lines" poem, which he prefaced "by saying that one friend who had put on immortality, but who really never seemed to have put it off — frequently read this poem to her sister":

No coward soul is mine
No trembler in the world's storm-troubled sphere
I see Heaven's glories shine
And Faith shines equal arming me from Fear

O God within my breast
Almighty ever-present Deity
Life, that in me hath rest
As I Undying Life, have power in Thee

At the close of the service, the honorary pallbearers carried the casket out the rear door of the Homestead. By Emily's instructions, it was then "borne by the faithful workmen of the grounds, Dennis Scannell, Steve Sullivan, Pat Ward, . . . Dennis Cashman, Dan Moynihan, Tom Kelly." Emily had seen "& talked to, occasionally, up to the last" each of these men. They led the way, and the cortege of mourners followed, across the Homestead lawn, through the hedge, and then along "the ferny footpaths to the little cemetery."

Having "forded the Mystery" at last, Emily Dickinson had passed to her "Rendezvous of Light." Within a few short years, her poetry would begin to "Make Summer." And so it still does.

A Note on the Sources

EMILY DICKINSON'S PUBLISHING HISTORY reads like a biography itself; it is the story of twins separated at birth. Because of the animosity surrounding relations between Austin Dickinson's wife and the woman with whom he carried on a twelve-year affair, Emily Dickinson's unpublished poems were divided, less than a decade after her death, between two families, with Susan Dickinson and Martha Dickinson (Bianchi) having control of one portion and Mabel Loomis Todd and Millicent Todd (Bingham) possessing the other lot. Todd and Thomas Wentworth Higginson were the first to edit and publish Dickinson's work; they produced the first edition in 1890, with the second series following in 1891, and a third series in 1896. Bianchi published different editions of her aunt's poems in 1914, 1929, 1935, and 1937. In 1945, Bingham published one further edition of Dickinson's poems.

Only after extensive legal wrangling were the scattered poems edited and the poetic family reunited in a single edition in 1955. Thomas Johnson edited the three-volume *The Poems of Emily Dickinson* (Cambridge: The Belknap Press of Harvard University Press, 1955). Without its scholarly apparatus, the Johnson edition is available in a single volume, *The Complete Poems of Emily Dickinson* (Boston: Little, Brown, 1958). Ralph W. Franklin is currently editing a new edition of the poetry to be published by Harvard University Press.

The manuscript study of Emily Dickinson was revolutionized when Ralph Franklin edited *The Manuscript Books of Emily Dickinson* (Cambridge: The Belknap Press of Harvard University Press, 1981). Franklin's text consists of reproductions of the forty fascicles and fifteen unbound sets of handwritten poems that Dickinson left behind at death; this edition continues to spark debate about Dickinson's artistic intentions and the history of Dickinson publishing. Finally, William Shurr has edited *New Poems of Emily Dickinson* (Chapel Hill: University of North Carolina Press, 1993); this book consists of almost five hundred selections from her letters that the editor has arranged in stanza form.

The history of Dickinson's letters is also tied up with the Dickinson-Todd dispute. Different, incomplete editions of the letters appeared over six decades before Thomas Johnson and Theodora Ward edited the three-volume *The Letters of Emily Dickinson* (Cambridge: The Belknap Press of Harvard University Press, 1958). Ralph Franklin has produced a helpful edition of *The Master Letters of Emily Dickinson* (Amherst: Amherst College Press, 1986). A vital addition to Dickinson scholarship was the publication of Richard Sewall's *The Lyman Letters: New Light on Emily Dickinson and Her Family* (Amherst: University of Massachusetts Press, 1965).

The other indispensable primary sourcebook on the life of Emily Dickinson is Jay Leyda's two-volume *The Years and Hours of Emily Dickinson* (New Haven: Yale University Press, 1960). In this remarkable work, which proceeds chronologically through Dickinson's life, Leyda has collected an exhaustive array of selections from primary and secondary sources. All biographers and Dickinson scholars are in Leyda's debt. Though some new sources and biographical information have come to light since he published this work in 1960, it remains unsurpassed as a Dickinson resource.

Biographies of Dickinson began to appear in the 1920s, when it became evident that interest in the poet was not about to wane. Martha Dickinson Bianchi published two biographical studies, *The Life and Letters of Emily Dickinson* (Boston: Houghton Mifflin, 1924) and *Emily Dickinson Face to Face* (Boston: Houghton Mifflin, 1932); though both works display shoddy editorial work with the poems and offer dubious conjectures about Dickinson's love interests and seclusion, they also contain useful information on the Dickinson family and its circle of friends. Josephine Pollitt's *Emily Dickinson: The Human Background of*

Her Poetry (New York: Harper, 1930) and Genevieve Taggard's *The Life and Mind of Emily Dickinson* (New York: Alfred A. Knopf, 1930) are badly outdated studies of the life.

The serious biographical study of Emily Dickinson began with George Frisbie Whicher's *This Was a Poet: A Critical Biography of Emily Dickinson* (New York: Scribner's, 1938; reprint, Amherst: Amherst College Press, 1992). Though he had to work with incomplete primary sources, Whicher was able to provide the first account of the poet's life that situated her accurately in her time and place and explored her poetry with lasting insight. Thomas Johnson produced a companion biography to go along with his edition of the poems, *Emily Dickinson: An Interpretive Biography* (Cambridge: Harvard University Press, 1955). The definitive biography appeared in 1974, when Richard Sewall capped almost thirty years of work on Dickinson with *The Life of Emily Dickinson,* 2 vols. (New York: Farrar, Straus and Giroux, 1974; single volume edition, 1980). Sewall's biography was the first treatment of Dickinson that was able to take account of the enormous volume of materials produced by Mabel Loomis Todd; it was from Sewall that we first learned of the nature of Todd's relationship to Austin Dickinson and the full implications of that affair for Emily Dickinson's publishing history. While his extensive treatment of the affair skews the biography in places, in general Sewall has produced a thorough and balanced study of the poet. Cynthia Griffin Wolff's *Emily Dickinson* (New York: Alfred A. Knopf, 1987) is strong on the family background to the poet's life.

Near the end of her life, Millicent Todd Bingham published three highly useful studies on different aspects of Dickinson. *Ancestors' Brocades: The Literary Debut of Emily Dickinson* (New York: Harper, 1945) details the early publishing history of Dickinson's poems and contains illuminating information, especially from Austin and Vinnie, about her life; *Emily Dickinson: A Revelation* (New York: Harper, 1954) marked the first publication of Dickinson's letters to Otis Phillips Lord and contained important background information on the texts; and *Emily Dickinson's Home: Letters of Edward Dickinson and His Family* (New York: Harper, 1955) provided extensive historical and cultural contexts for the poet's life. In addition to Bingham's works on the Dickinsons, two other works deserve mention. One is Polly Longsworth's *Austin and Mabel: The Amherst Affair and Love Letters of Austin Dickinson and Mabel*

Loomis Todd (New York: Farrar, Straus and Giroux, 1984). Longsworth reprints portions of the voluminous correspondence between Austin Dickinson and Mabel Loomis Todd and provides informative background studies of the Todd and Dickinson marriages. In a similar manner Vivian Pollak has edited, with commentary, *A Poet's Parents: The Courtship Letters of Emily Norcross and Edward Dickinson* (Chapel Hill: University of North Carolina Press, 1988).

Numerous nineteenth-century sources deepen our understanding of Dickinson's cultural and theological context. They include Noah Webster, *A Plea for a Miserable World* (Boston: Ezra Lincoln, 1820); Samuel Fowler Dickinson, *An Address Delivered at Northampton Before the Hampshire, Hampden and Franklin Agricultural Society* (Amherst: J. S. and C. Adams, 1831); Mary Lyon, *Fifth Anniversary Address Before the Mount Holyoke Female Seminary* (Amherst: J. S. and C. Adams, 1843); William Gardner Hammond, *Remembrance of Amherst: An Undergraduate's Diary, 1846-1848,* ed. George Frisbie Whicher (New York: Columbia University Press, 1946); Edward Hitchcock, *The Religion of Geology and Its Connected Sciences* (Boston: Phillips, Sampson, 1852; reprint, Hicksville: Regina Press, 1975); Edward Hitchcock, *The Power of Christian Benevolence Illustrated in the Life and Labors of Mary Lyon* (Northampton: Hopkins, Bridgman, 1852); Thomas Wentworth Higginson, "Letter to a Young Contributor," *Atlantic Monthly* 9 (April 1862): 401-11; William S. Tyler, *History of Amherst College During Its First Half Century* (New York: Frederick H. Hitchcock, 1895); *Reunion of the Dickinson Family at Amherst, Mass.,* August 8th and 9th, 1883 (Binghamton: Binghamton Publishing Company, 1884); and *An Historical Review: One Hundred and Fiftieth Anniversary of the First Church of Christ in Amherst, Massachusetts* (Amherst: Press of the *Amherst Record,* 1890).

For additional historical background, the Dickinson collections at the Houghton Library (Harvard University) and the Jones Library (Town of Amherst) are most helpful; the Houghton has extensive materials from Emily Dickinson, including her library, while the Jones Library has exhaustive primary resources covering nineteenth-century Amherst. Two works that provide additional information on the history of Amherst are *Essays on Amherst's History* (Amherst: Vista Trust, 1978) and Daniel Lombardo, *Tales of Amherst: A Look Back* (Amherst: Jones Library, 1986). The following essay offers a rich historical assessment of Dickinson's solitude: Robert A. Gross, "Lonesome in Eden: Dickinson, Thoreau and the Problem of Community in Nineteenth-Century New England," *Canadian Review of American Studies* 14 (1983): 1-17. Also informative is Joseph Conforti, "Mary Lyon, the Founding of Mount Holyoke College and the Cultural Revival of Jonathan Edwards," *Religion and American Culture* 3 (1993): 69-89.

George S. Merriam's two-volume work *The Life and Times of Samuel Bowles* (New York: Century, 1885) offers valuable insight into a man who was of central importance to Emily Dickinson and her family. Perhaps the best firsthand account we have of Amherst College is John W. Burgess, *Reminiscences of an American Scholar* (New York: Columbia University Press, 1934). Another memoir of interest was written by the son of the Dickinsons' favorite pastor: MacGregor Jenkins, *Emily Dickinson: Friend and Neighbor* (Boston: Little, Brown, 1939). For further anecdotal information about the Dickinson era, see Alfred A. Stearns, *An Amherst Boyhood* (Amherst: Amherst College Press, 1946).

One weakness of much Dickinson scholarship has been a general slighting of the political, cultural, and theological context for her life and art. (The study of nineteenth-century gender issues is one exception; there is a rich, diverse body of secondary material on this topic.) This oversight seems particularly regrettable, when one considers the excellent quality of recent historical scholarship on eighteenth- and nineteenth-century American religion and culture. At the beginning, of course, there is Jonathan Edwards; both *Freedom of the Will*, ed. Paul Ramsey (New Haven: Yale University Press, 1957), and *A Jonathan Edwards Reader*, ed. John E. Smith, Harry S. Stout, and Kenneth P. Minkema (New Haven: Yale University Press, 1995), proved important for establishing Dickinson's theological context. Of the many historical studies of the period, I found the following to be particularly informative and insightful: Sydney E. Ahlstrom, *A Religious History of the American People*, 2 vols. (New Haven: Yale University Press, 1972; reprint Garden City: Image, 1975); Richard Bushman, *The Refinement of America* (New York: Alfred A. Knopf, 1992; New York: Vintage, 1993); Charles Cashdollar, *The Transformation of Theology, 1830-1890: Postivism and Protestant Thought in Britain and America* (Princeton: Princeton University Press, 1989); Allen C. Guelzo, *Edwards on the Will: A Century of American Theological Debate* (Middletown: Wesleyan University Press, 1989); Daniel Walker Howe, *The Political Culture of the American Whigs* (Chicago: University of Chicago Press, 1979); Bruce Kuklick, *The Rise of*

American Philosophy: Cambridge, Massachusetts, 1860-1930 (New Haven: Yale University Press, 1977), and *Churchmen and Philosophers: From Jonathan Edwards to John Dewey* (New Haven: Yale University Press, 1985); George Marsden, *The Soul of the American University: From Protestant Establishment to Established Nonbelief* (New York: Oxford University Press, 1994); Edmund Morgan, *Visible Saints: The History of a Puritan Idea* (New York: New York University Press, 1963; Cornell Paperbacks edition, Ithaca: Cornell University Press, 1965); Richard Rabinowitz, *The Spiritual Self in Everyday Life* (Boston: Northeastern University Press, 1989); Louise Stevenson, *Scholarly Means to Evangelical Ends: The New Haven Scholars and the Transformation of Higher Learning in America, 1830-1890* (Baltimore: Johns Hopkins University Press, 1989); and James Turner, *Without God, Without Creed: The Origins of Unbelief in America* (Baltimore: Johns Hopkins University Press, 1985).

For the broad context of intellectual history, I benefited from the following works: M. H. Abrams, *Natural Supernaturalism: Tradition and Revolution in Romantic Literature* (New York: W. W. Norton, 1971); W. H. Auden, *The Dyer's Hand* (New York: Random House, 1962; reprint, New York: Vintage, 1989); Andrew Delbanco, *The Death of Satan: How Americans Have Lost the Sense of Evil* (New York: Farrar, Straus and Giroux, 1995); John Patrick Diggins, *The Promise of Pragmatism: Modernism and the Crisis of Authority* (Chicago: University of Chicago Press, 1994); Leszek Kolakowski, *Modernity on Endless Trial* (Chicago: University of Chicago Press, 1990); Robert Langbaum, *The Poetry of Experience: The Dramatic Monologue in Modern Literary Tradition* (New York: Random House, 1957; reprint, Chicago: University of Chicago Press, 1985); Richard Rorty, *Contingency, Irony, and Solidarity* (Cambridge: Cambridge University Press, 1989); Charles Taylor, *Sources of the Self: The Making of the Modern Identity* (Cambridge: Harvard University Press, 1989); and Max Weber, *The Protestant Spirit and the Ethic of Capitalism* (New York: Scribner's, 1958).

General studies on the question of gender in the nineteenth century are essential reading for the situating of Dickinson's life and work. Three of these studies that are still among the best of their kind were first published in the 1970s: Nancy F. Cott, *The Bonds of Womanhood: "Woman's Sphere" in New England, 1780-1835* (New Haven: Yale University Press, 1977); Ann Douglas, *The Feminization of American Culture* (New York: Alfred A. Knopf, 1977; New York: Avon, 1978); and

Sandra M. Gilbert and Susan Gubar, *The Madwoman in the Attic: The Woman Writer and the Nineteenth-Century Literary Imagination* (New Haven: Yale University Press, 1979).

Emily Dickinson's poetry needs to be situated in the history of Christian thought and of Protestantism in particular. In considering the theological significance of her work, I profited from the following works: Saint Augustine, *On Christian Doctrine* (Indianapolis: Bobbs-Merrill, 1958); John Calvin, *Institutes of the Christian Religion*, 2 vols., ed. John T. McNeill (Philadelphia: Westminster, 1960); John Dillenberger and Claude Welch, *Protestant Christianity: Interpreted Through Its Development* (New York: Scribner's, 1954); *Martin Luther's Basic Theological Writings*, ed. Timothy Lull (Minneapolis: Fortress, 1989); and Reinhold Niebuhr, *The Nature and Destiny of Man*, 2 vols. (New York: Scribner's, 1943). For understanding the implications of Dickinson's Christology and for setting her romantic secularity in perspective, my most important resources were the first two volumes of Helmut Thielicke's systematic theology, *Evangelical Faith* (Grand Rapids: Eerdmans, 1974, 1977).

For assessing the theoretical dimensions of Dickinson's work, I found, as always, the work of Bakhtin, Gadamer, and Ricoeur to be provocative and illuminating: M. M. Bakhtin, *The Dialogical Imagination*, ed. Michael Holquist (Austin: University of Texas Press, 1981); Gary Saul Morson and Caryl Emerson, *Mikhail Bakhtin: Creation of a Prosaics* (Stanford: Stanford University Press, 1990); Hans-Georg Gadamer, *Truth and Method*, 2nd rev. ed. (New York: Crossroad, 1989); and Paul Ricoeur, *The Symbolism of Evil* (Boston: Beacon Press, 1967).

My approach to Dickinson depends to a good extent upon comparisons of her poetry with the work of her greatest American literary contemporaries. The major nineteenth-century primary texts cited in this volume are drawn from the Library of America editions of the authors' works. The following authors are important for understanding Dickinson in her American literary context: Henry Adams, *Democracy, Esther, Mont Saint Michel, Chartres, The Education of Henry Adams* (New York, 1983); Ralph Waldo Emerson, *Essays and Lectures* (New York, 1983); Herman Melville, *Redburn, White-Jacket, Moby-Dick* (New York, 1983); Henry David Thoreau, *A Week on the Concord and Merrimack Rivers, Walden, The Maine Woods, Cape Cod* (New York, 1985); and Walt Whitman, *Poetry and Prose* (New York, 1982).

In 1960, Dickinson scholar Charles Anderson proudly announced, in his own study of the poet, "I have read everything that has been published on Emily Dickinson." To that point, there had been fewer than 1,000 books and articles on the poet printed in the seventy years since the first publication of her poems. No one could make Anderson's claim today, because each year sees scores of articles and books published on the poet. Dickinson criticism is one of the major industries of American literary studies. In my cataloguing of the literary criticism covering Dickinson, I will attempt to highlight the main texts as well as works of particular relevance to the poet's biography.

In the past several decades, there have been many outstanding articles published on Dickinson as a poet and religious thinker. The best of these have been reprinted in several different collections, the most recent of which is *Emily Dickinson: A Collection of Critical Essays,* ed. Judith Farr (Upper Saddle River: Prentice Hall, 1996). In the Farr volume are included, among others, the following essential texts on Dickinson's religious views and aesthetic practices: Jane Donahue Eberwein, "Emily Dickinson and the Calvinist Sacramental Tradition"; Dorothy Huff Oberhaus, " 'Tender Pioneer': Emily Dickinson's Poems on the Life of Christ"; Judy Jo Small, "A Musical Aesthetic"; and Richard Wilbur, "Sumptuous Destitution." For a study of Dickinson's vocabulary see William Howard, "Emily Dickinson's Poetic Vocabulary," *PMLA* 72 (1957): 225-48. A medical analysis of Dickinson's eye ailment is offered in Martin Wand and Richard Sewall, " 'Eyes Be Blind, Heart Be Still': A New Perspective on Emily Dickinson's Eye Problem," *New England Quarterly* 52 (1979): 400-406. What Daniel Lombardo calls "the most significant Emily Dickinson revelation to come to light in recent years" is documented in Karen Dandurand, "New Dickinson Civil War Publications," *American Literature* 56 (1984): 17-27, and Dandurand, "Another Dickinson Poem Published in Her Lifetime," *American Literature* 54 (1982): 434-37. Dandurand's dissertation, "Why Dickinson Did Not Publish" (Massachusetts, 1984), is the best study we have of the poet's attitude toward publication. On the general subject of publishing in nineteenth-century America, see William Charvat, *The Profession of Authorship in America 1800-1870* (Columbus: Ohio State University Press, 1968; reprint, New York: Columbia University Press, 1992).

Of the countless critical studies on Emily Dickinson, the two that have been the most influential in my own thinking are Jane Donahue Eberwein, *Dickinson: Strategies of Limitation* (Amherst: University of Massachusetts Press, 1985), and Albert Gelpi, *Emily Dickinson: The Mind of the Poet* (Cambridge: Harvard University Press, 1966). Eberwein offers analyses of many Dickinson poems in a treatment that is especially well balanced in its discussion of the religious dimensions of the poetry. Elegantly written and impressively nuanced, Gelpi's study is perhaps the most philosophically astute reading of her work to date. Other important treatments include, but are by no means limited to, the following: Charles Anderson, *Emily Dickinson's Poetry: Stairway of Surprise* (New York: Holt, Rinehart and Winston, 1960); Wendy Barker, *Lunacy of Light: Emily Dickinson and the Experience of Metaphor* (Carbondale: Southern Illinois University Press, 1987); Paula Bennett, *Emily Dickinson: Woman Poet* (Iowa City: University of Iowa Press, 1990); Sharon Cameron, *Choosing Not Choosing: Dickinson's Fascicles* (Chicago: University of Chicago Press, 1992); Jack Capps, *Emily Dickinson's Reading 1836-1886* (Cambridge: Harvard University Press, 1966); Joanne Feit Diehl, *Dickinson and the Romantic Imagination* (Princeton: Princeton University Press, 1981); Susan Howe, *My Emily Dickinson* (Berkeley: North Atlantic Books, 1985); Karl Keller, *The Only Kangaroo among the Beauty: Emily Dickinson and America* (Baltimore: Johns Hopkins University Press, 1979); Cristanne Miller, *Emily Dickinson: A Poet's Grammar* (Cambridge: Harvard University Press, 1987); David Porter, *Dickinson: The Modern Idiom* (Cambridge: Harvard University Press, 1981); Barton Levi St. Armand, *Emily Dickinson and Her Culture* (Cambridge: Cambridge University Press, 1984); and Daneen Wardrop, *Emily Dickinson's Gothic: Goblin with a Gauge* (Iowa City: University of Iowa Press, 1996).

In addition to the works discussed above, the following books and articles are also cited in the notes to this biography: *The Articles of Faith and Government of the First Church in Amherst, Mass.*, adopted February 13, 1834; W. H. Auden, *A Certain World: A Commonplace Book* (New York: Viking Press, 1970), and *Forewords and Afterwords* (New York: Random House, 1973); Harold Bloom, ed., *Romanticism and Consciousness* (New York: W. W. Norton, 1970); Leo Braudy, *The Frenzy of Renown: Fame and Its History* (New York: Oxford University Press, 1986); Elizabeth Barrett Browning, *The Poetical Works of Elizabeth Barrett Browning* (London: John Murray, 1914); *The Complete Poems of Emily Brontë*, ed. Philip Henderson (London: Folio Society, 1951); Emil Brunner, *The*

Christian Doctrine of Creation and Redemption (Philadelphia: Westminster Press, n.d.); Gerald Bruns, *Hermeneutics, Ancient and Modern* (New Haven: Yale University Press, 1992); *The Portable Coleridge,* ed. I. A. Richards (New York: Viking Press, 1950); Isak Dinesen, *Seven Gothic Tales* (New York: Vintage Books, 1991); Lillian Federman, "Emily Dickinson's Letters to Sue Gilbert," *Massachusetts Review* 28 (1977); *William Wordsworth,* ed. Stephen Gill (Oxford: Oxford University Press, 1984); Erich Heller, *Thomas Mann: The Ironic German* (South Bend: Regnery/Gateway, 1979); Thomas Wentworth Higginson, preface to *Poems,* 1890, reprinted in *Collected Poems of Emily Dickinson* (New York: Gramercy Books, n.d.); Helen Hunt Jackson, *Mercy Philbrick's Choice* (New York: AMS Press, 1970); C. S. Lewis, *An Experiment in Criticism* (Cambridge: Cambridge University Press, 1961), and *The Discarded Image: An Introduction to Medieval and Renaissance Literature* (Cambridge: Cambridge University Press, 1964); Abraham Lincoln, *Lincoln: Speeches, Letters, Miscellaneous Writings, Presidential Messages and Proclamations* (New York: Library of America, 1989); Henry May, *The Enlightenment in America* (New York: Oxford University Press, 1976); James McPherson, *Battle Cry of Freedom: The Civil War Era* (New York: Oxford University Press, 1988); H. Richard Niebuhr, *The Kingdom of God in America* (New York: Harper and Brothers, 1935); Jean Paul Friedrich Richter, *Flower, Fruit and Thorn Pieces* (Boston: James Munroe and Co., 1845); Helmut Thielicke, *I Believe: The Christian's Creed* (Philadelphia: Fortress Press, 1968); Frederick Waite, *Western Reserve University: The Hudson Era* (Cleveland: Western Reserve University Press, 1943); *The Journal of John Winthrop,* 1630-1649, ed. Richard S. Dunn and Laetitia Yeandle (Cambridge: Harvard University Press, 1996).

Notes

By far the largest number of citations that follow are drawn from two sources: the three-volume *The Letters of Emily Dickinson* and Jay Leyda's two-volume work, *The Years and Hours of Emily Dickinson*. See "A Note on the Sources" for more information on these volumes.

NOTES TO THE INTRODUCTION

Page 3 "On subjects of which . . ." (ED to Otis Phillips Lord, April 30, 1882), *Letters of ED*, 3:728.

5 "An inexhaustible inner domain . . . ," Taylor, *Sources of the Self*, 390.

NOTES TO CHAPTER 1

7 "Memory is a strange Bell . . ." (ED to Elizabeth Holland, December, 1882), *Letters of ED*, 3:830.

9 "We are entered . . . ," Winthrop, *Journal of John Winthrop*, 9, 10.

9 "He appears to have dominated . . . ," Bianchi, *ED Face to Face*, 74.

9 "Threatened to choke out . . . ," Sewall, *Life of ED*, 18.

9 "Our names outnumber . . . ," Bianchi, *Amherst Record*, July 19, 1933, 1.

11 "The conversion of the world . . . ," Tyler, *History of Amherst College*, 122.

11 "Natural men are held . . . ," Edwards, "Sinners in the Hands of an Angry God," *A JE Reader*, 95.

12 "How does religion . . . ," Guelzo, *Edwards on the Will,* 223.
12 "With passing decades . . . ," Turner, *Without God,* 88.
13 "Whiggery stood for . . . ," Stevenson, *Scholarly Means,* 5-6.
13 "To blend the activist . . . ," Howe, *Political Culture of American Whigs,* 159-60.
14 "That of educating . . . ," Webster, *Plea for a Miserable World,* 7, 8, 11.
14 "His large-heartedness . . . ," *Reunion of the Dickinson Family,* 173-74.
15 "What may be my determination . . ." (Samuel Fowler Dickinson to Edward Dickinson, September 4, 1821), Houghton Library.
15 "His experience was insufficient . . . ," Waite, *Western Reserve,* 315.
16 "A virtuous life . . ." (Edward Dickinson to Emily Norcross, October 29, 1826), Pollak, *A Poet's Parents,* 53.
16 "The most interesting of all . . ." (Edward Dickinson to Emily Norcross, March 19, 1828), Pollak, *A Poet's Parents,* 196.
16 "As Treasurer of Amherst College . . . ," Tyler, *History of Amherst College,* 540.
16 "No Dickinson, at least . . . ," Sewall, *Life of ED,* 38.
17 "I am lost . . ." (Austin Dickinson to Mabel Loomis Todd, November 7, 1887); "No boy let out . . ." (Austin Dickinson to Mabel Loomis Todd, November 13, 1887); "Just a great, nasty, horrid . . ." (Austin Dickinson to Susan Gilbert Dickinson, November 13, 1887); "Which one's respect . . ." (Austin Dickinson to Mabel Loomis Todd, November 24, 1887), Longsworth, *Austin and Mabel,* pp. 299, 301.
17 "If she never felt want . . ." (T. W. Higginson to Mary Higginson, August 15, 1870), *Letters of ED,* 2:474.
17 "To shut our eyes is Travel . . ." (ED to Elizabeth Holland, October 1870), *Letters of ED,* 2:482.
17 "I do not go away . . ." (ED to T. W. Higginson, 1881), *Letters of ED,* 3:716.
18 "I like travelling . . . ," *Years and Hours,* 1:14.

NOTES TO CHAPTER 2

20 "Amherst was hardly more . . . ," Bingham, *ED's Home,* 64.
20 "Scanning with a keen . . . ," Jackson, *Mercy Philbrick's Choice,* 48, 49, 50-51.
21 "[Emily] Elizabeth called it *the fire* . . . ," *Years and Hours,* 1:20-22.
22 "Father used to take me . . ." (ED to Louise and Frances Norcross, November 1873), *Letters of ED,* 2:515; "When a few . . ." (ED to T. W. Higginson, June 1877), *Letters of ED,* 2:583; "We said she said . . . ," *Letters of ED,* 3:920; "Two things I have lost . . . ," *Letters of ED,* 3:928-29.
23 "A connoisseur of epitaphs . . . ," Bruns, *Hermeneutics Ancient and Modern,* 165.
23 " 'But they are dead . . . ,' " "We Are Seven," *William Wordsworth,* 84-85.
25 "Peculiar burden was to be . . . ," Gelpi, *ED: Mind of the Poet,* 91.
25 "It is my nature . . ." (ED to Abiah Root, June 26, 1846), *Letters of ED,* 1:34.
26 "The two most terrifying . . . ," Longsworth, *Austin and Mabel,* 73.
26 "I visited her often . . ." (ED to Abiah Root, March 28, 1846), *Letters of ED,* 1:32.
26 "I have just seen . . ." (ED to Abiah Root, January 12, 1846), *Letters of ED,* 1:24.
27 "Yesterday as I sat . . ." (ED to Abiah Root, March 28, 1846), *Letters of ED,* 1:31.

27 "The domestication of death . . . ," Douglas, *Feminization of American Culture*, 240-72; "Dying was a way . . . ," St. Armand, *ED and Her Culture*, 52.

27 "The air was as silent . . . ," Douglas, *Feminization*, 250-51.

28 "It seems as if . . ." (ED to Abiah Root, September 8, 1846), *Letters of ED*, 1:36.

28 "We take no note of time . . ." (ED to Abiah Root, September 8, 1846), *Letters of ED*, 1:38.

29 "If roses had not faded . . ." (ED to Elizabeth Holland, August 1856), *Letters of ED*, 2:329.

29 "Consider man's involvement . . . ," Niebuhr, *Nature and Destiny*, 2:2.

29 "A clear relation between . . . ," Brunner, *Christian Doctrine of Creation and Redemption*, 129.

29 " 'Whom he loveth . . .' " (ED to Elizabeth Holland, November 1871), *Letters of ED*, 2:492.

30 "I am in the class . . ." (ED to Jane Humphrey, May 12, 1842), *Letters of ED*, 1:7.

31 "Very distinct and pleasant impressions . . . ," *Years and Hours*, 1:81.

31 "The whole earth is to be subdued . . . ," S. F. Dickinson, *Address Delivered at Northampton*, 19, 24.

32 "Taught her to look . . . ," Whicher, *This Was a Poet*, 48.

32 References to science are detailed in Howard, "ED's Poetic Vocabulary."

32 "All former changes . . . ," quoted in Ahlstrom, *Religious History*, 2:228.

33 "If geology or any other science . . . ," Hitchcock, *Religion of Geology*, 1-2.

33 "Hitchcock compromise opened . . . ," Ahlstrom, *Religious History*, 2:228.

33 "When Flowers annually died . . ." (ED to T. W. Higginson, 1877), *Letters of ED*, 2:573.

33 "Was to open her eyes . . . ," Sewall, *Life of ED*, 354.

34 "Purposive adaptation by God . . . ," Wright, *Religion of Geology*, 4m.

34 "Mrs Dr Stearns called . . ." (ED to Otis Phillips Lord, April 30, 1882), *Letters of ED*, 3:728.

35 "Recognizes himself and his own finiteness . . . ," Gadamer, *Truth and Method*, 132.

35 "Insight into the limitations . . . ," Gadamer, *Truth and Method*, 357.

36 "They sang most *beautifully* . . . ," Hammond, *Remembrance of Amherst*, 168.

36 "[Mary Lyon] sought not merely . . . ," quoted in Sewall, *Life of ED*, 362.

37 "Infinitely more precious . . . ," Lyon, *Fifth Anniversary Address*, 4, 3, 21, 26, 28, 29, 36, 39, 44.

38 "Looms up in the future . . . ," Lyon, *Fifth Anniversary Address*, 26.

39 "A communal alternative . . . ," Conforti, "Mary Lyon," 79.

39 "Love of *benevolence* . . . ," Edwards, "Nature of True Virtue," in *A JE Reader*, 247.

39 "At 6. oclock, we all rise . . ." (ED to Abiah Root, November 6, 1847), *Letters of ED*, 1:54-55.

40 "Demonstration of saving grace . . . ," Morgan, *Visible Saints*, 90.

40 "That they have beene wounded . . . ," quoted in Morgan, *Visible Saints*, 90.

40 "Free consent as the basis . . . ," Morgan, *Visible Saints*, 29.

41 "There were real ogres . . . ," *Years and Hours*, 1:131.

41 "Cramped, curbed, repressed . . . ," Bianchi, *Life and Letters of ED*, 25.

41 "Legend of Emily's insurrection . . . ," Bianchi, *Life and Letters of ED*, 25-26.

41 "I attended another meeting . . . ," *Years and Hours,* 1:135; "Still *appears* unconcerned . . . ," *Years and Hours,* 1:136.

42 "All who had decided . . . ," *Years and Hours,* 1:136; "There is a great deal . . ." (ED to Abiah Root, January 17, 1848), *Letters of ED,* 1:60.

42 "Such sermons I never heard . . ." (ED to Austin Dickinson, February 7, 1848), *Letters of ED,* 1:64.

43 "Fate will be sealed . . ." (ED to Abiah Root, May 16, 1848), *Letters of ED,* 1:67-68.

43 "Primitive naiveté . . . ," Ricoeur, *Symbolism of Evil,* 351, 349.

44 "The disenchanting of the world . . . ," Weber, *Protestant Ethic,* 221-22, 104-6.

44 "I may not hope to win . . . ," Coleridge, "Dejection: An Ode," in *Portable Coleridge,* 170; "Once we lived . . . ," Emerson, "Experience," Library of America edition, 487.

44 "About two hundred years ago . . . ," Rorty, *Contingency, Irony, and Solidarity,* 5, 6.

46 "Do I know myself . . . ," Gelpi, *ED: Mind of the Poet,* 153.

46 "Beyond the desert . . . ," Ricoeur, *Symbolism of Evil,* 350-52.

NOTES TO CHAPTER 3

48 "Was almost persuaded to be a christian . . ." (ED to Abiah Root, January 31, 1846), *Letters of ED,* 1:27-28, 29.

49 "As to his knowledge . . . ," *Articles of Faith,* 7.

50 "Notably fuller and more solemn . . . ," Colton, *An Historical Review,* 77-78.

51 "The Whig personality ideal . . . ," Howe, *Political Culture of American Whigs,* 302.

51 "Reared in an era . . . ," Bennett, *ED: Woman Poet,* 381-82; "It seems clear . . . ," Sewall, *Life of ED,* 381-82.

52 "How lonely this world . . . ," (ED to Jane Humphrey, April 3, 1850), *Letters of ED,* 1:94; "Calmer, but full of radiance . . ." (ED to Abiah Root, May 7, 1850), *Letters of ED,* 1:98.

53 "It *certainly* comes from God . . ." (ED to Jane Humphrey, April 3, 1850), *Letters of ED,* 1:94.

53 "I tell each of you . . . ," Austin Dickinson, "Confession of Faith," Houghton Library.

54 "Became the Word of God . . . ," Dillenberger and Welch, *Protestant Christianity,* 50.

54 "It is not this or that . . . ," Langbaum, *Poetry of Experience,* 21.

54 "For the principle . . . ," Auden, *Dyer's Hand,* 318.

56 "Sewing Society has commenced . . ." (ED to Jane Humphrey, January 23, 1850), *Letters of ED,* 1:84.

57 "Quite a trimming . . ." (ED to Austin Dickinson, April 2, 1853), *Letters of ED,* 1:237.

57 "Can we understand reverie . . . ," Rabinowitz, *Spiritual Self,* 175.

57 "Sweet silver moon . . ." (ED to Susan Gilbert, October 9, 1851), *Letters of ED,* 1:143-44.

58 "Take heed to thy heart . . . ," quoted in Turner, *Without God,* 111.

58 "Notion of liberty . . . ," Edwards, *Freedom of the Will*, 1:5, 164.

NOTES TO CHAPTER 4

62 "What shall we do . . ." (ED to Abiah Root, May 7, 1850), *Letters of ED*, 1:98.

63 "I am glad you are *not* delighted . . ." (ED to Austin Dickinson, June 15, 1851), *Letters of ED*, 1:113.

63 "A dozen compositions . . . ," *Years and Hours*, 1:182.

63 "Home is a holy thing . . ." (ED to Austin Dickinson, October 25, 1851), *Letters of ED*, 1:150-51.

65 "The New London Day . . ." (ED to Austin Dickinson, June 5, 1853), *Letters of ED*, 1:254.

65 "I saw Mr. Dickinson . . ." (T. W. Higginson to Mary Higginson, August 17, 1870), *Letters of ED*, 2:475.

66 "It must have been . . . ," quoted in Bingham, *Ancestors' Brocades*, 231-33.

66 "He cracks a few walnuts . . ." (ED to Austin Dickinson, March 18, 1853), *Letters of ED*, 1:231; "Father says your letters . . ." (ED to Austin Dickinson, July 6, 1851), *Letters of ED*, 1:122.

67 "For all you differ . . ." (ED to Austin Dickinson, November 10, 1853), *Letters of ED*, 1:269; "I do think it's so funny . . ." (ED to Austin Dickinson, March 18, 1853), *Letters of ED*, 1:231.

67 "Tutor Howland was here . . ." (ED to Austin Dickinson, June 8, 1851), *Letters of ED*, 1:111.

67 "One day sitting down . . . ," Bingham, *ED's Home*, 112.

67 "Father sat all the evening . . ." (ED to Austin Dickinson, July 6, 1851), *Letters of ED*, 1:121.

68 "Father was very severe . . ." (ED to Austin Dickinson, April 2, 1853), *Letters of ED*, 1:237; "[Father] buys me many Books . . ." (ED to T. W. Higginson, April 25, 1862), *Letters of ED*, 2:404.

68 "My father seems to me . . . ," *Lyman Letters*, 70-71.

68 "Father, too busy with his Briefs . . ." (ED to T. W. Higginson, April 25, 1862), *Letters of ED*, 2:404; "My father only reads on Sunday . . ." (T. W. Higginson to Mary Higginson, August 16, 1870), *Letters of ED*, 2:473.

69 "Preached about death and judgment . . ." (ED to Josiah and Elizabeth Holland, November 26, 1854), *Letters of ED*, 1:309.

70 "*That* God must be a friend . . ." (ED to Elizabeth Holland, October 1881), *Letters of ED*, 3:713.

70 "Congeniality was religious . . . ," Sewall, *Life of ED*, 600.

70 "While Hon. E.D. of Amherst . . . ," *Years and Hours*, 1:178; "A grand type . . . ," Sewall, *Life of ED*, 60n.6.

71 "A quiet, sweet, practical . . . ," Sewall, *Life of ED*, 268.

71 "Their mother, quiet gentle little lady . . . ," Bingham, *Ancestors' Brocades*, 8.

71 "Was as usual . . . ," *Years and Hours*, 1:81; "Mrs. Edward Dickinson . . . ," *Years and Hours*, 2:7; "Mrs. Edward Dickinson . . . ," *Years and Hours*, 2:81.

71 "I never had a mother . . ." (T. W. Higginson to Mary Higginson, August 17,

1870), *Letters of ED*, 2:475; "I always ran Home to Awe . . ." (ED to T. W. Higginson, January 1874), *Letters of ED*, 2:517-18.

72 "Father and mother sit . . ." (ED to Austin Dickinson, November 16, 1851), *Letters of ED*, 1:157; "Mother feels quite troubled . . ." (ED to Austin Dickinson, October 25, 1851), *Letters of ED*, 1:151; "Mother went out with Father . . ." (ED to Austin Dickinson, February 18, 1852), *Letters of ED*, 1:180.

72 "In Emily's day . . . ," Bingham, *ED's Home*, 112.

72 "I have retired to my chamber . . . ," *Years and Hours*, 1:17.

72 "We were never intimate . . ." (ED to Elizabeth Holland, December 1882), *Letters of ED*, 3:754-55.

NOTES TO CHAPTER 5

74 "Ah John — *Gone*" (ED to John Graves, 1856), *Letters of ED*, 2:330.

74 "It is a beautiful, warm morning . . . ," *Lyman Letters*, 12.

75 "The last week . . ." (ED to William Cowper Dickinson, February 14, 1849), *Letters of ED*, 1:76; "Amherst is alive with fun . . ." (ED to Joel Norcross, January 11, 1850), *Letters of ED*, 1:80.

75 "We had a Shakespeare Club . . . ," *Years and Hours*, 2:478.

76 "A tiny figure in white . . . ," *Years and Hours*, 2:273.

76 "I have never met . . ." (ED to Edward Everett Hale, January 13, 1854), *Letters of ED*, 1:282-83.

77 "A beautiful copy . . ." (ED to Jane Humphrey, January 23, 1850), *Letters of ED*, 1:84; "All can write autographs . . . ," *Years and Hours*, 1:158.

77 "My dying Tutor . . ." (ED to T. W. Higginson, June 7, 1862), *Letters of ED*, 2:408; "When a little Girl . . ." (ED to T. W. Higginson, April 25, 1862), *Letters of ED*, 2:404.

77 "Will you be my Preceptor . . ." (ED to T. W. Higginson, June 7, 1862), *Letters of ED*, 2:409; "Now my ascended Playmate . . ." (ED to Susan Gilbert Dickinson, October 1883), *Letters of ED*, 3:799.

78 "Tutor [Newton] died . . ." (ED to T. W. Higginson, April 25, 1862), *Letters of ED*, 2:404.

78 "Perhaps Death — . . ." (ED to T. W. Higginson, February 1863), *Letters of ED*, 2:423; "Why should we censure Othello . . ." (ED to Mabel Loomis Todd, 1885), *Letters of ED*, 3:889.

79 "I'd strike the sun . . . ," Melville, *Moby Dick*, Library of America edition, 967.

80 "Beside ourselves in a sane sense . . . ," Thoreau, *Walden*, Library of America edition, 429-30.

81 "Nice times . . . ," (ED to Austin Dickinson, January 5, 1854), *Letters of ED*, 1:281; "My thoughts are far from idle . . ." (ED to Susan Gilbert, February 28, 1855), *Letters of ED*, 2:317.

81 "Comes down here . . ." (ED to Austin Dickinson, April 2, 1853), *Letters of ED*, 1:238.

81 "Social calls to be numbered . . . ," Sewall, *Life of ED*, 415.

81 "She sat in my lap . . . ," *Lyman Letters*, 50-51.

82 "A gay party of us . . . ," *Lyman Letters*, 17-18.

82 *"A storm arose* in the house . . . ," *Years and Hours,* 1:196.

82 "If Vinnie had been fit . . . ," *Lyman Letters,* 49, 53.

83 "Emily you see is platonic . . . ," *Lyman Letters,* 48-49.

83 "Secrets are interesting . . ." (ED to Perez Cowan, October 1869), *Letters of ED,* 2:463.

84 "The War between the Houses . . . ," Sewall, *Life of ED,* 157.

84 "This strange feud . . . ," Stearns, *Amherst Boyhood,* 77-78.

85 "Confidence [told by Emily] to her Sister Sue . . . ," Bianchi, *Life and Letters of ED,* 46-48.

86 "Emily sent word to her lover . . . ," Taggard, *Life and Mind,* 108.

86 "Of that chapter . . . ," Bianchi, *Life and Letters of ED,* 46-47.

86 "Revelation [of George Gould . . .]," Taggard, *Life and Mind,* 110.

87 "He told me about her . . . ," Bingham, *Ancestors' Brocades,* 12.

87 " 'It was in Washington' . . . ," Bingham, *Ancestors' Brocades,* 319.

88 "Emily never had any love disaster . . . ," Sewall, *Life of ED,* 153.

88 "As she passed on . . . ," *Years and Hours,* 2:473.

89 " 'So poor that the neighbors . . . ,' " Longsworth, *Austin and Mabel,* 69.

89 "With whom she was . . . ," Federman, "ED's Letters to Sue Gilbert," 205.

89 "The dishes may wait . . ." (ED to Susan Gilbert, February 6, 1852), *Letters of ED,* 1:175, 176; "Oh Susie, I would nestle . . ." (ED to Susan Gilbert, February 1852), *Letters of ED,* 1:177; "Nobody loves me here . . ." (ED to Susan Gilbert, April 5, 1852), *Letters of ED,* 1:193.

90 "The people who love God . . ." (ED to Susan Gilbert, February 1852), *Letters of ED,* 1:181; "When I was gone to meeting . . ." (ED to Susan Gilbert, April 1852), *Letters of ED,* 1:201; "The Roman Catholic system . . ." (ED to Susan Gilbert, June 27, 1852), *Letters of ED,* 1:216.

91 "Real life is private life . . . ," Gross, "Lonesome in Eden," 11.

91 "From nature to redeemed nature . . . ," Bloom, *Romanticism and Consciousness,* 5-6.

92 "Some things are to be enjoyed . . . ," Augustine, *On Christian Doctrine,* 9, 10.

92 "An unfit partner . . . ," Heller, *Mann: Ironic German,* 111.

93 "Deprivation of 'Spiritual converse' . . . ," *Years and Hours,* 1:316.

93 "The loveliest sermon . . ." (ED to Frances Norcross, 1873), *Letters of ED,* 2:502-3.

93 "I've not written to you . . ." (ED to Susan Gilbert, August 1854), *Letters of ED,* 1:304.

93 "Sue — you can go or stay . . ." (ED to Susan Gilbert, 1854), *Letters of ED,* 1:305-6.

95 "Not one word comes back . . ." (ED to Susan Gilbert, January 1855), *Letters of ED,* 2:315.

95 "Ah John — Gone? . . ." (ED to John Graves, 1856), *Letters of ED,* 2:330.

96 "To live is so startling . . ." (ED to T. W. Higginson, 1872), *Letters of ED,* 2:500.

96 "As for Emily . . . ," Bingham, *ED's Home,* 413-14.

NOTES TO CHAPTER 6

98 "Jerusalem must be . . ." (ED to Mary and Samuel Bowles, June 1858), *Letters of ED*, 2:334.

98 "The golden days . . . ," Kate Anthon to Susan Dickinson, Houghton Library.

98 "Much has occurred . . ." (ED to Joseph Sweetser, 1858), *Letters of ED*, 2:335; "Good-night! I can't stay . . ." (ED to Elizabeth and Josiah Holland, November 6, 1858), *Letters of ED*, 2:341; "Blessed Aunt Lavinia now . . ." (ED to Lavinia Dickinson, April 1860), *Letters of ED*, 2:361-62.

99 "I had a terror . . ." (ED to T. W. Higginson, April 25, 1862), *Letters of ED*, 2:404; "You were not aware . . ." (ED to T. W. Higginson, June 1869), *Letters of ED*, 2:460.

99 "Dickinson did not write . . . ," Franklin, *Master Letters of ED*, 5.

99 In dating the "Master" letters, I accept Ralph Franklin's revision of the dates assigned to the three letters in Thomas Johnson's authoritative edition of the Dickinson letters. The many following citations from the letters come from Johnson's edition: *Letters of ED*, 2:333, 391-92, and 373-75.

101 "While in all probability . . . ," Pollak, *ED: Anxiety of Gender*, 101-2.

102 "He said that at different times . . . ," Bingham, *ED's Home*, 374.

102 "One of his favorite resorts . . . ," Merriam, *Life of Samuel Bowles*, 2:79.

102 "Wanted to have a salon . . . ," Sewall, *Life of ED*, 264; "Flirtations with delightful Sam Bowles . . . ," Sewall, *Life of ED*, 281; "Was glad to be spared . . . ," Merriam, *Life of Samuel Bowles*, 2:79.

103 "I am much ashamed . . ." (ED to Samuel Bowles, August 1860), *Letters of ED*, 2:366.

103 "The hand that wrote . . . ," *Poems of ED*, 6.

103 "I cant explain it . . ." (ED to Samuel Bowles, 1860), *Letters of ED*, 2:363.

104 "Thank you. 'Faith' is a fine . . ." (ED to Samuel Bowles, 1861), *Letters of ED*, 2:364.

104 "We pray for your new health . . ." (ED to Samuel Bowles, February 1861), *Letters of ED*, 2:371.

105 "Been in a savage, turbulent state . . . ," *Years and Hours*, 2:77.

105 "To the girls & all . . . ," *Years and Hours*, 2:76.

105 "If I amaze[d] your kindness . . ." (ED to Samuel Bowles, 1862), *Letters of ED*, 2:393. For the suggested reconstruction of the text of this incomplete letter — its outside edges are torn away — I am indebted to Dandurand, *Why Dickinson Did Not Publish*.

106 "I smile when you suggest . . ." (ED to T. W. Higginson, June 7, 1862), *Letters of ED*, 2:408.

106 "A Soldier called . . ." (ED to Samuel Bowles, August 1862), *Letters of ED*, 2:416.

106 "Title divine — is mine! . . ." (ED to Samuel Bowles, 1862), *Letters of ED*, 2:394.

108 "By an article . . . ," Dandurand, *Why Dickinson Did Not Publish*, 128.

108 "To be remembered . . ." (ED to Mary Hills, 1871), *Letters of ED*, 2:487.

108 "I have known little of you . . ." (ED to Louise Norcross, January 4, 1859), *Letters of ED*, 2:345. "Could I make you and Austin — proud — . . ." (ED to Susan Gilbert Dickinson, 1861), *Letters of ED*, 2:380.

109 "We might call her . . . ," Braudy, *Frenzy of Renown*, 472.

110 "The home was gradually emptied . . . ," Bushman, *Refinement of America*, 422.
110 "Dear Mr Bowles . . ." (ED to Samuel Bowles, 1862), *Letters of ED*, 2:252.
110 "On April 16, 1862 . . ." (T. W. Higginson), *Letters of ED*, 2:403.
110 "Higginson and Hawthorne . . . ," *Years and Hours*, 2:79.
111 "It is the habit to overrate . . . ," Higginson, "Letter to a Young Contributor," 401-11. All citations of this essay are taken from the text of its original publication in the April 1862 *Atlantic Monthly*.
113 "Are you too deeply occupied to say . . ." (ED to T. W. Higginson, April 15, 1862), *Letters of ED*, 2:403.
113 "Was in a handwriting so peculiar . . . ," *Years and Hours*, 2:55.
113 "Thank you for the surgery . . ." (ED to T. W. Higginson, April 25, 1862), *Letters of ED*, 2:404-5; "Will you tell me my fault . . ." (ED to T. W. Higginson, July 1862), *Letters of ED*, 2:412.
114 "Two Editors of Journals . . ." (ED to T. W. Higginson, April 25, 1862), *Letters of ED*, 2:404-5.
114 "I have had few pleasures . . ." (ED to T. W. Higginson, June 7, 1862), *Letters of ED*, 2:408.
115 "Writes primarily to exploit . . . ," Charvat, *Authorship in America*, 108, 109-10.
116 "O soul, made white . . . ," quoted in Dandurand, *Why Dickinson Did Not Publish*, 21.
116 "Would you have time . . ." (ED to T. W. Higginson, June 7, 1862), *Letters of ED*, 2:409.
116 "You are true . . ." (ED to T. W. Higginson, July 1862), *Letters of ED*, 2:412.
116 "Often, when troubled with entreaty . . ." (ED to T. W. Higginson, 1877), *Letters of ED*, 2:573.
117 "The stimulus of Loss . . ." (ED to Susan Gilbert Dickinson, September 1871), *Letters of ED*, 2:489.
118 " 'Matty, child, no one . . . ,' " Bianchi, *ED Face to Face*, 65-66.
118 "Purpose in going . . . ," Thoreau, *Walden*, Library of America edition, 338.
118 "Humanity at the limits . . . ," Sewall, *Life of ED*, 491.

NOTES TO CHAPTER 7

120 "Sorrow seems more general . . ." (ED to Louise and Frances Norcross, 1864), *Letters of ED*, 2:436.
121 "Combinations too powerful to be suppressed . . . ," Lincoln, "Proclamations Calling Militia," Library of America edition, 232.
121 "The heather is on fire . . . ," quoted in McPherson, *Battle Cry*, 274.
121 "A rousing sermon in the college chapel . . . ," *Years and Hours*, 2:26.
121 "I never knew Amherst . . . ," *Years and Hours*, 2:26.
121 "An elegant national banner . . . ," *Years and Hours*, 2:26, 27.
122 "Had news of the death . . ." (ED to Louise Norcross, December 31, 1861), *Letters of ED*, 2:386.
123 "An exciting day for Amherst . . . ," *Years and Hours*, 2:46.
123 "Dear Children, 'tis least . . ." (ED to Louise and Frances Norcross, March 1862), *Letters of ED*, 2:397-98.

123 "The news from Newbern . . . ," *Years and Hours,* 2:49.

123 "Austin is chilled . . ." (ED to Samuel Bowles, March 1862), *Letters of ED,* 2:399.

124 "Friends are nations in themselves . . ." (ED to Samuel Bowles, November 1862), *Letters of ED,* 2:420.

124 "I should have liked to see you . . ." (ED to T. W. Higginson, March 1863), *Letters of ED,* 2:423-24.

124 "God might be . . . ," Adams, *Education,* Library of America edition, 983.

125 "Sorrow seems more general . . ." (ED to Louise and Frances Norcross, 1864), *Letters of ED,* 2:436.

125 "They are religious . . ." (ED to T. W. Higginson, April 25, 1862), *Letters of ED,* 2:404.

126 "A house where each member . . ." (T. W. Higginson to Mary Higginson, August 16, 1870), *Letters of ED,* 2:473.

126 "She [Emily] is the quintessence . . . ," quoted in Bingham, *Ancestors' Brocades,* 169-70.

127 "She makes all the bread . . ." (T. W. Higginson to Mary Higginson, August 16, 1870), *Letters of ED,* 2:475.

127 "1 Quart Flour . . . ," *Letters of ED,* 2:493.

127 "If Emily Dickinson gradually withdrew . . . ," Lombardo, *Tales of Amherst,* 102.

128 "Carlo died . . ." (ED to T. W. Higginson, January 1866), *Letters to ED,* 2:449.

128 "He is not willing I should write . . ." (ED to Lavinia Dickinson, May 1864), *Letters of ED,* 2:430; "Emily may not be able . . ." (ED to Lavinia Dickinson, November 1864), *Letters of ED,* 2:434.

128 "A woe, the only . . . ," *Lyman Letters,* 76.

129 "Elijah . . . in the Wilderness . . ." (ED to Lavinia Dickinson, July 1864), *Letters of ED,* 2:433; "I have been sick so long . . ." (ED to Lavinia Dickinson, November 1864), *Letters of ED,* 2:435; "For caring about me . . ." (ED to Lavinia Dickinson, 1864), *Letters of ED,* 2:435.

129 "Going home[,] I flew . . . ," *Lyman Letters,* 76.

129 "I shall go Home . . ." (ED to Lavinia Dickinson, November 1864), *Letters of ED,* 2:435.

130 "Vinnie was there . . . ," *ED's Home,* 412.

130 "She abhorred the commonplace . . . ," Sewall, *Life of ED,* 131; "Her fiercest denunciations . . . ," Bingham, *Ancestors' Brocades,* 298.

130 "Vinnie is sick . . ." (ED to Elizabeth and Josiah Holland, September 1859), *Letters of ED,* 2:353; "She has no Father . . ." (ED to Elizabeth and Josiah Holland, 1873), *Letters of ED,* 2:508.

131 "I find ecstasy in living . . ." (T. W. Higginson to Mary Higginson, August 61, 1870), *Letters of ED,* 2:474.

132 "The forces that Dickinson felt conspired . . . ," Barker, *Lunacy of Light,* 32.

132 "I felt that I was . . ." (ED to Abiah Root, January 31, 1846), *Letters of ED,* 1:27-28.

133 "I am uncertain of Boston . . ." (ED to T. W. Higginson, 1866), *Letters of ED,* 2:450.

135 "The medieval universe . . . ," Lewis, *Discarded Image,* 98-99.

136 " 'We have been amateurs . . . ,' " Dinesen, *Seven Gothic Tales,* 267.

137 "Insight into the limitations . . . ," Gadamer, *Truth and Method,* 357.

137 "Certainty that death . . . ," Auden, *Forewords and Afterwards*, 173.
138 "The laureate and attorney . . . ," Wilbur, "Sumptuous Destitution," *ED: Collection*, 130.
138 "Emblem is immeasurable . . ." (ED to T. W. Higginson, April 1883), *Letters of ED*, 3:773; "Remoteness is the founder . . ." (ED to Louise and Frances Norcross, April 1873), *Letters of ED*, 2:504.
138 "Not choosing in Dickinson's . . . ," Cameron, *Choosing Not Choosing*, 21, 24.
139 "On subjects of which . . ." (ED to Otis Phillips Lord, April 30, 1882), *Letters of ED*, 3:728.
139 "Several consciousnesses meet . . . ," Morson and Emerson, *Bakhtin: Creation*, 238-39.

NOTES TO CHAPTER 8

140 "I had no Monarch . . ." (ED to T. W. Higginson, August 1862), *Letters of ED*, 2:414.
141 "Belong emphatically to what Emerson . . . ," Higginson, preface to *Poems*, *1890*.
141 "Revolution in literature . . . ," Emerson, "New Poetry," Library of America edition, 1169-70.
143 "We sang tune after tune . . . ," as cited in Small, "Musical Aesthetic," 220.
143 "She did not have to step . . . ," Johnson, *ED: Interpretive Biography*, 85.
143 "Now Brother Pegasus . . ." (ED to Austin Dickinson, March 27, 1853), *Letters of ED*, 1:235.
143 For a catalog of Dickinson rhyme patterns, see Johnson, *ED: Interpretive Biography*, 87.
145 "The splendor of divine glory . . . ," Calvin, *Institutes*, 1.11.3.
145 "Because men misused . . . ," Luther, *Heidelberg Disputation*, #20, in *Luther's Theological Writings*, 43.
148 "The known unbelievers . . . ," Turner, *Without God*, 44, 4.
149 "When I try . . . ," Kolakowski, *Modernity on Endless Trial*, 13.
151 "Until the time . . . ," Kuklick, *Rise of American Philosophy*, 19-20.
153 "Nature is the opposite . . . ," Emerson, "The American Scholar," Library of America edition, 56.
154 "The soul must go . . ." (ED to Elizabeth Holland, November 1866), *Letters of ED*, 2:455.
155 "Nature, seems it to myself . . ." (ED to T. W. Higginson, June 9, 1866), *Letters of ED*, 2:454.
155 "Morning of [a] spring day . . . ," Thoreau, *Walden*, Library of America edition, 575.
156 "In the history . . . ," Gelpi, *ED: Mind of the Poet*, 89, 91.
157 "They bore mites . . . ," Whitman, *Song of Myself*, Library of America edition, 233.
159 "Your wickedness makes you . . . ," Edwards, "Sinners in the Hands," *A JE Reader*, 96.
160 "Dickinson wants to follow language . . . ," Wardrop, *ED's Gothic*, 133.

161 "Series of windows . . . ," Lewis, *Experiment in Criticism*, 138.

162 "Doctrine of poetry as message . . . ," Sewall, *Life of ED*, 711.

162 "The Giant in the Human Heart . . ." (ED to Elizabeth Holland, 1873), *Letters of ED*, 2:514.

163 "Thank you for the Affection . . ." (ED to Elizabeth Holland, January 1875), *Letters of ED*, 2:537.

164 "Distillation — despite its . . . ," Eberwein, *ED: Strategies*, 138.

166 "The significance of the Mass . . . ," Auden, *Certain World*, 134.

168 "The Son [or] the Sayer . . . ," Emerson, "The Poet," Library of America edition, 449.

168 "In that only sense . . . ," Emerson, "Lord's Supper," Library of America edition, 1137; "Alone in history . . . ," Emerson, "Divinity School Address," Library of America edition, 80.

172 "Obtaining but his own extent . . ." (ED to James Clark, 1882), *Letters of ED*, 3:745.

174 "When Jesus tells us . . ." (ED to Mary Hills, 1882), *Letters of ED*, 3:837.

176 "Traditional concepts, schemes, and values . . . ," Abrams, *Natural Supernaturalism*, 13.

176 "History is an impertinence . . . ," Emerson, "Self-Reliance," Library of America edition, 270.

177 "Naturally one of [Emily's] favorite authors . . . ," Capps, *ED's Reading*, 119; "My purpose in going . . . ," Thoreau, *Walden*, Library of America edition, 338.

NOTES TO CHAPTER 9

179 "A Letter always feels . . ." (ED to T. W. Higginson, June 1869), *Letters of ED*, 2:460.

180 "The social leader . . . ," Burgess, *Reminiscences*, 60, 61, 62.

180 "The total number . . . ," Johnson, *Letters of ED*, 2:448.

180 "Would we could mail . . ." (ED to Louise and Frances Norcross, 1868), *Letters of ED*, 2:459.

181 "Within a generation . . . ," Ahlstrom, *Religious History*, 2:191.

181 "Liberal Protestantism without Protestantism . . . ," Marsden, *Soul of American University*, 406, 424.

182 "Night of terror . . . ," Burgess, *Reminiscences*, 28-29.

182 "Sweetest, kindest, most sympathetic natures . . . ," Burgess, *Reminiscences*, 57-58.

183 "Was the most suggestive . . . ," Burgess, *Reminiscences*, 52, 55, 54.

183 "It seemed to be . . . ," Burgess, *Reminiscences*, 141.

183 "College as a place . . . ," Burgess, *Reminiscences*, 147-48.

185 "The valuation is now . . . ," Taylor, *Sources of Self*, 187.

185 "Seemed almost inspired . . . ," Burgess, *Reminiscences*, 61-62.

186 "It was long ago . . . ," *Years and Hours*, 2:479.

186 "The Dickinson home . . . ," *Years and Hours*, 2:483; "An elderly lady . . . ," *Years and Hours*, 2:482-83.

187 "Emily saw no one . . . ," *Years and Hours*, 2:120.

187 "Lady whom the people call . . . ," *Years and Hours*, 2:357, 376.

187 "She would walk . . . ," *Years and Hours*, 1:xxix-xxx; "E[mily] D[ickinson] had to be . . . ," *Years and Hours*, 1:xxx.

188 "It is extraordinary . . . ," Jenkins, *ED: Friend and Neighbor*, 133.

188 "G. F. Bailey & Co's . . . ," *Years and Hours*, 2:113; "To distract our . . . ," Burgess, *Reminiscences*, 59; "Friday I tasted life . . ." (ED to Elizabeth Holland, May 1866), *Letters of ED*, 2:452.

188 "There is that which is called . . ." (ED to Louise and Frances Norcross, April 1873), *Letters of ED*, 2:505-6.

189 "[Emily's] father felt . . . ," Jenkins, *ED: Friend and Neighbor*, 82.

189 "There was a legend . . . ," *Years and Hours*, 2:133.

190 "Dear Cousins . . ." (ED to Louise and Frances Norcross, July 1879), *Letters of ED*, 2:644.

192 "Sue, it is the only thing . . . ," Bianchi, *ED Face to Face*, 28; "I read Miss Prescott's . . ." (ED to T. W. Higginson, April 25, 1862), *Letters of ED*, 2:404.

192 "Wonder at your self-forgetting . . ." (ED to Elizabeth Holland, December 1881), *Letters of ED*, 3:721; "As Emily Brontë . . ." (ED to Elizabeth Holland, 1883), *Letters of ED*, 3:802-3.

193 "Though Earth and man . . . ," *Poems of Emily Brontë*, 247.

193 "Hawthorne appalls, entices . . ." (ED to T. W. Higginson, December 1879), *Letters of ED*, 2:649.

194 " 'What do I think of *Middlemarch?*' . . ." (ED to Louise and Frances Norcross, April 1873), *Letters of ED*, 2:506; "My George Eliot . . ." (ED to Louise and Frances Norcross, 1881), *Letters of ED*, 3:750.

194 "Vinnie is eager to see . . ." (ED to Elizabeth Holland, 1881), *Letters of ED*, 3:693.

195 "By the way . . . ," Browning, *Aurora Leigh*, 1:455-65, *Poetical Works*, 358.

196 "While Shakespeare remains . . ." (ED to T. W. Higginson, November 1871), *Letters of ED*, 2:491; "After long disuse . . ." (T. W. Higginson to Mary Higginson, August 17, 1870), *Letters of ED*, 2:476; "How my blood bounded! . . . ," *Lyman Letters*, 76; "Had I a trait . . ." (ED to Franklin Sanborn, 1873), *Letters of ED*, 2:516.

196 "I . . . have known little of literature . . ." (ED to T. W. Higginson, February 1879), *Letters of ED*, 2:635; "With the exception of Shakespeare . . ." (ED to Susan Gilbert Dickinson, 1882), *Letters of ED*, 3:755.

197 "We hope that you . . ." (ED to Josiah Holland, 1878), *Letters of ED*, 2:605-6.

198 "There is no account . . ." (ED to Abiah Root, January 12, 1846), *Letters of ED*, 1:24.

201 "To encourage laughter . . . ," Bakhtin, *Dialogic Imagination*, 72.

201 "In modern times . . . ," Bakhtin, *Dialogic Imagination*, 71, 77.

202 "As to the 'innocent' . . . ," Bingham, *Ancestors' Brocades*, 166-67.

202 "Although it may have been true . . . ," Bingham, *Ancestors' Brocades*, 167.

202 "Take all away from me . . ." (ED to Mary and Eben Jenks Loomis, January 2, 1885), *Letters of ED*, 3:855.

203 "A Letter always feels . . ." (ED to T. W. Higginson, June 1869), *Letters of ED*, 2:460.

203 "Shiver to hear . . . ," *Years and Hours*, 2:478; "Could consent to publish . . . ," Bingham, *Ancestors' Brocades*, 166.

203 "The Risks of Immortality . . ." (ED to T. W. Higginson, October 1870), *Letters of ED*, 2:480.

204 "Of Miss P———— I know but this . . ." (ED to Louise Norcross, 1872), *Letters of ED*, 2:500.

205 "[Vinnie] has no Father and Mother . . ." (ED to Elizabeth Holland, 1873), *Letters of ED*, 2:508; "It seemed peculiar . . ." (ED to Elizabeth Holland, January 1875), *Letters of ED*, 3:537; "Austin seldom calls . . ." (ED to Elizabeth Holland, December 1882), *Letters of ED*, 2:756.

206 "Power to ramble . . ." (ED to Elizabeth Holland, September 1877), *Letters of ED*, 2:593; "Mother does not yet stand . . ." (ED to Elizabeth Holland, October 1879), *Letters of ED*, 2:648.

206 "Austin and I were talking . . ." (ED to Elizabeth Holland, July 1880), *Letters of ED*, 3:667.

206 "When a Child . . ." (ED to Elizabeth Holland, May 1874), *Letters of ED*, 2:524-25; "The Fiction of 'Santa Claus' . . ." (ED to Elizabeth Holland, December 1882), *Letters of ED*, 3:756; "I suppose he is . . ." (ED to Elizabeth Holland, May 1877), *Letters of ED*, 2:582.

207 "Why the Thief ingredient . . ." (ED to Elizabeth Holland, January 1871), *Letters of ED*, 2:485; "Science will not trust us . . ." (ED to Elizabeth Holland, September 1873), *Letters of ED*, 2:511; "How unspeakably sweet . . ." (ED to Elizabeth Holland, June 1878), *Letters of ED*, 2:612-13.

207 "Our hearts have flown . . ." (ED to Elizabeth Holland, October 1881), *Letters of ED*, 3:712-13; "Panting to help . . ." (ED to Elizabeth Holland, October 1881), *Letters of ED*, 2:712-13.

208 "After a while, dear . . ." (ED to Elizabeth Holland, October 1881), *Letters of ED*, 3:713; "How sweet that he rose . . ." (ED to Elizabeth Holland, October 1881), *Letters of ED*, 3:714.

209 "EMILY. 'Things are not . . . ,'" *Lyman Letters*, 69.

209 "Seems to me often . . . ,'" *Lyman Letters*, 70.

209 "An inexhaustible inner domain . . . ,'" Taylor, *Sources of the Self*, 390.

210 "But Susan is a stranger . . . ,'" *Poems*, 3:971.

210 "So I conclude . . . ,'" *Lyman Letters*, 70-71.

210 "To reading the Old . . . ,'" *Lyman Letters*, 73.

211 "We used to think . . . ,'" *Lyman Letters*, 78.

212 "I had promised . . ." (ED to T. W. Higginson, 1866), *Letters of ED*, 2:450; "I must omit Boston . . ." (ED to T. W. Higginson, June 9, 1866), *Letters of ED*, 2:453.

212 "Their strange power . . ." (T. W. Higginson to ED, May 11, 1869), *Letters of ED*, 2:461.

213 "Could it please your convenience . . ." (ED to T. W. Higginson, June 1869), *Letters of ED*, 2:460.

213 "Large county lawyer's house . . ." (T. W. Higginson to Mary Higginson, August 16, 17, 1870), *Letters of ED*, 2:473-76.

214 "The impression undoubtedly . . . ," Higginson, quoted in *Letters of ED*, 2:476.

215 "Away from paternalism . . . ," Howe, *Political Culture of American Whigs*, 302.

215 "The belief that human virtue . . . ," R. Niebuhr, *Nature and Destiny*, 1:108.

215 "A God without wrath . . . ," H. R. Niebuhr, *Kingdom of God*, 193.

216 "That general habit of thought . . . ," quoted in Cashdollar, *Transformation of Theology*, 18.

216 "The hundredth year . . . ," Wolff, *Emily Dickinson*, 537.

216 "Truth is such a *rare* thing . . ." (T. W. Higginson to Mary Higginson, August 16, 1870), *Letters of ED*, 2:474.

NOTES TO CHAPTER 10

218 " 'This tabernacle' is . . ." (ED to Elizabeth Holland, 1878), *Letters of ED*, 2:609.

218 "Trying to restore . . . ," Johnson, in *Letters of ED*, 2:448.

219 "I saw the sunrise . . ." (ED to Elizabeth Holland, November 1866), *Letters of ED*, 2:455; "I cooked the peaches . . ." (ED to Louise Norcross, May 1870), *Letters of ED*, 2:471; "Life is the finest secret . . ." (ED to Elizabeth Holland, October 1870), *Letters of ED*, 2:482.

221 "The Dyings have been too deep . . ." (ED to Rebecca Mack, 1884), *Letters of ED*, 3:843; "The doctor calls it . . ." (ED to Louise and Frances Norcross, August 1884), *Letters of ED*, 3:826.

221 "Father steps like Cromwell . . ." (ED to Louise and Frances Norcross, 1870), *Letters of ED*, 2:470; "Father was very sick . . ." (ED to Louise Norcross, 1871), *Letters of ED*, 2:486.

222 "The last Afternoon . . ." (ED to T. W. Higginson, July 1874), *Letters of ED*, 2:528.

222 "We were eating . . ." (ED to Louise and Frances Norcross, 1874), *Letters of ED*, 2:526.

222 "Because she was sure . . . ," *Years and Hours*, 2:225; "I thought Vinnie's character . . . ," *Years and Hours*, 2:226.

222 "Austin leaned over . . . ," *Years and Hours*, 2:224; "Terror at my father's grief . . . ," Bianchi, *ED Face to Face*, 13; "Austin is . . . the most shocked . . ." *Years and Hours*, 2:226.

223 "And where was Aunt Emily?" Bianchi, *ED Face to Face*, 13; "We take him the best flowers . . ." (ED to Louise and Frances Norcross, 1874), *Letters of ED*, 2:526.

223 "Heart was pure . . ." (ED to T. W. Higginson, July 1874), *Letters of ED*, 2:528.

223 "Mother is asleep . . ." (ED to Elizabeth Holland, January 1875), *Letters of ED*, 2:537.

224 "Home itself is far . . ." (ED to Sarah Tuckerman, March 1875), *Letters of ED*, 2:538.

225 "I suppose even God . . ." (ED to T. W. Higginson, 1876), *Letters of ED*, 2:551.

225 "Since my Father's dying . . ." (ED to T. W. Higginson, June 1877), *Letters of ED*, 2:583.

226 "To them both . . . ," Bianchi, *ED Face to Face*, 85-86; "Will be even more respected . . . ," *Years and Hours*, 2:224-25.

227 "It is a condition . . . ," *Years and Hours*, 2:226-27.

227 "Full fathom five . . . ," *The Tempest*, act 1, scene 2, lines 397-402.

228 "She was on her way . . . ," *Years and Hours*, 1:lvi.

228 "I have seen [a lady] . . ." (T. W. Higginson to ED, May 11, 1869), *Letters of ED*, 2:461.

228 "Have I a word . . ." (ED to Helen Hunt Jackson, October 1875), *Letters of ED*, 2:544; "This is *mine* . . ." (Helen Hunt Jackson to ED, March 20, 1876), *Letters of ED*, 2:544.

229 "A little manuscript . . ." (H. H. Jackson to ED, March 20, 1876), *Letters of ED*, 2:544-45.

229 "Surely, in the shelter . . ." (H. H. Jackson, August 20, 1876), *Letters of ED*, 2:563.

229 "Are you willing . . ." (ED to T. W. Higginson, October 1876), *Letters of ED*, 2:562-63.

230 "It is always hard . . ." (T. W. Higginson to ED, October 22, 1876), *Letters of ED*, 2:564.

230 "[I feel] as if I . . ." (H. H. Jackson to ED, October 1876), *Letters of ED*, 2:565.

230 "It was not stories . . ." (ED to T. W. Higginson, October 1876), *Letters of ED*, 2:566; "Often, when troubled . . ." (ED to T. W. Higginson, 1877), *Letters of ED*, 2:573.

231 "I will copy them . . ." (H. H. Jackson to ED, April 29, 1878), *Letters of ED*, 2:624.

231 "Now — will you send . . ." (H. H. Jackson to ED, October 25, 1878), *Letters of ED*, 2:625.

231 "For want of a known sponsor . . ." (Thomas Niles to ED, January 15, 1879), *Letters of ED*, 2:626.

232 "If I could help you? . . ." (ED to T. W. Higginson, September 1877), *Letters of ED*, 2:590.

232 "I know we shall certainly see . . ." (ED to Catharine Sweetser, February 1870), *Letters of ED*, 2:469.

232 "He who finds Christ . . . ," Thielicke, *I Believe*, 11.

233 "That the Divine . . ." (ED to Richard Mather, November 1877), *Letters of ED*, 2:594-95.

233 "I went to the Room . . ." (ED to Samuel Bowles, 1877), *Letters of ED*, 3:589-90.

234 "To remember our own . . ." (ED to Mary Bowles, January 16, 1878), *Letters of ED*, 3:599.

234 "The last song that I heard . . ." (ED to T. W. Higginson, January 19, 1878), *Letters of ED*, 3:599.

235 "His name was Future . . ." (ED to Susan Gilbert Dickinson, January 1878), *Letters of ED*, 3:600.

235 "I hasten to you, Mary . . ." (ED to Mary Bowles, 1878), *Letters of ED*, 2:601.

235 "I have thought of you often . . ." (ED to Maria Whitney, 1878), *Letters of ED*, 3:602-3.

236 "Anthropological over-compensation . . . ," Thielicke, *Evangelical Faith*, 2:386.

237 " 'Christ! is there no God?' " Richter, "Speech of Dead Christ," 234ff.

238 The Common Sense "credo," May, *Enlightenment in America*, 358.

238 "Under its feet any divinity . . . ," Guelzo, *Edwards on the Will*, 277.

239 " 'This tabernacle' is a blissful trial . . ." (ED to Elizabeth Holland, 1878), *Letters of ED*, 3:609.

NOTES TO CHAPTER 11

241 "I have only a moment, exiles . . ." (ED to Louise and Frances Norcross, Sep-

tember 1880), *Letters of ED*, 3:675; "The responsibility of Pathos . . ." (ED to Elizabeth Holland, September 1880), *Letters of ED*, 3:675.

241 "Mother pines for you . . ." (ED to Elizabeth Holland, September 1877), *Letters of ED*, 2:593; "Very improper . . ." (ED to Elizabeth Holland, July 1880), *Letters of ED*, 3:667.

242 "Mother asked me last Sabbath . . ." (ED to Jonathan Jenkins, August 1878), *Letters of ED*, 2:618.

242 "Best friend . . . ," Bingham, *Revelation*, 3; "Rock bed of old conservative . . . ," Susan Dickinson, "Annals of Evergreens," Houghton Library; "Abstinence from Melody . . ." (ED to Benjamin Kimball, 1885), *Letters of ED*, 3:861.

243 "Little 'Playthings' . . ." (ED to Otis Phillips Lord, April 30, 1882), *Letters of ED*, 3:727.

243 "Aunt Emily and he enjoyed . . . ," Bianchi, *ED Face to Face*, 36; "Their enjoyment of the comedy . . . ," Bianchi, *Life and Letters of ED*, 69-70.

244 "My lovely Salem . . ." (ED to Otis Phillips Lord, 1878), *Letters of ED*, 2:614-15.

244 "Dont you know . . ." (ED to Otis Phillips Lord, 1878), *Letters of ED*, 2:617.

245 "I do — do want you tenderly . . ." (ED to Otis Phillips Lord, May 1, 1882), *Letters of ED*, 3:728.

245 "Meanwhile Tom [Kelley] had come . . ." (ED to Otis Phillips Lord, May 14, 1882), *Letters of ED*, 3:730.

245 "Emily 'Jumbo!' Sweetest name . . ." (ED to Otis Phillips Lord, November 1882), *Letters of ED*, 3:747; "You said with loved timidity . . ." (ED to Otis Phillips Lord, December 3, 1882), *Letters of ED*, 3:753.

246 "You will not allow . . . ," *Years and Hours*, 2:376.

246 "Their mystification when they read . . . ," *Years and Hours*, 1:lix; "Take it away . . . ," Bingham, *Revelation*, 23.

246 "I have written you . . ." (ED to Otis Phillips Lord, December 3, 1882), *Letters of ED*, 3:753.

246 "The withdrawal of the Fuel . . ." (ED to Otis Phillips Lord, 1883), *Letters of ED*, 3:786.

247 "I feel like wasting . . ." (ED to Otis Phillips Lord, 1883), *Letters of ED*, 3:786.

248 "Intimacy of many years . . ." (ED to James Clark, August 1882), *Letters of ED*, 3:737-38.

248 "I knew him . . ." (ED to James Clark, 1882), *Letters of ED*, 3:744; "In illustrating such phrases . . . ," Sewall, *Life of ED*, 451.

249 "I am speechlessly grateful . . ." (ED to James Clark, February 1883), *Letters of ED*, 3:762.

249 "He was a dusk Gem . . ." (ED to James Clark, 1882), *Letters of ED*, 3:745.

249 "The dear Mother . . ." (ED to Elizabeth Holland, November 1882), *Letters of ED*, 3:746; "Both benumbed . . ." (ED to Nellie Sweetser, November 1882), *Letters of ED*, 3:748.

250 "She was scarcely the aunt . . ." (ED to Louise and Frances Norcross, November 1882), *Letters of ED*, 3:749-50.

250 "As we bore . . ." (ED to James Clark, 1882), *Letters of ED*, 3:752; "I cannot conjecture . . ." (ED to Otis Phillips Lord, December 3, 1882), *Letters of ED*, 3:753; "I have thought of you . . ." (ED to Elizabeth Holland, December 1882), *Letters of ED*, 3:754.

251 "Mother has now been gone . . ." (ED to Elizabeth Holland, December 1882), *Letters of ED*, 3:754-55.

251 "All is faint indeed . . ." (ED to Maria Whitney, 1883), *Letters of ED*, 3:771.

252 "My wife's tavern . . . ," Sewall, *Life of ED*, 191; "A man with an expensive family . . . ," *Years and Hours*, 2:450.

253 "Be true to yourself, Mattie . . ." (ED to Martha Dickinson, October 1884), *Letters of ED*, 3:845.

253 "Ned put most of the blame . . . ," Sewall, *Life of ED*, 193.

254 "Could *I* — then . . ." (ED to Susan Gilbert Dickinson, 1861), *Letters of ED*, 2:381.

254 "*Private* I have intended . . . ," Houghton Library.

254 "Austin seldom calls . . ." (ED to Elizabeth Holland, December 1882), *Letters of ED*, 3:756; "My Brother is with us . . ." (ED to James Clark, March 1883), *Letters of ED*, 3:765; "I have two or three little visits . . . ," Sewall, *Life of ED*, 765; "The tie between us . . ." (ED to Susan Gilbert Dickinson, 1885), *Letters of ED*, 3:893.

255 "I make no special mention . . . ," Sewall, *Life of ED*, 193; "There was in him . . . ," Sewall, *Life of ED*, 124.

255 "Miss Emily Dickinson . . . ," *Years and Hours*, 2:406; "Emily received a nervous shock . . . ," Sewall, *Life of ED*, 146.

256 "The Vision of Immortal Life . . ." (ED to Susan Gilbert Dickinson, October 1883), *Letters of ED*, 3:799.

256 "The Physician says . . ." (ED to Elizabeth Holland, 1883), *Letters of ED*, 3:802; "I hardly dare to know . . ." (ED to Louise and Frances Norcross, March 1884), *Letters of ED*, 3:817.

257 "Eight Saturday noons ago . . ." (ED to Louise and Frances Norcross, August 1884), *Letters of ED*, 3:826-27.

258 "Open the Door . . ." (ED to Elizabeth Holland, 1883), *Letters of ED*, 3:803; "The prance that crossed . . ." (ED to Susan Gilbert Dickinson, 1884), *Letters of ED*, 3:828.

259 "Summer in a Chair . . ." (ED to Helen Hunt Jackson, September 1884), *Letters of ED*, 3:840; "I have not been strong . . ." (ED to Rebecca Mack, 1884), *Letters of ED*, 3:843.

259 "Twice been very sick . . ." (ED to Louise and Frances Norcross, March 1886), *Letters of ED*, 3:897; "I came down to go . . . ," *Years and Hours*, 2:461; "Emily is quite sick . . . ," Yale University Library.

259 "I have been very ill . . ." (ED to T. W. Higginson, 1886), *Letters of ED*, 3:903; "I am better . . ." (ED to Charles Clark, April 1886), *Letters of ED*, 3:901.

259 "Little Cousins, Called Back . . ." (ED to Louise and Frances Norcross, May 1886), *Letters of ED*, 3:906.

259 "Emily seemed to go off . . . ," *Years and Hours*, 2:471.

260 "He is terribly oppressed . . . ," Yale University Library.

260 "It was settled before . . . ," *Years and Hours*, 2:471-72.

260 "Old-fashioned times . . . ," *Years and Hours*, 2:472-73.

262 "Deliciously brilliant sunny afternoon . . . ," *Years and Hours*, 2:476.

262 "An atmosphere of its own . . . ," *Years and Hours*, 2:474-75.

262 "By saying that one friend . . . ," *Years and Hours*, 2:475, 474.

Index of First Lines

The poem number in brackets is the one assigned in the Johnson edition of Dickinson's poetry. An asterisk indicates that the poem is cited in full. The following index does not include those instances in which poems have been cited within the text of a Dickinson letter; in those cases, the end notes give the volume and page reference for the letter in which the poem appears.

Index of Names and Subjects

Permissions

The author and publisher gratefully acknowledge permission to reprint material from the following:

The poetry of Emily Dickinson is reprinted by permission of the publishers and the Trustees of Amherst College from *The Poems of Emily Dickinson*, Thomas H. Johnson, ed., Cambridge, Mass.: The Belknap Press of Harvard University Press, Copyright © 1951, 1955, 1979, 1983 by the President and Fellows of Harvard College and from *The Complete Poems of Emily Dickinson*, edited by Thomas H. Johnson, Copyright © 1929, 1935 by Martha Dickinson Bianchi; Copyright © renewed 1957, 1963 by Mary L. Hampson, by permission of Little Brown and Company, Boston.

The letters of Emily Dickinson are reprinted by permission of the publishers from *The Letters of Emily Dickinson*, edited by Thomas H. Johnson, Cambridge, Mass.: The Belknap Press of Harvard University Press, Copyright © 1958, 1986 by the President and Fellows of Harvard College.

The citation of material from the Dickinson family papers, shelf mark bMS Am 1118.95, is by permission of the Houghton Library, Harvard University.

The citation of material from the Todd-Bingham family papers is by permission of the Yale University Library.